THE AMERICAN ASSOCIATION FOR STATE AND LOCAL HISTORY * * * 1940 * * *

Using Local History in the Classroom

Fay D. Metcalf
and
Matthew T. Downey

The American Association for State and Local History
Nashville, Tennessee

Library of Congress Cataloguing-in-Publication Data

Metcalf, Fay D., 1928–
    Using local history in the classroom.

    Includes bibliographical references and index.
    1. United States—History, Local—Study and teaching (Secondary)   2. United
States—History, Local—Study and teaching (Higher)   I. Downey, Matthew T.   II. Title.
E175.8.M47   973'.07'1273   81–19098
ISBN 0–910050–56–2   AACR2

*Publication of this book was made possible in part by funds from the sale of the Bicentennial State
Histories, which were supported by the National Endowment for the Humanities.*

Designed by Gary Gore

Acknowledgments

Author and publisher make grateful acknowledgment to the following for permission to use in this book the materials listed below.

To Davis Bitton, for quotations from his "Family History: Therapy or Scholarship?" paper delivered at the annual meeting of the Society of American Archivists, Salt Lake City, Utah, October 6, 1977.

To the *Boulder* (Colorado) *Daily Camera*, for the George Fonda obituary in figure 4.2 and for plates 5.3 and 5.4.

To the Boulder (Colorado) Historical Society, for plate 3.6 and figure 8.2; to the L. Paddock Collection of the Boulder Historical Society for plate 3.7.

To the Chicago Metro History Fair, for material from pages 30–31 and 68–70 of *Chicago Metro History Fair: A Handbook for Teachers*, by Prudence Moylan and Walter Kelly. Copyright © 1978 by the Chicago Metro History Fair.

To the State Historical Society of Colorado, for plates 1.5, 5.1, 5.6, and 6.2.

To the Denver Public Library, Western History Department, for plates 4.1, 4.2, 4.3, 5.2, 5.5, 6.1, 6.3, 6.4, 6.5, and 6.6.

To Thomas L. Dynneson, for excerpts from pages 2–3 of his *Planning Local History Projects for Elementary and Secondary Students* (n.p.: West Texas Council for the Social Studies, 1976).

To *Early Man, Magazine of Modern Archeology*, for figure 3.5 and 3.6 and plate 3.15, from "Death-Heads, Cherubs, and Shaded Urns," by Felicia A. Holton, *Early Man*, Autumn 1979, page 6; and for figure 3.11, also from *Early Man*.

To Education Systems Research, for figure 1.4.

To Ginn and Company, for material adapted from pages TG–8 and TG–9 of *In Search of America*, annotated edition, by Martin W. Sandler. Copyright © 1975 by Ginn and Company (Xerox Corporation).

To Harvard University Press, for material from pages 290–292 of *The Other Bostonians: Poverty and Progress in the American Metropolis, 1880–1970*, by Stephan Thernstrom, copyright © 1973 by Harvard University Press; for figures 6.1, 6.2, and 6.3, from *The People of Hamilton, Canada West: Family and Class in a Mid-Nineteenth-Century City*, by Michael B. Katz, copyright © 1975 by Harvard University Press; and for material from

v

Immigrant Milwaukee, by Kathleen Neils Conzen, copyright © 1976 by Harvard University Press.

To Harvard-Danforth Center for Teaching and Learning, for quotations from "Graven Images," by Stephen Botein et al., in *Experiments in History Teaching*, copyright © 1977 by Harvard-Danforth Center for Teaching and Learning.

To Merrimack Valley Textile Museum, for figure 5.2, insurance survey of the Shaw Manufacturing Company.

To the Minnesota Social History Project, funded by the National Endowment for the Humanities, at Saint Mary's College, Winona, Minnesota, for project materials in tables 1.1, 1.2, 5.3, and 5.4, and for figure 4.4.

To the National Council for the Social Studies, for material from pages 89–90 of "Organizing and Evaluating Information," by Alice Eikenberry and Ruth Ellsworth, in *Skill Development in the Social Studies*, edited by Helen McCracken, copyright © 1963 by the National Council for the Social Studies; and for material from pages 188–189 of "Pre-Writing and Rewriting to Learn," by Barry Beyer, in *Social Education*, copyright © 1979 by the National Council for the Social Studies.

To the State Education Department of the University of the State of New York, for material from pages 40–41 of *Teaching the Age of Homespun: A Guide for Seventh-Grade Social Studies*. Copyright © 1965 by the State Education Department of the University of the State of New York.

To the University of North Carolina Press, for material from "Buildings as Sources: Architecture and the Social Studies," by Gerald A. Danzer, in *The High School Journal* 57, no. 5, February 1974. Copyright © 1974 by the University of North Carolina Press. Reprinted by permission of the publisher.

To Old Sturbridge Village, for material adapted from page 15 of *Building Collaborative Programs: Museums and Schools*, by Alberta Sebolt, copyright © 1980 by Old Sturbridge Village; for the "Pliny Freeman Family" data, from the Old Sturbridge Village packet "Households and Families"; and for figures 4.3, 5.1, 5.3, and 5.4.

To Richard J. Riley, for materials and plates 3.13 and 3.14, on the Hancock Cemetery Restoration Project, in Quincy, Massachusetts.

To Sonoran Heritage, a Learning Library Program funded by the National Endowment for the Humanities, at the Tucson Public Library, for materials from *Making Connections: A Family History Workbook*, developed for Sonoran Heritage in 1979 and edited by Karen Dahood.

To Catherine Taylor, for materials from the curriculum package "Two Boulder Neighborhoods," developed for the Boulder Valley (Colorado) Schools in 1977.

To Celeste Woodley, for material from an interview, "Memories of a Depression Childhood."

Contents

Preface

The past ten years have seen a remarkable growth of interest among teachers in the use of local history as a classroom resource. We became involved in this development in the early 1970s, when we began to assign local history projects to students in our United States history courses at Boulder High School and at the University of Colorado at Boulder. Later on, each of us developed separate local history courses, as well. At the time, we were not aware of the number of teachers becoming involved in this kind of activity. At the Anglo-American History Teachers' Conferences at Pasadena in 1973 and at York in 1974, we did find out how successfully British teachers were exploiting local history source materials with their students. But it was not until two years later, when the ERIC Clearinghouse for Social Studies/Social Science Education asked us to prepare a "tips and resources" publication on local history, that we discovered how extensively teachers in the United States were using local history. A search for articles, papers, and syllabi related to the classroom uses of local history in the ERIC system produced a thick print-out of bibliographical entries. The ERIC pamphlet, *Teaching Local History: Trends, Tips, and Resources*, published in 1977 as a result of that search, described the "state of the art" at that time.

The thought of writing a more comprehensive manual for teachers, based upon our own experience as well as what we had discovered that other teachers were doing with local history, occurred to us while we were working on the ERIC pamphlet. There seemed to be a clear need for such a publication, despite the existence of several excellent manuals on the subject of local history. The existing books were either manuals about researching and writing local history, addressed to the amateur historian, or they were publications for teachers, calling attention to the value of local history without spelling out precisely what should be done with it. Consequently, we welcomed the opportunity suggested by Rollie Adams, Education Director for the American Association of State and Local History, to write a practical manual on the use of local history for classroom teachers.

The book that we have written is an attempt to provide both secondary school and college history teachers with a how-to-do-it manual on the use of local history in the classroom. We have tried to include projects and activities suitable for a wide range of students, and we assume that teachers will use the book both selectively and creatively. Some of the activities described herein are clearly more suitable for secondary school students than for college students. Others obviously require the resources of a research library more typically found on a university campus. We hope that teachers will use those activities that they find suitable for their students and adapt to their own needs those that are not too far off the mark.

This book is also a collaborative effort in the broadest sense of that term. In the first place, the authors have worked closely together. During the past decade, the two of us have consistently benefited from each other's experience in using local history. We have shared materials and ideas and have helped out in one another's classrooms. We have also taken advantage of the experience of a great number of other history teachers. We have included in the book many activities developed by other teachers with whom we have talked and corresponded or whose descriptions of classroom projects we have read.

We have also incurred a number of other personal debts that we would like to acknowledge here. As we have already mentioned, it was Rollie Adams's interest that made this project possible, in the first place. We are also indebted to Gary G. Gore, Publications Director of the American Association for State and Local History, for his guidance, assistance, and patience during the preparation of the manuscript. Peter O'Connell of Old Sturbridge Village deserves special mention. His probing comments have again and again caused us to rethink our decisions about the best way to put together a manual for teachers. We were also fortunate to have as our typist Ginny Jones, who is both a skilled typist and a thoughtful social studies teacher. We benefited from the many pertinent questions that she asked as the manuscript progressed.

FAY D. METCALF
MATTHEW T. DOWNEY

Using Local History in the Classroom

Introduction:
Why Local History?

DURING the past decade, history teachers all across the United States have rediscovered the value of the local community as a resource for teaching history. Their students, armed with cassette recorders and note pads, have visited senior citizens' centers to interview elderly residents about a great variety of history topics. In some schools, students have worked together for a semester to write a local history; in others they have published magazines devoted to local history and folk culture. Some teachers have prepared architectural walking tours to help students look more knowingly at turn-of-the-century office buildings, cast-iron store fronts, and gingerbread trim. Activities and units on local history have been introduced into a variety of history and social studies courses. A teacher of German in a high school in San Antonio even used a local history investigation to help her students learn to read German script. Clearly, there is under way a major revival of interest in local history, and it is not happening only in the schools and colleges.[1]

The growing importance of local history in the school and college curriculum is a reflection of a much more inclusive interest in community history that has been developing in society at large in recent years. It is a cultural as well as a pedagogical phenomenon. "Local and community history may well be one of the fastest-growing popular intellectual persuits in the United States today," David A. Gerber has recently written. "At a time when history languishes in the schools, many Americans are engaged in separate searches into their 'roots'—writing histories of their towns, families, ethnic communities and parish churches."[2] The inclusion of families and ethnic and religious groups in

1

Gerber's list is significant, for the interest in local history is rooted in something deeper than an affection for a particular locality. The local neighborhood, town, or city, much like the family or the ethnic group to which one belongs, are social realities that help provide individuals with a sense of identity. They have always performed such a role for all but the most rootless of Americans, but never in recent years has that role seemed so important to so many.

Has community history finally developed a loyal following in the United States, or is it just a passing fad? In some respects it may be a casual and passing interest. Some of the interest in local history stimulated by the decision to celebrate the nation's bicentennial in a decentralized fashion with historical projects and pageants organized in communities throughout the United States may dissipate, over time. In other respects the interest in community history seems to be more deeply rooted. The village smithies and spreading chestnut trees of local history have always had a nostalgic appeal for Americans. In the wake of Vietnam and Watergate, when our sense of national purpose and our perception of national character seemed unclear and confused, local roots became more important than ever before. It is also important to note that local history not only became more popular during the 1970s; it also gained an intellectual respectability that it had traditionally lacked. Academic historians who once dismissed local history as necessarily provincial and antiquarian recognized the extraordinary value of a growing body of work by scholars who had used individual communities as case studies in social history investigations.

Whatever the explanation for this pervasive interest in community history, history teachers have been quick to take advantage of it. And they have done so with good reason. Introducing local history into the curriculum helps to redress a serious imbalance in the way history has traditionally been taught. The American history courses that most secondary school and college students take are largely concerned with people and events that had national significance. Yet American history involves a great deal more than laws enacted by Congress and decisions made by captains of industry and leaders of labor unions and reform movements. The everyday experiences of ordinary men, women, and children in countless towns and neighborhoods also helped give shape to the past. Local history, family history, and the history of ethnic communities provide avenues into the history of ordinary people and everyday events. Moreover, students seem to find that kind of history interesting. It is less remote from their own interests and concerns, more concrete, easier to grasp. Finally, the sources of local history have provided innovative teachers with an abundant supply of new teaching materials. For most communities, local history sources are plentiful, readily exploitable, and easily tailored to the interests of individual students.

Local History in Historical Perspective

It is important to note that the decade of the 1970s was not the first time that teachers have discovered that the local community can be a rich resource for teaching history. Serious interest in the use of local history in the classroom dates back at least to the 1890s, that decade which saw such intense interest in secondary school curriculum reform. Indeed, as early as 1885, Herbert Baxter Adams noted in the first methods book for history teachers published in the United States that "one of the best introductions to history that can be given . . . is through a study of the community in which the school is placed." [3] More important was the appeal of local history to those teachers and writers of the 1890s who were beginning to question the central role of the textbook in history instruction. Advocates of the "source method," as the major alternative teaching approach was called, emphasized the importance of having students work with primary materials.[4] While "source-textbooks" were becoming available for American and European history courses, the local community was seen as the fullest repository of primary sources for the vast majority of students. Among the curriculum recommendations proposed in 1893 by the "Madison Conference" of the National Education Association's Committee of Ten was a twelfth-grade course devoted to a year's intensive study of a historical topic or of "some considerable phase of local history." [5] The curriculum reformers of the 1890s were largely unsuccessful in their effort to install either the source method or local history into the curriculum of the schools. They were unable to find sufficient support from teachers or from the historical profession to displace the narrative textbook from its already dominant position.

Although local history did not come to occupy a significant place in the school curriculum, it did continue to find advocates during the next several decades. Educators and state legislators who began to promote the teaching of state history during the 1920s usually said they wanted more "state and local history" taught in the schools. Although the words "state and local history" were fused in the educational jargon of the time, the local history component in state history courses was probably minimal.[6] By the eve of World War II, local history found new advocates among social studies educators. Perhaps the most influential among them were the proponents of a community-centered approach to social studies education. These educators emphasized the importance of using the community to help students understand American culture, to appreciate democratic values, and to become more competent citizens. While these people primarily had in mind the study of the contemporary community, they provided a ready-made rationale for the use of local history, as well. The 1939 yearbook of the National Council for the Social Studies, which was entitled *Utilization of Community Resources in the Social Studies* and which publicized this approach, contained two chapters on the use of the community as a historical resource.[7] Local history was also of interest by the late 1930s to those educators involved in the propaganda analysis movement. They recommended the use of local history sources to help students develop critical-thinking skills.[8] While various social studies educators endorsed the use of local history during these years, it was never their principal concern. Not until after World War II did local history again find the kind of commitment and support that it had had at the turn of the century.

Shortly after the end of the war, a local history movement got under way whose leaders were fired with a reforming zeal unmatched among history educators since the source-method movement of half a century before. Most of the active leaders of the local history movement were state historical society officials, state historians, and secondary school people. Chief among them were Mary E. Cunningham of the New York State Historical Association and S. K. Stevens, Pennsylvania State Historian and president of the American Association for State and Local History. Under the auspices of the AASLH, they founded in 1947 a new journal, *American Heritage*, devoted exclusively "to the techniques of teaching local, community history in our schools, historical societies, museums, and similar agencies." [9] Although not conspicuous in the leadership of this movement, professional historians did give it important support. The principal professional association for American historians, the Mississippi Valley Historical Association, devoted a day-long program at its 1948 annual meeting to community history. By the end of that year, it seemed to Mary E. Cunningham, who served as the first editor of *American Heritage*, that the movement was sweeping the country. "Papers on the subject seem to have bloomed in every historical journal, in nearly every teaching periodical. No historical society worth its salt seems to meet these days without a session on teaching community history. State and local history courses in the colleges have doubled, tripled. Workshops have been initiated." [10] She reminded her readers that almost all of that had been accomplished in just two years.

Like the source-method movement of fifty years before, the local history movement of the 1940s did not have the impact that its advocates had hoped it would have. "In view of the vast potentialities in this field of teaching," a teacher from Philadelphia noted in 1951, "one may well express surprise that the secondary schools should not have made more progress in adapting it to their uses." [11] President David D. Henry of Wayne State University also noted that year that while social science teachers had successfully used community resources, "we have not done as well in the study of history, although the same educational principle applies." Henry saw little change in the high school curriculum as a result of the local history movement. "A casual glance at the typical curriculum of the secondary school will show that world history, western civilization, or history of the United States have an exclusively dominant place." [12] Perhaps the most significant results were several how-to-do-it manuals for teachers and a series of "localized history" pamphlets published by historians involved in the movement. [13] The movement also helped to publicize the

Junior History Program, a program with somewhat earlier roots that has continued to be active in several states. In the 1940s it consisted of statewide student organizations composed of local chapters supported, usually, by the state historical society. The state organization sponsored conferences and contests, encouraged local chapters to present school and community history programs, and usually published a junior historians' magazine that printed the students' work. The emphasis was usually on local history.[14]

This brief glance backward at previous periods of enthusiasm for the use of local history in the classroom will help place the current revival of interest in a useful historical perspective. Obviously, this is not the first time that teachers have discovered that local history sources can be valuable teaching tools. And it is not the first time that students have enthusiastically responded to the invitation to explore the history of their own community. More than sixty years ago, students at Fairmont High School in Marion County, West Virginia, collected information and wrote a history of their county, and even that may not be the earliest example of students involved in a local history project.[15] Yet despite this long-standing interest in local history, local resources have never played a very large role in the history curriculum. Why has local history failed to make a larger impact in the past, and what are the implications of that for the future?

Not least among the several possible explanations is lack of strong support from the historical profession itself for those teachers and historians who have advocated the use of local history in the classroom. It was partly the opposition in 1897 from the American Historical Association's influential Committee of Seven that prevented the source-method movement, and local history along with it, from gaining ground at the turn of the century.[16] That prestigious committee's recommendations restored the place of the textbook to the center of instruction and reduced primary sources to the role of illustrative supplementary material. The report of the Committee on American History in the Schools and Colleges, the so-called Wesley Committee, did recommend in 1944 the use of regional, state, and local history, but only as sources of examples to enrich the content of the

United States history course.[17] The report stopped far short of suggesting that local history materials should occupy any significant part of the students' time. The professional historians regarded local history with considerable suspicion and kept it at arm's length. The reasons for that need to be carefully examined.

Some Pitfalls in Using Local History and Ways to Avoid Them

The major and most serious reservation that historians have had about local history is the ease with which it becomes either parochial or filiopietistic. It is a concern that is well grounded. A great deal of local history has been written over the years that has little redeeming social or intellectual value. Much of it is the work of antiquarians, who were, as Allan J. Lichtman and Valerie French have noted, "unconcerned with historical issues, but enraptured by the task of recording community events and collecting local memorabilia. Too often, amateur local historians drone on for hundreds and hundreds of pages, providing neither analysis nor interpretation." [18] While that variety of local history may be boring, it does have the virtue of being innocuous. The local historians of early and mid-nineteenth-century New England who used town histories to extoll the virtues of their white Protestant ancestors were much less naive. They wrote local history with a pointed social purpose: to define patriotism and Americanism in terms of the values of their own ethnic group and class during a period of increasing immigration and threatening social change.[19] It is with considerable justification that professional historians, until very recently, have either considered local history to be synonymous with ancestor worship or have dismissed it as trivia.

Local history in the classroom is as susceptible to irrelevance and distortion as local history published in books. It can be put to uses that have no intellectual value and that misrepresent the historical truth. That is not to say that most teachers have anything in common with the antiquarian historian who drones on for pages or that they are given to ancestor-worshiping. Parochialism and filiopietism are simply dangers inherent in working with local history. Both need to be carefully guarded against.

Local history activities and projects do have a tendency to become narrow and parochial. That can happen when any local history topic is investigated "for its own sake"—that is, with such a narrow focus that one loses sight of the larger context of which it was a part. Individual students' projects that fall beyond the boundaries of the traditional content of textbook history are especially susceptible to this pitfall. For example, the history of a local theater, a natural disaster such as a flood or a fire, or the biography of an individual who was important only on the local scene are sometimes difficult to place in a broader historical context. Yet, when any historical event is viewed in isolation, it is essentially meaningless. The variety shows performed at the local theater in the 1890s will remain meaningless curiosities to the student who examines them out of context. But in the context of popular entertainment, Tin Pan Alley, and the vaudeville circuits of the 1890s, the billing at the local theater will have much to tell the student about American society and culture of that time. Otherwise the local history project may well be a waste of the student's time.

Filiopietism—ancestor worship—also has a modern-day counterpart that teachers using local history must take care to avoid. Its modern form is the celebration of locality, ethnicity, or family, indulged in more for therapeutic purposes than for the purpose of historical understanding. The current popular interest in community history may well be part of a cultural backlash to the traumatic national events of the Vietnam and Watergate era. It does seem to contain elements of nostalgic retreat from that larger, national community to which we belong toward a simpler and partly mythical past in which local communities played a larger role in people's lives. Those Americans who are turning to local history in search of comfort and solace may insist on finding what they are looking for. There are even more obvious possibilities for ancestor worship in ethnic group history and family history. It is never easy to be objective about one's ancestors. It is especially difficult in a cultural environment that places a premium on ethnic consciousness.

How does a teacher venturing into the domain of local history avoid the pitfalls of parochialism and ancestor worship? The only certain formula for avoiding ancestor worship is to make sure that every local history investigation is governed by that spirit of critical-mindedness and intellectual honesty central to any kind of scholarly endeavor. Let the chips fall where they may. Parochialism can be avoided by making sure that every local investigation is conducted within some larger intellectual framework. Curiosity and personal interest in a topic may lead a student into a local history investigation, but these alone will not guarantee that the student will come away with historical understanding. It is the teacher's responsibility to help the student develop the topic within some broader historical or conceptual framework. Fortunately, recent developments within the historical profession have made the solution to both these problems easier than before. Models do exist now for community studies that investigate significant historical questions. As a result of several new directions of historical scholarship, the historical profession's perception of local history has also begun to change.

During the past two decades, local historical studies have gained an unprecedented academic prestige. Historians in England, Europe, and the United States have virtually redefined the field of social history through local case studies of family structure, social mobility, and community organization. Among the pioneering studies undertaken in the United States were books on family and community organization in American colonial towns. Studies in nineteenth-century social history defined *community* somewhat differently, concentrating on immigrant neighborhoods, black ghettos, and the changing social geography of American cities. Whatever the focus, these case studies broke sharply from the parochial local histories of earlier times. They were not concerned about local communities as places with a unique history important for its own sake. These social historians were concerned, rather, about social processes that could be examined in a microscopic fashion at the community level, but that operated throughout the larger society. Those larger questions that they were concerned about provided the context that gave these local investigations historical significance and meaning. In the process, they have opened many new avenues for the use of local history in the classroom that avoid the problems of parochialism and filiopietism.

Local History, the Teacher, and the Curriculum

Even in the midst of that enthusiasm for local history that she saw sweeping across the educational landscape in the late 1940s, Mary E. Cunningham had reminded her friends that "the battle is by no means won. Only the first hilltop." She was well aware of two obstacles that the local history advocates of that time had not yet even begun to overcome. The first was the lack of teachers trained to use local history sources. Although a course in state and local history was required or generally offered in the majority of states by that time, only eight states required training of any kind in community history for teacher certification. Mary E. Cunningham realized that the dearth of teachers who knew how to locate and exploit local history materials would severely limit the use of local history in the schools. But that was not the only problem. "Nor is this the worst," she continued. "Not only is there a woeful paucity of teachers' courses in community history but the very tools with which such courses may be built are lacking. There is little or no adequate research on the basic requirements, the basic implications of curriculum building in state and local history." [20] These were problems that the promoters of local history in the postwar years were unable to solve. Led primarily by public historians who were neither teachers nor teacher educators, the local history movement of that generation made little headway in training teachers and stopped far short of curriculum reform.

The failure to overcome those two obstacles that Mary E. Cunningham identified helps to explain why local history has never been widely used in school and college classrooms. Despite the recurring waves of enthusiasm, local history has never quite found its place in the curriculum. It is perhaps the classic example of a teaching technique that has periodically received wide publicity, but has never been widely adopted. Part of the explanation surely is that using local history requires skills and interests of a different kind on the teachers' part from the more traditional textbook-centered approach to teaching history. Teachers as well as students must learn to locate and exploit materials that lie beyond the walls of the school. Until very recently, neither the departments of history nor the schools of education that together train history teachers have placed much emphasis upon the development of such skills. Departments of history have emphasized mastery of content; professional schools have focused on the techniques of classroom management. The curriculum in teacher-training institutions was not designed to prepare teachers to use primary historical resources, and the curriculum in the schools was not sufficiently flexible to accommodate this unorthodox approach to teaching history. As a result, the circle of teachers who used local history never expanded much beyond those self-trained teachers who were also the principal publicists of this method. The future of local history as a teaching technique may still depend very much upon what happens in those closely related areas of teacher-training and curriculum.

In the area of teacher-training and curriculum change in teacher-training institutions, there is some cause for optimism. Students who have been trained as teachers in many colleges and universities during the past decade have had advantages not available to the teachers of Mary E. Cunningham's generation. The inquiry approach popularized by the New Social Studies movement has received a great deal of attention in teacher-training programs throughout the United States. Prospective teachers are encouraged to involve students actively in the process of learning through a variety of activities and materials that encourage student participation. While these teaching strategies are usually introduced in conjunction with commercially produced materials, many of them are also applicable to the source materials of local history. An increasing number of departments of history during the past decade or so have also introduced courses that involve students (among them future teachers) in local and family history research. Thus the opportunities for students to receive training in historical research methods have increased somewhat. A growing number of students in university history courses are also presumably being exposed to the literature on community history, which provides indispensable background knowledge for local history investigations. While the prospects for teachers who are currently being trained have improved somewhat, in-service training in the use of local source materials is still minimal and inadequate.

The vast majority of teachers now in the classrooms have received no formal training whatsoever in local history research. To use local history materials effectively, teachers will either have to train themselves or arrange for their school districts to provide a more formal in-service training program. Manuals such as this one may make the former somewhat easier to do, but they are poor substitutes for local institutes and workshops that can introduce the participants to the source materials available in each community. That kind of training should be made available for history teachers. Even if teachers who are now in the classroom do receive adequate help in locating and using local history sources, the question of how to integrate local history into the school curriculum still remains unanswered.

The answer to that question depends very much upon why a teacher wishes to use local history. What is the point of teaching with local history? What educational value does it have? While teachers have answered these questions in different ways over the past several decades, the basic rationale for using local history in the classroom has remained remarkably stable. Two of the most fundamental and persistent reasons were stated by Mary Sheldon Barnes in 1895: "In local history alone can the teacher most nearly bring [a] pupil face to face with all the sources, and give . . . the best training that history has . . . in accuracy, the nice weighing of evidence, the sympathetic interpretation of the past. In the second place, through local history the citizen finds a close and intimate connection with the great whole." [21] In other words, local history provides training in critical thinking, and it is an avenue into larger areas of historical experience. Other reasons that are sometimes mentioned tend to fall within the general area of citizenship education. It is said that local history investigations help students understand the problems of the local community and will make students more aware of local social and political institutions. Whether or not local history investigations will make students better citizens when they become adults is another question; but the principal reasons that teachers have given have always been that local history helps students understand larger historical developments and that it is useful for developing skills. These two basic reasons have very different implications for the curriculum.

If local history is to be used primarily to help students develop research and critical-thinking skills, it must be used in a course that can function as a research seminar much of the time. The students will not benefit much from the casual assignment of an out-of-class term paper to be completed with minimum supervision. The haphazard use of some poorly developed skills should not be confused with skills development. To accomplish the latter will require a course in which a great deal of time can be devoted to that purpose. Class time should be spent teaching students how to use bibliographies and indexes before they go to the library. Oral history manuals stress the importance of students conducting practice interviews before they go out to interview their subjects.[22] Class time is also needed to give students individual attention as they define their research topics and develop a strategy for research. The teacher will have to spend still more time helping them with writing skills when the students submit the early drafts of their written reports.

Although segments of an existing course could be set aside for such a purpose, the ideal situation would be a one-semester elective course in local history. Such a course would also provide sufficient time for the students to learn about the history of the community in some breadth while also investigating one topic in depth. The local history course developed by one of the authors at Boulder High School, for example, includes visits to the classroom and talks by local historians, historical slide presentations, architectural-history walking tours, and other class sessions in which all of the students are learning about the history of the town. During other sessions the students are working with the teacher individually or are independently pursuing their own research. Making room for a research project in a more traditional course in which other content has to be covered would probably lead to a more narrowly focused treatment of local history and research projects of less value for skills development.

Can an elective course in local history be justified, given the demands that already exist upon the students' time and an already overcrowded social studies curriculum? Are the skills to be developed worth such a substantial investment of time? Are they more important than knowledge that might be gained from other social studies courses that these students will not have time to take? These are questions that must be confronted by any school district that is considering the addition of a local history course to its curriculum. British curriculum developers justify the time students spend on local historical studies partly as preparation for later leisure-time activities. Whether American educators can assume that very many of their students will make a hobby of local history in later years is another question. Skills used in locating, organizing, and reporting information do have practical value beyond historical research. They are likely to be essential skills for college students or for college-bound secondary students, especially those majoring or planning to major in humanities and social science disciplines. From a purely utilitarian point of view, a local history course might be easier to justify for some students than for others.

Adding a local history course to the curriculum is not the only way to use local history in the classroom. It has been used most often in the service of another history or social science course. In the colleges these courses are invariably history courses. At the secondary school level, they include history, American studies, and various social science courses. Used as a component of another course, the principal purpose of local history usually is to illustrate some aspect of course content.

Teachers have discovered a great variety of ways in which local history can be used for that purpose. The most obvious use is as a source of illustrations for courses in United States history or state history. Surely every teacher has made offhand reference to some local example of industrialization or urbanization or of the New Deal's public works program. While these are not very sophisticated uses of local history, they may add concreteness to a history lecture. It is far more valuable to have students actively involved in using the materials of local history. The use of oral history techniques is one way that can be done. For example, students in

American history courses have gone out to interview local residents about the Great Depression.[23] Walking tours and brief excursions to sites of historical interest are frequently used by teachers in American history and other social studies courses. Some focus on local architecture or industrial sites; others on neighborhoods or districts within the community that reflect larger social and economic changes.[24] Teachers have also brought data from local city directories or manuscript census returns to class to let students test hypotheses about social mobility or examine ethnic migration patterns.[25] The possibilities are virtually unlimited.

While such local history activities place less responsibility upon the students than do independent research projects, they make substantial demands upon the teacher's time. Assignments that require students to go out into the community to examine buildings or neighborhoods of historical importance require careful preparation and considerable historical research. Social history activities may require the teacher to collect data from the federal census and from city directories. A slide collection of historical photographs is virtually indispensable for activities that focus on the history of important districts and neighborhoods of the community. Finally, the integration of new material into an old course will require that time be spent reorganizing parts of the course and bringing the teacher's historical knowledge up to date.

The great advantage of such use of local history is that it can be done by the teacher on a very selective basis and does not need to be done all at once. New activities can be introduced and further developed over a period of several semesters. Moreover, nothing much is lost if a one- or two-day classroom activity is not entirely successful the first time around. That is decidedly not true of a separate local history course. A substantial failure there represents the waste of an entire course.

The concreteness of local history examples can also be an important aid to conceptual learning. Local social history projects, for example, can be used to explain a variety of sociological concepts. The Minnesota Social History Project developed a model activity based on manuscript census data about two local families. The material shows in a simple but impressive way the migration route of each family, ethnic differences, changing household structure and family size, extent of upward social mobility, and changing economic roles of women.[26] Such economic concepts as industrialization, specialization of labor, or obsolescence of skills can likewise be illustrated by census or city directory data about the occupations of local residents. Insurance maps, city zoning ordinances and master plans, and city directories enable one to explore the many facets of the idea of segregation—economic, functional, ethnic, or racial. Local election data has similar and obvious uses for illustrating concepts from political science.

In the chapters that follow, we have tried to develop in much greater detail the curricular implications for both of these major uses of local history. We have divided the book into three major sections. Part 1 deals with the methods and sources commonly used in teaching local history. Chapter 1 is primarily concerned with the skills that can be developed through the use of local history sources and research methods that students can use to develop those skills. Chapter 2 describes major sources of local history. Chapter 3 presents techniques for using material culture as local history sources. In Part 2, we have described a variety of local history activities that can be used in history and social studies courses, either to make larger historical developments more concrete or to help make abstract ideas more understandable. Chapter 4 describes family history activities; chapter 5 presents activities dealing with economic history; chapter 6 suggests activities to be used in dealing with social history; and chapter 7 discusses the use of local history sources in teaching about political history. Finally, Part 3, chapter 8, describes techniques one might use to set up a local history course.

Part 1
Methods and Sources

1

Methods, Skills, and Techniques for Doing Local History

L OCAL history activities have a great many possibilities for helping students develop useful skills. That potential is partly inherent in the materials of local history and partly in the processes in which they are used. Even the most simple activities usually involve students in the use of primary sources, with historical data being organized, evaluated, interpreted, or manipulated in one way or another. Of course, some kinds of projects demand more of students than others. Those that engage students directly in historical research have extraordinary possibilities and can be deliberately exploited for that purpose.

Most research projects in local history can help students develop greater proficiency in the use of a library. Students will need to do more than find their way to the card catalogue. Researching a local history topic will bring them into contact with the reference librarian, the government documents section, the microfilmed-newspaper collection, and the local history or manuscripts section, should the library have one. Students will have the opportunity to learn how to use finding guides, historical bibliographies, and various indexes to historical literature. They should come away with a much fuller understanding of the library as a complex system for locating and retrieving information and an increased ability to use it. And for many projects, that will be only the beginning.

Tracking down elusive information that is not in the library will give students experience in dealing with a variety of agencies and people. The local historical society, the historical museum, and the municipal and county government offices housing estate records and wills, property transfer and tax records, and plats and maps are major repositories of historical information. The bureaucratic procedures of some of these agencies can be rather intimidating to the inexperienced. Indeed, in some parts of the country, students may find it virtually impossible to get access to some of these records. Even if they are only partially successful, learning to deal with these gatekeepers of public information will be no small or insignificant accomplishment. Seeking out people for oral history interviews, learning to ask good questions and to listen well may help students develop other skills. Still other opportunities will be created, once the research is completed.

The information that student researchers have compiled will have to be evaluated, organized, and put together in some meaningful way. It will have to be subjected to that critical process by which data about the past is transformed into meaningful history. Is the information accurate? Is the source reliable? Was the author biased? Is the information sufficient for the student's purpose? Can questionable facts be verified? What is the best way to organize the data? What does it all mean? In the process, a number of so-called critical-thinking skills are brought into play; or at least the opportunity is there for students to gain some experience in using data in a critical way. If a written report is called for, still other skills will be involved. Students will get practice in organizing their thoughts and in constructing coherent paragraphs and grammatically correct sentences.

In actual practice, many of the methods, skills, and techniques needed for doing local history projects will be overlapping. In this chapter, however, we will try to describe systematically the several kinds of skills normally involved at each stage in a local history project. These stages will include research, evaluation, critical analysis and synthesis of data, and the reporting of the results to others.

Research in the Sources of Local History

Typically, a variety of sources are used in historical research for projects. Different kinds of projects require different sources and methods of research. Here we shall describe five kinds of sources that students are likely to use and some of the research methods appropriate to each.

Written Sources

Sources in the school and university libraries. Research using written sources, published or unpublished, is the most traditional kind of historical investigation. It is the basis for most of the historical literature that has been produced over the years and no doubt always will be the dominant mode of historical research. Most students will have done a report, if not a term paper, and they will have some proficiency in the use of what are typically called library skills.

As part of the orientation to research, the teacher might wish to develop a worksheet for students to use as they start their library work. Besides alerting students to the fact that something appears in print about their community, however great or little that might be, a worksheet provides the teacher an opportunity to determine which students need help with simple, basic research skills, and which students may be turned out to work on their own. A sample library tour-guide for secondary school students is included in the appendix, along with instructions for developing a research strategy suitable for college-level students.

Most school and university libraries now have part of their periodical collection on microfilm or microfiche. If students have not had practice using these machines, teachers might also devise a worksheet that requires their use; some students, like some adults, are "machine shy," and they will often skip such research if they can. Three or four questions to be answered from the contents of a particular newspaper or historical society magazine will ensure that they at least have some practice running the machine.

After students have used the library tour-guide and have had some experience working their way around the library, they should begin the task of finding appropriate sources for their own projects. Certainly, the first step should be the bibliographical search utilizing finding guides, historical bibliographies, guides to manuscript collections, newspaper files, and pamphlet and clipping files. Sometimes there will also be an index for a photo-

Plate 1.1.   Students quickly become proficient at using the microfiche reader.

graphic collection and a special reference collection of maps. A few students will also need to be told of the browsing or serendipity method of finding materials. Most libraries have some areas of open stacks. If a student has located a book that seems useful, he should look at the books on either side of that volume. Since books are catalogued by subject matter, it is likely that such browsing will add several sources to the bibliography. It must be pointed out that some students use this as their *only* method of search, and that of course must be discouraged.

When the basic sources have been identified by the bibliographic search, the student must then exploit those sources. That does not just mean copying on note cards information pertinent to the topic, but noting other bibliographic leads found in footnotes and elsewhere. That needs to be made explicit. Note-taking techniques are taught in English classes, and it is not necessary to become a teacher of writing, except for those few students who claim never to have had such training or who "forget" from year

Plate 1.2. The Readers' Guide to Periodical Literature *can be a useful tool for research.*

to year. It is a simple matter to run off copies of proper bibliographic citation forms for books, periodicals, interviews, and public documents. It is also helpful to provide examples of properly identified note cards. Any good handbook of English usage or guide to historical methods will provide such examples.

Sample note cards will show students that proper note-taking will eventually help them in the organization of their data. Cards can be sorted and resorted as one works through a tentative outline for the presentation of materials. That procedure also allows students to determine very quickly what part of the research might be considered complete, and which aspects require further work or must be discarded because of the lack of enough information to make that particular section of the project worthwhile.

Other libraries and data repositories. Public and municipal libraries and historical societies have many local history materials that are seldom found even in the best of school and university librar-

Plate 1.3. Note-taking is an essential step in the research process.

ies. Such holdings may include business and city directories, insurance maps, files of clippings, pamphlets and other ephemera,
collections of photographs and drawings, tape recordings, manuscript collections, diaries and journals, and, frequently, local and
federal government documents such as records of the fire and
police departments and state and federal manuscript census
records.

Other repositories of useful data include various city and
county offices. Assessors' offices will have such records as the
names and addresses of the owners of property, appraisors' records, and maps. County offices will hold records of all property
transactions and estate records. The office responsible for city
planning and city engineering is a good source for maps and
building permits, and a useful source for descriptions of buildings
is often the local historic preservation office.

Finally, local newspaper offices frequently have libraries open

Plate 1.4.   A library's vertical file may also be a rich source of information.

to the public. Their files can be of great use to students in the research phase of their projects. Research methods to be used in these libraries or repositories will be substantially the same as those used in the school or university libraries, but finding guides and indexes will be specialized and the librarian or clerk in charge will explain the proper procedure for their use to students.

Oral History Research

Oral history can be an important method for collecting information for local history projects. Oral history is not an end in itself, but just another method of research. The tapes will be only as valuable as the questions asked, and the questions depend upon the particular purposes of the research. In that sense, the oral history method of research is similar to traditional methods of research. The same kinds of questions are raised about the subject; the same search for sources is conducted; in fact, the same kinds of basic research is done. Willa Baum makes that point very clearly:

> Oral history is not a substitute for this basic research. It is, rather, a second chance to pick up information that has never been saved in any other form, or it might be used to obtain vivid eye-witness accounts of important events. It might be used to validate data found in other sources, to collect up-to-date information, to obtain opinions reflecting different points of view or simply to acquire background or perspective on a topic of research. The novel aspect of oral history is that it is just one other aspect of researching—the asking of questions from a human rather than a printed source.[1]

If the oral history is to be a useful part of the research, then the interview must be as carefully planned as the basic research was conducted. The first step is for students to analyze the already-gathered materials and then determine what kinds of questions they still have about the topic. These questions should be organized in outline form for use during the actual interview or series of interviews.

Locating the people who have first-hand knowledge about the topic is the second step. Many students will have family members, neighbors, or friends who might be interviewed, or they may know of someone with knowledge of a particular topic; but the teacher should also be prepared to provide the names of some of these human resources. Local historical societies are usually of great help. They may have had oral history projects of their own; many of their members may be knowledgeable about specific topics. Individuals interested in local history can make suggestions. Fraternal and church organizations often have elderly members who know the community well. Senior citizens' clubs and retirement villages usually have members or residents who are delighted to be asked to participate. It takes only a couple of hours to set up a file listing the names of such people and the subjects they feel competent to discuss. Each student who does an oral history project or a series of interviews should add his information to such a file.

Most students will need some practice before they become competent interviewers. That can be accomplished by dividing the class into groups of three, with each group using a portable cassette recorder. Choose any topic of current interest in the school and have each group develop a series of questions that will illuminate the topic. Then have one person interview another, while the third member of the team observes the process and jots down notes on good techniques for asking questions. Each person should have an opportunity to be interviewed, to interview, and to act as critic. When all the students have completed this task, the teacher should listen to the tapes and pick out sections for the class to listen to the next day. As that is done, teachers should make critical comments: "Why was this a good question?" "Why was this a clever follow-up question?" "Note how this student changed the direction of the conversation." "Note how this student picked up on a comment that seemed to be an aside, but proved to be more useful than the original topic at hand."

After this initial experience, students should do at least one more practice interview, perhaps five or ten minutes long. This practice interview should be done outside the classroom. We have found it useful to allow some latitude in choice of subject and interviewee, but we also suggest that, if all students interview a family member on perceptions of the local community, we will have an interesting session when these tapes are played back for the class. Students are often surprised to hear the many different perspectives that people have on their community. The teacher has an important responsibility at this point: although it takes a long time and can be very dull, the teacher really should listen to each completed practice tape and write a detailed response to it. It is very much the same procedure one uses when students turn in rough drafts of term papers. Constructive criticism at this point can make a good deal of difference in the completed project.

It is usually helpful to give students a typed list of the tips for doing an interview. Such a list can be used as a reference when the class listens to the practice tapes, and it can act as a useful review when students go out to do a project tape. One might tape a copy to the lid of the tape recorder, along with the directions for running the machine. There are any number of good manuals on the methods of oral history; many of them are described in chapter 2. Most contain checklists similar to this one, which is excerpted and slightly adapted from Willa Baum's classic work.

Tips for Interviewers

1. An interview is not a dialogue. The whole point of the interview is to get the narrator to tell *his* story. Limit your own remarks to a few pleasantries to break the ice, then ask brief questions to guide him along.

2. Ask questions that require more of an answer than yes or no. Start with *Why, How, Where, What kind of . . . .* Instead of "Was Henry Miller a good boss?" ask "What did the cowhands think of Henry Miller as a boss?"

3. Ask one question at a time. Sometimes interviewers ask a series of questions all at once. Probably the narrator will answer only the first or last one. You will catch this kind of questioning when you listen through the tape after the session, and you can avoid it the next time.

4. Ask brief questions. . . . It is unlikely that the narrator is so dull that it takes more than a sentence or two for him to understand the question.

5. Start with noncontroversial questions; save the delicate questions, if there are any, until you have become better acquainted.

6. Don't let periods of silence fluster you. Give your narrator a chance to think of what he wants to add before you hustle him along with the next question. Relax, write a few words on your note pad. The sure sign of a beginning interviewer is a tape where every brief pause signals the next question.

7. Don't worry if your questions are not as beautifully phrased as you would like them to be for posterity. A few fumbled questions will help put your narrator at ease as he realizes that you are not perfect, and he need not worry if he isn't, either. It is unnecessary to practice fumbling a few questions; most of us are nervous enough to do that naturally.

8. Don't interrupt a good story because you have thought of a question, or because your narrator is straying from the planned outline. If the information is pertinent, let him go on, but jot down your question on your note pad so you will remember to ask it later.

9. If your narrator does stray into nonpertinent subjects
. . . try to pull him back as quickly as possible: "Before we move
on, I'd like to find out. . . . "

10. It is often hard for a narrator to describe persons. An easy
way to begin is to ask him to describe the person's appearance.
From there, the narrator is more likely to move into character
description.

11. Try to establish at every important point in the story
where the narrator was or what his role was in the event under
discussion, in order to indicate how much is eye-witness information and how much is based on reports of others. "Where were
you at the time of the mine disaster?" "Did you talk to any of the
survivors later?" . . . Work around these questions carefully, or
you can appear to be doubting the accuracy of the narrator's
account.

12. Do not challenge accounts you think may be inaccurate.
Instead, try to develop as much information as possible that can
be used by later researchers in establishing what probably happened.

13. Don't switch the recorder off and on. It is much better to
waste a little tape on irrelevant material than to call attention to
the tape recorder by constant on-off operation. . . . Of course you
can turn off the recorder if the telephone rings or if someone
interrupts your session.

14. Interviews usually work out better if there is no one present except the narrator and the interviewer. [If two of you go to
an interview, have one person take notes while the other asks the
questions. You may switch roles in the middle of the interview if
you wish. Interviewees can find it confusing to have two people
asking questions.]

15. Do end the interview at a reasonable time. An hour and a
half is probably maximum.

16. Don't use the interview to show off your own knowledge,
vocabulary, charm, or other abilities. Good interviewers do not
shine; only their interviews do.[2]

To that list, one might wish to add one more item, if students
are interviewing older people. It very often happens that, in the
process of talking about the past, some unpleasant or sad memories are brought to the mind of the narrator. If the student thinks
that might be happening, he should spend a little time after the

interview has been concluded, talking about present-day events of a pleasant nature—the interviewee's garden, a cherished pet, a present hobby, and so on.

Students will usually have some experience with the operation of a tape recorder, but often they are not nearly so expert as they think. Do have them practice using the machine. Many otherwise good interviews have been ruined by the neglect of a few simple rules.

Tips for Using the Tape Recorder

1. Use tapes of the best quality available.
2. To avoid machine noise, place the machine and the microphone on different surfaces (unless of course you are using a machine with a built-in mike; then try to place the machine on a padded surface).
3. Place the microphone on a padded surface on a table between you and the narrator.
4. Turn the machine on immediately and let it run as you and the narrator become acquainted. Before you begin the actual interview, play back what has been recorded to make sure that the machine is working properly and that the volume control is correctly set.
5. Keep an eye on the tape so that you will remember to turn it over.
6. Leave enough blank tape so that you can make a formal introduction later. Do not make the narrator nervous by doing it at the time of the interview.
7. *Always* take an extension cord with you.[3]

Documentation

Just as one expects students to observe proper form in written work, one must expect them to follow the proper protocol in dealing with oral history. Students must always obtain permission from the person interviewed to use the information on the tape. They should bring a release form to the interview, explain its purpose, and ask the interviewee to sign it. The release form used at Boulder High School, based on the form used at the Bancroft Library at the University of California at Berkeley,[4] is reproduced

Boulder High School: Local History

I hereby give and grant to the Local History class of Boulder High School as a donation for scholarly and educational purposes as the class shall determine the tape recordings and their contents listed below.

_____

Name of Narrator

_____

Address of Narrator

_____

Name of Interviewer

_____

Date of Agreement

Subject of Tape(s):

If you would like any additional information on this project, please contact Fay Metcalf at Boulder High School.

Fig. 1.1.   Release form used by Boulder High School students taping oral history interviews.

in figure 1.1. To help catalogue the completed tape, the student should also fill out an acquisition form such as that in figure 1.2.

Research Using Three-Dimensional Objects

Buildings, museum artifacts, and other three-dimensional objects can also be valuable sources for local history. Students are less likely to have the skills necessary to use such materials, since in most cases their training will have been greater in the area of

Boulder High School Local History Tape Collection

General Topic of Interview_____

Date_____ Place_____ Length_____

Personal Data:

Narrator   *Interviewer*

Name_____   Name_____

Address_____   Address_____

Name, address of relative, friend

_____   _____

_____   _____

Birthplace_____

_____

Birth date_____   What was the occasion of the interview

Occupation(s)_____   _____

_____   _____

_____   _____

INTERVIEW DATA

Side 1   Subjects covered, in approximated ord

Side 2   (Please spell out the names of persons

Estimated time on tape   and places mentioned.)

_____   _____

_____   _____

_____   _____

_____   _____

_____   _____

_____   _____

_____   _____

_____   _____

_____   _____

Fig. 1.2.   Sample acquisition form to help in cataloguing an oral history interview tape.

printed materials. The methods and skills necessary for utilizing the sources of architecture, sculpture, tools and weapons, and other realia are primarily those we associate with visual literacy. Basically, visual literacy may be defined as the ability to decode nonverbal messages. Such decoding can be done only if two conditions are met: first, students must be taught the language of vision. The eye must perceive light, shape, movement, color, texture, lines, patterns, similarities, and contrasts. But physical perception is not enough. The second condition is that students must be taught to bring to the object to be decoded information from other sources. To "read" *visually* is similar to reading *verbally*; the completeness and quality of the "reading" relates directly to the completeness and quality of the reader's stored information. We see what we want to see, and we see in terms of what we already know or believe. That is, we see what we are looking for—what we have been trained to see.

There are a number of approaches one might take to help students increase their visual literacy. One can help them learn the language of vision and extend their stored knowledge by having them practice reading artifacts. One very useful guide is supplied by Fred Schroeder in his technical leaflet, *Designing Your Exhibits: Seven Ways to View an Artifact*.[5] The local museum may be able to set up a series of exhibits for you and your students to practice on, or the teacher may wish to adapt the following set of statements to established exhibits in the local museum. This list is adapted from Schroeder's work:

1. Reading with your hands. This technique involves more than having students handle specific items. It also involves their attempts to create the object. Trying to dip candles, spin wool into yarn, or flake a flint—any such activity done before a trip to a museum—will make the artifacts to be examined more meaningful. They will *know* how an artifact will *feel*.

2. How was it used? This method concentrates on the practical function of the artifact. The questions students should ask are "How is/was it used?" and "Why *this* artifact and *this* use at *this* time and in *this* place?" The physical act of using the artifact—even if only carried part-way—can make the student more sensitive to the artifact and to other things like it. Students cannot heat a flatiron on a coal stove, but they can try to press a fabric with it.

3. What was its environment? As Schroeder states, sickles and hayforks did not exist in museums, but in fields. If the museum you will be visiting cannot place such items in a fabricated environment, the teacher can do so before or after the museum visit.

Either book illustrations or student-drawn murals can produce the sense of "realness" that may not be felt at a museum.

4. Development through time. With this method, one is attempting to relate an artifact to its relatives in the developmental history of the object. One thinks again of the flatiron and its modern form of electric steam iron. This time dimension adds the value of comparison and detail to the examination of artifacts. If the museum itself does not make such comparisons, the teacher may provide them for the student. Prior experience—that is, knowledge of the evolution of an item—can enhance the students' understanding.

5. Cross-cultural comparisons. Here comparison is also used, but rather than a chronology of development, the emphasis is on analogues in different cultures. Toys are obvious examples. Values of a culture can often be determined from toys. Other general classes of items that could be examined cross-culturally would include cooking utensils, weapons, light sources, musical instruments, and agricultural implements.

6. Noting the influences. Far more abstract than the other methods, this technique examines the influences that can be discerned in the design and decoration of the artifact. Students who have studied influences in the arts will enjoy this method, but it is appropriate for other areas as well. Architecture is an obvious example. Every city in America has examples of Greek, Roman, or Gothic style motifs. The museum building itself is a good place to start pointing out influences. A less obvious example is the design influence from wagon to automobile. Overall design tends to remain constant, even when function changes. Consider the numerous types of hammers: claw hammers for pulling nails, lightweight hammers to be used when balloon-frame construction developed, hammers especially used by shoemakers, upholsterers, masons, and auto-body specialists. Other designs might work as well, but hammers are still recognized as influenced by the original hammer.

7. Functional meanings or values. Most religious items would fall into this category. There are images that serve as media between the viewer and greater truths and meanings and values. But the "wish book" mail order catalog can also illustrate this type of artifact. Whenever people express feelings about a thing, the function of that thing is more than practical. It will have to do

with deeply rooted value systems, aesthetic, mythical, and iconological.

A second useful approach to the examination of artifacts is a model designed by E. McClung Fleming. He suggests that there are five basic properties through which any artifact can be examined. These properties include history, material, construction, design, and function. Each item has a *history*. One asks, where and when was it made? By whom? For whom and why? Have there been any changes made in condition or function? It is important to know who owned it? What is its *material*? Is it made of wood? Ceramics? Glass? Fibers? Metals? What can one make of the *construction*? Is it machine-made? Hand-made? Does it show careful workmanship? What are its parts? How can they be put together? What is the *design*? What can one say about structure? Form? Style? Ornamentation? Symbols used? What is the *function* of the object? How was it intended to be used? To what other purposes might/has it been put? Was it meant to be utilitarian? Used for pleasure? To be simply looked at and enjoyed?[6]

The analysis, the making sense of this data, uses the properties described above through a series of steps that will help organize the data. Fleming's steps are similar to those used by art historians and include identification or factual description, evaluation or judgment, cultural analysis—relationship of the artifact to its culture—and interpretation or significance. One can use these or similar operations with the students. The object of using either Schroeder's or Fleming's approaches to the examination of artifacts is twofold. First, it makes students realize that, just as there is a step-by-step approach to researching written sources—bibliography search, utilizing finding guides, and so on—so is there a methodology involved in closely examining artifacts, be they tools, weapons, houses, statutes in front of the courthouse, or tombstones in the local cemetery.

Research Using Photographs

Photographs are among the most used and most useful sources for studying local history. They can recreate the atmosphere of a main street, show the manner in which tasks were performed at some time in the past, illustrate particular architectural detail, indicate styles of clothing in a particular era; and, when used in conjunction with other sources, they may even be used to illustrate social class or sex roles at some particular time or place. Unless students are taught the techniques of analyzing photographs, however, they tend to see nothing more than "interesting" or "pretty" pictures.

To use photographs effectively, teachers and students must keep in mind two basic points. First, pictures do not really speak for themselves except in the most superficial way. Students must be trained to study photographs carefully and to pull from them the information contained. Second, the amount and types of evidence that can be extracted from the photograph depends upon how much the viewer already knows about the topic depicted. The more knowledge brought to bear upon it, the richer the photograph becomes.

> One viewer looking at a lithograph . . . of a busy intersection in New York City in the 1870s may see it as little more than a prototype of a modern traffic jam. To another observer who has some knowledge of architectural history, of nineteenth-century fashion design, and of the history of transportation and construction technology, the picture will be a highly informative historical document. It is largely because of the demands that pictures make upon the viewer that they are such useful learning tools.[7]

How can one help students learn to "read" photographs? Robert U. Akeret suggests that one can "Learn to read any photo as you would read a book, from left to right, then downward. Go over it again and again, each time trying to pick up something you have missed. Ask yourself more general questions, as many as you can think of." [8]

Other methods of observation are also useful. One might break the photograph down into smaller components (background, foreground, groups of objects or people, individual items, portions of the human body) and examine each carefully. One might use a worksheet like that designed for such a purpose by the Chicago Metro History Fair staff:

Studying a Photograph

Directions: Complete this chart and attach the photograph you have studied.

    1. First reactions: Jot down whatever first impressions you get about the photograph itself, the persons or objects in the photo, or your feelings.

    2. Detailed examination: List all the facts about the photo you can see.
Photograph itself: *People   Objects   Interior   Exterior*

    3. Facts known from other sources: Indicate here the actual place and date of the photo if not on the photo itself, the names of the people, etc.

    4. Characteristic expression or spatial relationships of persons or objects in the photo.

    5. Describe the mood of the photograph: Formal, candid, happy, unhappy, indifferent, etc..

    6. Considered reactions: Jot down how you feel about the photograph now that you have studied it and what unanswered questions you may have.[9]

Such tasks incorporate many of the skills involved in the mental process of reading photographs. Martin Sandler feels that these skills can be divided into five categories that ascend from low-level to high-level mental processes. He believes that, if one leads students through this series of skills a number of times, the process "can become second-nature to a student." Slightly modified, the skills he lists are:

1. Students *collect data* about the photograph itself. They make lists of such things as the number of people in the picture, types of action depicted, types of clothing, tools or weapons shown, etc.

2. Students *classify* or *sort data* into a matrix that uses the same general headings as in Step 1, but in more detail. For example, types of clothing (buckskins, uniforms) become *kinds* of clothing (hats, coats, footwear).

3. Students *make generalizations* about the data from the now-classified lists. Examples might include such statements as, "The people in the photograph represent members of the same social class (they are all dressed in similar finery)," or "The buildings along this street were built at different times (they reflect several styles of architecture)."

4. Students *draw inferences* or *make probability statements* about the photo. "People working on the assembly line are turning out large quantities of goods (they seem to be too busy to look up at the photographer and all of the peoples' hands are in motion)."

5. Students *make predictions* or *draw conclusions*. They go beyond the evidence to draw conclusions from unknowns. They learn to guess within reasonable boundaries, and to judge.[10]

One must be careful with this last point when photographs are being used as primary evidence. Other data should always be brought to bear to test out the predictions or conclusions drawn.

An example of a photograph that must be carefully examined lest wrong inferences be drawn is that of the picture of the ox team on the main street of a western town which appears in plate 1.5. What is happening? When is the event taking place? At first glance, students will say that they see a freight wagon parked along the street and that the time must be in the 1880s, since many of the buildings are known to have been built at that time. A closer look will reveal that clothing styles do not suit those times, and there is a telltale street light in the background. The actual event depicted was the celebration of fifty years of the town's existence, and the pageant shown was meant to show the "good old days."

Plate 1.5.   What is happening in this photograph? When was the photograph taken?—Colorado Historical Society; reprinted by permission.

There is one other skill that students must be taught if they are going to make their own photographs for projects, rather than just study them for information. They need to learn to keep careful records about the pictures they shoot. It is amazing how much detail about a particular frame can be forgotten between the time photographs are shot and time one views the contact sheet, a week or so later. For each photographing session, students should keep a data form that includes such things as film roll number, number of each shot on the roll, and a brief written description of each shot. That would include the address where the picture was made, the names, addresses, and telephone numbers of all the people who appear in the picture, the general appearance of buildings pictured, if they are the subject or appear in the background, and the angle from which the shot was made ("southeast corner of 12th and Main," for instance). And in some instances—if one is doing a series of buildings or other similar items—back-up sketches can be useful.

If one plans to use student-made photographs for classroom activities or for published materials, it is important that students obtain photograph-release forms from the people involved. These are needed whether one is photographing the people themselves or their possessions. Few persons would really object if one were to use a picture of their business or house, but it is wise to have documented permission. One can use a simple form such as that in figure 1.3.

Research Using Quantitative Data

The fundamental difference between the quantitative method and other approaches to historical study is the type of data used. As the name implies, quantification is used for information that can be counted or tabulated in some manner. The basic skills used are counting; rank ordering; averaging for central tendency (finding the mean, median, and mode); reading, interpreting and constructing tables and graphs; and working with standard deviation.[11] In most school and undergraduate projects, especially if the data must be manipulated by hand, the students will probably wish to use only descriptive statistics such as central tendency, categorizing by percentages and perhaps simple cross-tabulation. Examples of some of these uses can be found in tables 1.1 and 1.2.

Table 1.1 shows how such records were used to examine the number of people employed in twenty-five occupations. Developing a data sheet such as this would provide the students with practice in working with percentages and rank-ordering. One could then go on and use more of the census material to develop charts such as that shown in table 1.2, which uses the variables of sex and places of birth to show, among other things, that women of foreign birth fared much worse than men of foreign birth in holding jobs above the unskilled level.

Manipulating the data for charts such as those shown in tables 1.1 and 1.2 can be time-consuming. If one has access to the use of a computer, then the use of the Statistical Package for the Social Sciences can be helpful. It is available at most university computer centers or libraries. If one must deal with the data by hand, then

Photograph Release Form

I hereby give and grant to the Local History class at Boulder High School my permission for the photographs described below to be used for scholarly and educational purposes, including publication in published materials.

Subject and description of photograph(s)   Dates of photo, if known

_____   _____

_____   _____

_____   _____

_____   _____

_____   _____

_____   _____

_____   _____

_____   _____

_____   _____

Please list the full names of all people represented in the photographs (from left to right as one views the picture).

_____

_____

_____

_____

_____

_____   _____
Date of Agreement   Name of donor or model

                                _____
                                Address of donor or model

                                _____
                                Name of recipient of photos or
                                photographer

Fig. 1.3. Example of photograph release form.

TABLE 1.1

*Comparison of the Leading Twenty-Five Occupations
in Winona, Minnesota, 1880, 1905, by Number and Rank*

	1800			1905		
Occupation	*Number*	*Percent*	*Rank*	*Number*	*Percent*	*Rank*
Laborer	743	19.1	1	2056	24.0	1
Servant	413	10.1	2	798	9.3	2
Carpenter	187	4.8	3	239	2.8	6
Housekeeper	181	4.7	4	242	2.8	5
Dressmaker	117	3.0	5	243	2.8	4
Clerks	112	2.9	6	356	4.1	3
Railroad Workman	84	2.2	7	91	1.1	13
Teacher	72	1.9	8	236	2.7	7
Saw Mill Worker	69	1.8	9	6	0.07	150
Blacksmith	60	1.5	10	85	1.0	14
Painter	54	1.4	11	136	1.6	8
Tailor	54	1.4	11	48	0.6	24
Lumberyard Worker	45	1.2	13	31	0.4	53
Cooper	44	1.1	14	17	0.2	93
Teamster	43	1.1	15	102	1.2	11
Shoemaker	39	1.0	16	66	0.8	17
Grocer	39	1.0	17	34	0.4	48
Butcher	39	1.0	18	72	0.8	17
Hotel Owner	36	0.9	19	19	0.2	84
Farmer	33	0.9	20	66	0.8	17
Engineer	32	0.8	21	105	1.2	10
Machinist	31	0.8	23	98	1.1	11
Grocery Clerk	29	0.7	24	15	0.2	99
Saloon Keeper	28	0.7	25	40	0.5	40

SOURCE: *Manuscript of the Census of the United States, 1880, Population of the United States; Manuscript of the Census of Minnesota, 1905.* Reprinted from MISHAP 1 (December 1978), by permission of the Minnesota Social History Project, St. Mary's College, Winona, Minnesota.

one would tackle relatively simple analyses, and these can be done with the use of needle-sort cards (see figure 1.4). To use these cards, one simply codes each group of holes by notching them for particular characteristics (e.g., age, sex, occupation, place of birth). One must use a separate card for each person to be counted in the study. To retrieve information, one simply inserts a needle—a knitters' stitch-holder works well—into the hole that has been coded for the characteristic one is concerned with.

TABLE 1.2

*Occupational Rankings of the Workforce of Winona, Minnesota, 1880–1905
by Selected Places of Birth, Percentage by Sex*

	1880											
	Native		German		Polish		Irish		Norwegian		English	
	%M	%F	%M	%F	%M	%F	%M	%F	%M	%F	%M	%F
Professional, High White-Collar	4.0	0.2	1.4	0.0	0.0	0.0	1.3	0.0	0.0	0.0	3.6	0.0
Proprietor, Low White-Collar	30.9	17.5	17.0	8.4	8.9	4.2	11.6	10.3	13.1	1.4	25.3	13.3
Skilled	33.3	22.0	33.8	7.6	19.4	8.3	21.0	15.4	32.1	5.4	43.4	6.6
Specified, Unskilled	19.8	59.2	16.0	83.9	15.4	87.5	25.2	74.4	20.2	93.2	20.5	80.0
Unspecified, Unskilled	12.0	0.2	31.9	0.0	56.3	0.0	40.5	0.0	34.5	0.0	7.2	0.0
N =	1397	485	631	118	279	48	147	39	84	74	83	15

	1905											
	Native		German		Polish		Irish		Norwegian		English	
	%M	%F	%M	%F	%M	%F	%M	%F	%M	%F	%M	%F
Professional, High White-Collar	3.7	0.1	3.7	0.6	1.7	1.3	3.0	0.0	1.0	0.0	5.5	0.0
Proprietor, Low White-Collar	24.0	26.3	18.8	17.4	6.0	34.6	23.9	25.9	10.0	17.2	34.5	66.6
Skilled	30.7	17.0	32.2	21.5	13.0	5.1	30.0	0.0	49.0	17.2	30.9	0.0
Specified, Unskilled	15.6	48.8	14.9	50.6	8.1	52.6	17.9	59.3	14.5	48.3	16.4	33.3
Unspecified, Unskilled	25.9	7.8	30.4	9.9	71.0	6.4	25.4	14.8	24.5	17.2	12.7	0.0
N =	3285	2245	930	172	630	78	67	27	110	29	55	6

SOURCE: Reprinted from MISHAP 1 (December 1978), by permission of the Minnesota Social History Project, St. Mary's College, Winona, Minn.)

Perhaps an example will make this clear. If one asked the question, "How many people under the age of twenty-five were employed in the local shoe factory in 1880?" then one would insert the needle into the stack of cards three times. First, one would insert the needle in the hole coded for workers in the shoe fac-

Fig. 1.4. *This is a sample needle-sort card. Each set of holes represents a particular characteristic coded on the card (for example, land held, date of settlement, occupation).*—Reprinted by permission of Education Systems Research.

tory; all of these would fall off the needle and thus be sorted out. One would go through this smaller set of cards for the time period involved, and then through the last set of cards for people under age twenty-five. One could also determine how many of the factory workers were foreign-born or married. What is essential to keep in mind is that any data that one wished to retrieve must be punched into the cards. These cards and instructions for their use may be obtained from Education Systems Research, P.O. Box 157, Shrewsbury, Massachusetts 01545.

Many historians and many students find the use of such statistical data fascinating. The only real knowledge we have of some groups of people who lived in the past is this quantifiable data. Libraries and historical societies bulge with letters, journals, memoirs, and newspaper clippings that help us to reconstitute the lives of the elite of the community. The humble workman and his equally humble wife, children, relatives, and boarders may have left no personal documents concerning their lives. But it is nearly certain that there are public documents that give us some record of their existence. Birth and death records, marriage licenses, property transfer records, tax receipts, and state and federal census manuscripts are the types of documents that might be used to develop a profile of a particular group.

Public records are never free of error, of course. Clerks can misspell, miscount and misfile. The census enumerator sometimes "guessed" at the number of people living in a dwelling if he could not find them at home, or he may even have missed some dwellings altogether. Businessmen sometimes over- or underevaluated their assets, and so forth. There is also a further problem in the changing definitions of words. For example, *manufacturing* meant something very different in 1825 from what it meant in 1925. Sam Bass Warner, Jr., describes the problems involved in using data as census records and business directories:

> It is difficult to draw social generalizations from a detailed occupational list that goes on for pages in units of: 4 chocolate makers, 7 curriers, 1 engraver, 2 morocco workers, 4 willow-ware makers, 1 horse shoer, and so forth. On the other hand, old general categories like "at home," "laborer," "clerk," "mechanic," and so forth, cover so many conditions of life that it is hard to know what may lie beneath the general categories.
>
> These problems of definition, like the problems of the errors that can occur in the enumerations [of census data], require the local historian to regard his statistical material as an assembly of crude fragments out of which he must build his story in the same manner as any writer must. The statistical fragments, however carefully constructed, are an assembly to which only the historian's imagination can bring order.[12]

Teachers will want to keep such caveats in mind as they introduce students to the use of quantification in local history.

The local history projects to which quantifiable data is most useful are those concerning the characteristics of groups of people. What percentage of the laborers in the community were foreign-born? What was the usual rate of infant mortality in the community during the nineteenth century? What percentage of unskilled workers who remained in the community for a decade

or more moved up to white-collar occupations? Did voting precincts in ethnic neighborhoods tend to elect one political party's
candidates more regularly than another's? These are only a few
examples of the variety of local history topics that lend themselves
to research with quantifiable data.

Teachers who have not had personal experience using quantification for historical analysis may wish to examine the manual
for the Statistical Package for the Social Sciences (SPSS)[13] or to
consult one of the guides on the topic. A number of useful sources
are described in section 3 of chapter 2.

Evaluating, Analyzing and Organizing Researched Materials

While local history projects can help students develop a variety
of research skills, they can also bring into play those intellectual
processes used in organizing and interpreting information. They
are the essential ingredients in what historians call the historical
method. Educators sometimes refer to several of the processes as
"critical-thinking skills." By whatever name they are called, at least
the following processes are involved: evaluating and analyzing
information, organizing (synthesizing) information, and reporting information. Students can use all of these processes as they
prepare local history projects.

Evaluating and Analyzing Information

The critical evaluation of sources is the most essential element
of the historical method. It is this critical dimension, in all of its
ramifications, that distinguishes history from myth. Students must
be made constantly aware that the value of the information they
have collected is dependent upon the reliability of their sources.
And they must understand that all sources are suspect until
proven otherwise. At each step in the collection of their data, they
must examine materials using the skills of distinguishing fact
from opinion, recognizing bias and improper or unwarranted
assumptions, recognizing logical fallacies, and so on. Alice Eikenberry and Ruth Ellsworth provide a checklist that students might
use to examine information, whether it be from local histories,

personal interviews, eyewitness accounts, letters, personal diaries, public documents, or minutes from a school board meeting:

1. Who is the authority?
2. What is his background?
3. Is he speaking or writing on a subject on which he is a recognized authority?
4. What is the purpose of the material?
5. When and under what circumstances was the information recorded? Were primary sources used?
6. If a primary source, was the information written from memory or was it a direct account of what happened?
7. Is there corroboration of the facts from other sources?
8. Is the authority objective in the treatment of the material?
9. Is the material pertinent?[14]

For the evaluation of materials from sponsored sources or from public media, Eikenberry and Ellsworth suggest that these additional questions for evaluation be asked:

1. What organization is responsible for the materials?
2. What is the purpose of the materials?
3. Are the sources of information identified?
4. Does the conclusion seem justified on the basis of the facts presented?
5. Were all of the facts presented?
6. Does the authority distinguish between fact and opinion?
7. Do other sources agree with the presentation and interpretation of facts?[15]

In doing this sort of evaluation of sources, students have really begun the process of analysis. They are judging not only the source of the data, but the quality and significance of it, as well. But analysis involves much more. It also means to examine a document or photograph carefully to place it as accurately as possible in historical time, to identify correctly the various aspects or components of it, to get as much meaning as possible out of it. Much of the analysis will be done as students begin to organize their materials and plan the type of presentation they wish to make.

Organizing Information

Whether students are planning a narrative of the rise and demise of the local brewery, a study of the changing ethnic composition of a particular neighborhood or a photo-display of the changing styles of architecture in the business district of the city, they will have to decide on an effective way to organize their materials. If they have used checklists as they collected their data, they will find that most of the materials they have are germane to the topic. The next step they need to take is to come to some conclusions about the information gathered.

They should go through their stack of note cards, sorting them into smaller segments or aspects of the topic, and then read and reorganize the cards to make sense of the data and to see what conclusions can be drawn. From these conclusions the student will develop the thesis of the paper or project, which will also suggest how it should be organized. If students have little experience in writing papers or in presenting the results of research in other ways, they may need help in developing a plan for the organization of their data. Barry Beyer has developed a technique for helping students to do this. He calls his method a prewriting activity, and although it was developed for helping students produce a good written project, the technique is equally useful for other types of projects. Beyer suggests that the following set of questions might be used by students:

1. What is the problem or task facing you?
2. What main point do you wish/need to make?
3. What arguments can you use to support this point?
4. What evidence from the available data can you provide to support your arguments? What other evidence can you use?
5. What objections or questions might your readers raise? What might you say in response to these?
6. Why is (or ought to be) what you propose to write [say or show] important—to you? To your intended reader [audience]? To people in general? [16]

By writing out answers to these questions, students have in effect developed a rough outline that can be used as the basis for the more formal outline they may wish to develop before they actually write their papers or plan their presentations.

Reporting Information and Evaluating Projects

Students should be reminded that the first draft of a paper should always be considered a rough draft. The major task at this point is to present the basic information clearly and logically. When the first draft of the paper has been completed, they might go through the list of questions a second time to be sure that the material has been satisfactorily dealt with. Teachers should grade the rough drafts of the students' work. When papers are to be kept in the school files or are to be published in some way, it is important that they be as polished as possible.

Although rewriting can seem dull and pallid compared to the excitement of the research and the initial organization of the material, it is a most vital step if the project is to be good enough for students to feel real pride in their projects. Again, Beyer has some useful thoughts on this topic. Rewriting provides students an opportunity, he says:

> . . . to capitalize on what they have discovered about the topic . . . as they wrote their original drafts and to *re*-present these discoveries with greater clarity and completeness. The process of rewriting requires students to (1) evaluate the extent to which they accomplished their substantive goals; (2) revise their writing to improve the quality of their assertions and the logic of their arguments and to select more relevant information and evidence; and (3) repair (edit) errors in sentence structure, word usage, punctuation, and spelling.[17]

The above model for preparing a report is applicable to the traditional research paper. Similar procedures may be used in the writing of a script for a slide-tape presentation, an eight- or sixteen-millimeter film, or any other type of project presentation. Students need not be bound by traditional approaches in reporting on the data they have gathered and analyzed. One of the appeals of local history research is that it uses nontraditional approaches. The reporting of this research can be just as novel and students often choose a multimedia technique.

Because the scripting of an audiovisual presentation is a somewhat different task from that of writing an expository paper, however, students will perhaps need some special guidance. For teachers unfamiliar with such productions, Arthur L. Smith's

"Producing the Slide Show" [18] is helpful, as is Les Satterthwaite's *Graphics: Skills, Media and Materials.*[19] Satterthwaite's work is invaluable for teaching the skills needed in graphic projects of other kinds. The essential element for all types of reporting must always be the focus of the project and the careful consideration of the best ways of making the information clear to the anticipated audience.

This audience need not consist merely of classmates. Such civic groups as the Rotary Club, the Optimists, and the Sertoma Club of the local area are usually receptive to having students present slide-tape shows or short talks on the local history of the area. The local historical society or the public library staffs are often happy to allow students to set up photo-displays or exhibits of artifacts or models. Elementary and middle school teachers will usually welcome students who wish to make presentations to their classes. Charles Bennett and J. Michael Lenihan suggest several good reasons why projects concerning the community should be disseminated in this way:

> First, the project students are proud of their work, glad to show evidence of it, and enjoy the recognition that public programs provide. Second, the presentations help to make the project more a community effort than just a school project. . . . Third, these efforts awaken the curiosity of younger students and help to insure continued student interest in the project.[20]

Evaluating the Project

If the goals for the local history projects have been clearly defined before the students begin their work, then evaluation throughout the project should not be difficult to achieve. When checklists have been used as the students go through the various steps of research, analysis, and reporting, the evaluation has been continuous and has been an integral part of the work procedure. Teachers might also wish to require students to make periodic reports in which they list the progress made toward a definition of the project's contents, describe the methods of research they have used, list materials examined to that point, and note difficulties encountered in finding source materials and methods used to

Student's Name_____

Project Evaluation Form

	Points possible	Points granted
Bibliography and Note Cards (quantity, citation forms)	10	
Outline	5	
Mechanics of Writing (Capitalization, punctuation, sentence structure, usage, word choice)	10	
Quality of Content (Analysis, synthesis, flow of writing)	25	
Points possible	50	

Grading Scale:
    45—50 = A
    40—44 = B
    35—39 = C
    30—34 = D

COMMENTS:

Fig. 1.5.   Typical form for evaluating students' written projects.

overcome these difficulties. After teachers have read these progress reports, they will know which students need more individual
guidance and which students need only a suggestion or two to
keep them working productively.

The end products—the individual or group projects—must
also be evaluated. These can be graded as any other work in any

other course would be. A typical form for written projects is illustrated in figure 1.5.

However, evaluating a local history project involves more than the quality of the final report. There is also the question of how much each student learned in the process of doing it. The authors have both had students who turned in some rather poor projects that they knew did not reflect the value those projects had to the students as learning experiences. One should be equally concerned with individual students' growth. How one deals with that issue depends a good deal upon the level and the capacity of the students in the particular course and upon the teacher's own goals and philosophy of teaching.

2

Sources and Resources for
Local History

THIS chapter describes materials that students and teachers will find useful as they work on local history projects. It is neither a comprehensive finding guide for unpublished materials nor an exhaustive bibliography of published literature. Instead, it provides a description of commonly used unpublished resources available in most communities, a selected list of guides, manuals, and articles on aspects of local history and a description of possibilities for the collaboration of the schools with other agencies.

Local Sources for Local History

Many of the sources one needs to study local history are scattered among public agencies, local and state libraries and historical societies, and the files of local historians. Some are in the attics of long-time residents. Locating these materials can often be a difficult task. Unfortunately, there is no standard method for storing some of these useful records, and one must just keep asking until they are found. Sometimes, local libraries have developed finding guides for the study of a particular community.

One such work, *Guide to the Study of Lexington*, by Elizabeth G. Heath and Harry L. Taplin, was published by the Cary Memorial Library, Lexington, Massachusetts, in 1976. This book describes holdings of the library itself, the collections of the Lexington Historical Society, materials available at the governmental offices and departments of the town, and sources outside of the town proper.

Most certainly one would wish to see whether such a guide has been produced for his own community as a first step in materials collection. If no such publication exists, then one will wish to develop a finding guide of his own. As students complete projects each year, they should be encouraged to add the research information they have uncovered to a vertical file. After two or three years, one will have enough data to develop a finding guide for local materials. It is suggested that such a guide be kept in loose-leaf format, since additions will be made year after year.

Village, city, and county histories. Among the first sources one would wish to consult in developing a local history project of any kind are the already-published histories. Such histories usually describe the early years of settlement in detail. The founders of the community, the original economic base and the patterns of growth are often described with some thoroughness. Many of the early books or pamphlets were written on a subscription basis, and they often contain long and glowing accounts of the leading citizens. Although one must be cautious of obvious bias, the history may still contain important facts about the town's development. Other, more recent histories may have been carefully researched.

The earlier works may be difficult to locate. They were seldom printed in large quantities, and few have been reprinted—at least in their entirety. One should try the public library and local historical society first, then the state libraries or the rare-books room of the nearest university library. Persons who have lived in the community a long time and local history enthusiasts may have copies.

State or regional histories. Until the bicentennial, many state or regional histories were written as textbooks and tend to include more "significant" history than one is after, but they are often very useful for putting the local community into a regional or national perspective. They may be found at public libraries, university libraries, state libraries, or—more frequently—in the storerooms of the local school district.

There are also a number of popular histories available for each of the states. Funded by the National Endowment for the Humanities, the American Association for State and Local History, working with a distinguished editorial board, commissioned a bicentennial history for each of the states and the District of Columbia. These were written by scholars or by well-known historical writers. Most of these bicentennial state histories are very good, and they provide sensitive and thoughtful accounts of the unique qualities of the states.

A number of other state and regional books were developed for the bicentennial celebration. These vary in quality, but most of them are useful.

WPA American Guide Series and county surveys. The American Guide Series, written by members of the Writers' Program of the Works Projects Administration, are available for each of the forty-eight contiguous states. These books are a combination of essays on general subjects and detailed descriptive material on tours one could take around the state discussed. Although there are inaccuracies in some of the volumes, and the quality of the writing differs markedly from volume to volume, the American Guide books are a good introduction to a local community, since they provide regional background and a description of most towns and cities as they appeared in the late 1930s.

When they are available, the WPA County Record Surveys are an even richer source of information. They provide a complete list of county holdings as of the late 1930s, and they often include a number of manuscripts of oral interviews with people who were the older generation then. Unfortunately, many of these materials have disappeared over the years, but many county and state archivists are now attempting to survey collections extant. The state historical society or state archives are likely to have records of these collections.

Explorers and travelers' accounts. Since the sixteenth century, explorers and then travelers have written extensive accounts about the areas they passed through. Some described the physical setting of an area, and a few gave extensive inventories of the indigenous flora and fauna of a region. For example, western explorers Meriwether Lewis and William Clark spoke mostly of lands inhabited by native Americans, but later explorers such as John C. Frémont and Howard Stansbury described in detail the forts and other outposts they passed on their way to the western frontier. Works such as these have been reprinted a number of times, and they are available in most large public libraries, as well as in university libraries.

Some guides were written to persuade tourists to travel on the newly opened transcontinental railroads, and several works were published as gazetteers or sight-seeing tour guides. An example of these is Frederick Shearer's *The Pacific Tourist*, which described each mile of a trip along the Union Pacific Railroad. Most works of that type summarized important facts about each town in a particular state, and they are still useful introductions to a community's founding and early years. Early newspapers and weekly magazines often carried stories about trips and these were often pictorial in nature. *Leslie's Weekly* and *Harper's Weekly* are typical of these. Local and state librarians are likely to know of materials that describe a particular locality.

Novels and short stories. Many works of fiction have been written by regional writers who specialize in stories rich in local color. Some are so carefully detailed in describing the settings that they can help students reconstruct the appearance of a particular community at some time in the past. One thinks especially of writers such as Willa Cather, but there have been many others who have chronicled places as well. Local librarians are the best source for examples of a particular area.

Business histories and anniversary booklets. Banks, large mercantile establishments, and breweries were among the businesses that often published histories of the town and of the development of their own business. Typically, these marked fifty or a hundred years of operation, although a few have appeared at other times. Such publications often include human-interest items and a great many "then and now" photographs.

Some towns have periodically held celebrations, complete with pageants to celebrate their longevity. Lakota, North Dakota, for example, held such a celebration in 1958. The "Official Souvenir Booklet," *Lakota's 75 Years*, has a number of interesting articles, as well as a good collection of photographs from early days. One photograph series shows the original schoolhouse, the second school, a later photograph of the second school with a large addition, and finally, the "new" school, which shows the telltale signs of having been built in the 1930s. Among the reminiscences of early settlers are exciting stories of the devastating prairie fires and blizzards that frequently occurred in those days, as well as an extended account of the misadventures of a nearby site as an "end-of-the-track" town. Such works can provide some information for students and can be useful in suggesting subjects for further research.

Club yearbooks and school annuals. Most fraternal and civic organizations have a historian whose duty it is to record information important to that group each year. These annual accounts can be very important sources for photographs. Along with information about the members themselves, such yearbooks also include pictures of the group's buildings and the club's participation in community events.

School and university annuals also include much information beyond photographs of the graduates. Some print the course of study and the rules of the school. These can provide interesting detail about the changing educational system of the community.

Public school records. A school system's official files contain a wealth of additional information. Pupil permanent-record files and school attendance records can be used to identify the patterns of residential growth within a city, as well as population movement in and out of a city over a given time. Data from the files will allow one to determine such characteristics of the school population as who went to school; sex, national origin, religion, race, occupation of the parents; size of the family; and the number of years an individual attended school. Minutes of the meetings of the school board, rules and regulations governing the conduct of teachers and students, building plans, and calendars of the school year are among other types of information one can expect to find. Sometimes there are surprises. Students doing a history of one school in Colorado received permission to examine a great stack of old papers at the back of the basement vault. They discovered the original deeds of trust for the first three school properties in the district. It had been a well-kept secret by a succession of school administrators for more than one hundred years that these deeds had been lost. Anthony Penna, in his article cited in the section on guides, describes many practical uses for records such as these.

City and household directories, business directories, and telephone books. Specific individuals and businesses may be accounted for and traced over a number of years through various directories. Published annually, these types of references can often be used to trace the movements of a particular family or business enterprise as their fortunes rose or fell. R. L. Polk and Company publishes more than 1,400 city, county, state, and national directories. A typical city directory will include a brief section describing the history of the city, the major new business enterprises, and such statistics as the population, the mean annual temperature, the railroads servicing the area, and the total paved-street mileage. For more recent years, the directory is divided into four major sections. Section 1 is a buyer's guide, containing advertisements and business cards of local firms. Also included in this section is a Classified Business Section similar to the yellow pages of a telephone book. Section 2 is an alphabetical list of the names of residents and business and professional concerns of the city. The company tries to list the name, marital status, occupation, and address of each adult resident of the city. Although the listing is not always completely accurate, if one uses volumes that cover several years, one can check the validity of a particular reference. The third section is the directory of householders, including a street and avenue guide. This section can be especially useful if one is trying to trace the residents of a particular building, when the names of the people are not known. The final section of the directory is a numerical telephone directory. R. L. Polk and Company provide a Directory Library in more than 800 cities. These libraries are usually housed in Chamber of Commerce offices.

Telephone directories can be used to cross-check references in the city or business directory. They are often more convenient to use if all one is interested in is the address of a particular family at a particular time. Public libraries, state libraries, and historical societies usually have copies of city, county, and state business directories going back to the first published. Telephone companies and some historical libraries have collections of telephone directories.

Local newspapers. Area newspapers are among the most important sources for local history. They describe events as they happen, and they can provide much information about the economic and social life of a community, as well as the impact of state, national, and international events on the local area. Newspapers also include election notices, descriptions of public and private auctions, city ordinances, and legal announcements of such things as annexations and building permits, extensions of the water supply, the building of trolley lines, and the like. Many early newspapers contain highly biased articles, and the editors were frequently the prime boosters for the growth and prestige of the town. If there was more than one newspaper, the rivalry between papers, especially in local affairs, can make for interesting reading. Advertisements not only describe items in common use at a particular time, but they can also provide information important in tracing the change of a family's business fortunes, the changing trade areas of a city, or even the changing occupation of a particular historical person.

Many newspapers publish an anniversary issue each year or an expanded issue or special edition to mark such things as the fiftieth anniversary of its own existence or the centennial of the town's existence. These special editions usually have a special section devoted to the history of the community. Many have articles written by local historians, and these can be very useful. Most such issues are also profusely illustrated with old photographs from the newspaper's files. Students are often able to make copies of these photographs to use in their own projects.

Files of old newspapers can usually be found in public libraries and local historical societies. Occasionally, they may be found at the present newspaper office. Many state historical societies have microfilmed all of the papers that were ever published in the state. Newspapers are time-consuming to research, but more and more indexes are being prepared; one should inquire whether that has been done in his community.

Town, city, and county records. There are a great number of city and county offices and departments that maintain files useful for local history research. County offices hold records of all property transfers, abstracts of titles, and property deeds. These are usually filed by date of transaction, so one must begin the search with some previous knowledge. Estate records and wills may also be found at county offices. These records will list inheritors, and the records of the administrator of the will may include affidavits and correspondence, as supporting evidence. Such records may provide interesting insights into the life of the deceased. Frequently, inventories of personal property, including a list of home furnishings, are part of such records. If one is reconstructing the appearance of a house at a particular period of time, such information can be most useful. County offices also have lists of voters, poll books, and motor-vehicle registration records.

At city and county tax assessors' offices, one will find records of property that include the name and address of the owner; a legal description of the property, including lot, block number, and addition name; date of construction; floor plans; price last paid for the property; and tax assessment. Appraisers' records, which often include notes on structural peculiarities and violations of the building codes, may also be kept at the tax assessor's office.

City planning and city engineering offices are often good sources of maps that record additions to the city and quarter-section maps showing in large detail the streets, blocks, and lots of each addition to the city. Sometimes these maps are also found at an office with a title such as Building Department, which also will be the office that issues building permits. Permits usually list date, street address, legal description, architect (if there was one), contractor, and the nature of the building or improvement.

Other city and county offices can provide useful data. Birth, marriage, divorce, and death records may be kept at the county clerk's office or the city hall. Cemetery interment records may also be kept there. Such departments as the fire department, police department, animal control office, parks and recreation division, and the water and sewer department frequently maintain their own archives. The mayor's office may have records of public officials' speeches and proclamations, bulletins, newsletters, minutes of city council meetings, manuals and handbooks, constitutions and charters, press releases and reports. Some cities issue an annual social and economic report. These may be available from a Human Resources office, as well as from the mayor's office.

Some cities have found the accumulation of such records to be so large as to be beyond their means to catalogue and preserve them. In such instances, many cities have donated these materials to the public library. Students and teachers will want to check to see whether there is a special municipal reference section in the local library.

One other source for municipal information is booklets published periodically by the League of Women Voters. These booklets include information about the background of a city, a description of the organization of the city government, information on city budgets, services provided by the city government, and a number of maps and charts that include data on land use, school districts, and community development.

State and federal census records. Perhaps the most important state and federal records for use in local history are the various census records. Published Federal Census of Population, Agriculture, and Manufacturing can provide useful composite data, but for most local history projects, one would wish to obtain the manuscript versions. The manuscript versions of the population census are available on microfilm for the census years from 1790 to 1900, with the exception of the 1890 census, which was burned. The manuscript census consists of the actual handwritten entries of the census takers as they walked around the neighborhoods of the nation. The questions asked varied from decade to decade. The later censuses, for example, provide such information as who lived in each house on each street, family relationships in each dwelling, race, occupation, incidences of unemployment, childrens' school attendance, country or state of birth, and whether residents could read, write, or speak English.

Many states took mid-decade censuses; these were similar in nature to the federal questionnaires, but some of them are far more comprehensive. One guide to the state censuses is Henry J. Dubester's *State Censuses* (Washington, D.C., 1948), though this book is dated and incomplete. A better approach would be to check state archives or the state library. Even when these offices do not house the records, the librarians usually know where such materials are located. Some states have donated copies of their census records to the Genealogical Society of the Church of Jesus Christ of Latter-Day Saints in Salt Lake City, Utah. These records may be used by permission.

Federal census records are available for use at the several Federal Records Centers around the nation, or microfilm copies may be ordered by mail from the National Archives and Records Service (GSA), (Washington, D.C. 20408). To order, one must know the number of the reel or reels needed. Ordering information can be found in *Federal Population Censuses, 1790–1890*, or the supplement, *1900 Federal Population Census*. Both catalogues are available from the Publications Sales Branch (NEPS), General Services Administration, Washington, D.C. 20408. A soundex system (card index) is available for the 1880 and 1900 censuses. This system helps one discover listings for particular individuals.

Maps and bird's-eye views. Most cities have been recorded on insurance maps drawn up by national companies or by a local insurance board. Insurance maps and real estate atlases show every block and structure in a city at a given time, and they include information on the building materials used. Robinson, Baist, and Sanborn were the principal companies that prepared such maps. The Sanborn Map Company, later known as the Sanborn-Perris Map Company, drew maps that show the location and street address of a building, the construction materials used, including the roofing material, the number of stories of the building, the location of porches, the location of wells and outbuildings, and the use of the building. As these maps were updated as frequently as every two or three years, they show the constant change within a neighborhood.

Specialized maps of such things as climate regions, drainage systems of major rivers, electric transmission systems within a state, port and waterway data, and the physiographic divisions of a state or region are available in reproduction form from the National Archives and Records Service, General Services Administration. The finding guide for these maps is Special List 41, *Cartographic Records of the National Resources Planning Board*. It is available from the National Archives or from one of the National Resources Planning Board's field offices in Boston, Baltimore, Atlanta, Chicago, Omaha, Dallas, Denver, San Francisco or Portland. The U.S. Geological Survey makes available topographical maps of every section of land in the nation. These show the terrain, outlines of forests, roads, trails, and all other man-made improvements upon the land. In addition, the USGS has recently begun to publish some specialized maps that are particularly useful for local history. Historic-trail maps, for example, show not only the trail in question, but photographs and descriptions of early forts and landmark buildings in a particular area. These maps come under the heading of Miscellaneous Investigation Series, and they are published by the U.S. Geological Survey, Reston, Virginia 22092. The USGS is also the source of aerial photographs that provide still a different perspective for looking at a specific region.

Another type of map is the "bird's-eye view" of a city. During much of the nineteenth century, traveling artists drew these maps as panoramic views of a town or city, and it is possible to distinguish in them individual houses, business buildings, schools, and government buildings. One does need to use these maps with a bit of caution: the artist was hoping to sell a number of copies of these lithographs, and so the city is usually presented in the best possible mode. Some cities look much finer than they actually were.

Later, flying photographers did much the same thing with aerial photographs. These barnstorming pilots would take a number of panoramic photographs of a community or a large farm, have them enlarged into fine prints, and then sell copies to chambers of commerce, businessmen, and farm owners. Restaurants, banks, and historical societies seem to have the largest collections of these views of the city.

Lithographs, prints and photographs. Sometimes local or traveling artists were commissioned to do a drawing of a particular building—a grand house, or a commercial enterprise. Some of these drawings were lithographed for use as illustrations in local newspapers or as letterheads for stationery. *Harper's Weekly* sent artists along on excursions when new railroad lines were opened, and they frequently used illustrations of towns or parts of towns to describe the new route. Many of these were done "on the wing" and illustrate only what could be seen from the railroad depot, but they can be useful for determining the appearance of a building at a particular time or for dating specific buildings. Some town fathers, especially in the West, had streetscape paintings or photographs made of the business district; these may illustrate particular detail or give an impression of a whole block.

The Library of Congress has a vast collection of prints and photographs. The American Cities Collection contains more than 6,000 cloth-backed prints, mainly lithographs, and engravings from the eighteenth and nineteenth centuries. A particular example of the holdings is the Osborne Collection, 137 pencil drawings of early American architecture from nine different states. The well-indexed finding guide is entitled *Guide to the Special Collections of Prints and Photographs in the Library of Congress*. It may be obtained from the Superintendent of Documents, U.S. Government Printing Office, Washington, D.C.

Broadsides, ephemera and memorabilia. Local historical societies and sometimes public libraries have collections of broadsides and posters, used, especially in the nineteenth century, to advertise circuses, agricultural fairs, community events, or even patent medicine. Such materials can give flavor to a local history project. In addition, there may be collections of scrapbooks, family photograph albums, tools and implements, banners, badges, ribbons and medals, period clothing and accessories, children's toys and story books, invitations and visiting cards—all the keepsakes that were important to a particular family at one time. Students enjoy examining these artifacts. When they were donated by a family that a student is researching, or from a time period in which the students are especially interested, such materials can provide a good sense of what it was like to live during that time.

Diaries, letters, journals, and genealogies. Normally, it is the better-educated elite of a town who donate their personal papers to a historical society; occasionally, one may also find materials from or about others who have lived there. Such sources can be especially useful for intimate glances at people and events in the past. Seldom did people self-consciously plan for these materials to become historical sources, so, as a rule, they are breezy and informal in nature. One can learn about daily life, social customs, local scandals, economic problems, and the impact—or lack of impact—that national events made upon people in a given community.

People. Perhaps the most important source for working with local history projects is the people of the community itself. The recent past can be studied through interviews with parents, neighbors, and "old-timers" in the community. Many schools have developed lists of people who are available for students to interview. Some local historians and local history enthusiasts are willing to come to the classroom year after year to give lectures on their area of expertise or simply to tell stories about life in earlier days. Local newspapers are often willing to run articles asking for volunteers who will meet with students. Local historical societies and public libraries also often have lists of people who are willing to be interviewed. In addition, many of these agencies have large collections of oral histories, and these are available for student research.

Students themselves are often good resources. Many of them come from families that have lived in the area for a long time, and they are anxious to share with the rest of the class the information they have previously gathered.

Guidebooks to Local History

Teacher's guides and manuals. A number of curriculum guides and manuals for teachers suggest possible uses of local history in the schools. Such manuals usually include lists of commonly available source materials. Philip D. Jordan's *The Nature and Practice of State and Local History*, Publication no. 14 of the Service Center for Teachers of History (Washington, D.C.: American Historical Association, 1958), is a sensitively written introduction to the subject, addressed to teachers. Ralph Adams Brown and William G. Tyrrell's *How to Use Local History* (Washington, D.C.: National Council for the Social Studies, 1969) is an eight-page pamphlet in the National Council's "How-To-Do-It" Series. Although it is too brief to be very useful, it does include some helpful hints about incorporating local history into an American history course.

The manual that is probably the most widely used (at least, most frequently cited in the literature) is Clifford L. Lord's *Teaching History with Community Resources* (New York: Teachers

College, Columbia University, 1964). The book contains especially useful sections on developing school library and museum resources for local history programs and on strategies for involving in the program other academic departments and the community at large. It is also the introductory volume of the Localized History Series, which is edited by Lord. This series of student guides is devoted to the history of states, major cities, watersheds, and ethnic groups. Each volume contains a historical overview, a bibliography, and suggestions for field trips. The quality of the volumes varies considerably, but the field trip suggestions are very useful.

A number of curriculum guides produced by local school districts and state departments of education and other agencies provide directions for incorporating local historical research into social studies courses. One of the best is the guide entitled *Teaching the Age of Homespun: A Guide for 7th-Grade Social Studies* (Albany, N.Y.: State Education Department, 1965), which describes teaching activities and materials developed by Hazel Hertzberg. A publication with helpful hints on integrating local historical research into the social studies curriculum is Thomas L. Dynneson's *Planning Local History Projects for Elementary and Secondary Students* (n.p.: West Texas Council for the Social Studies, 1976).

For teachers in New England, a useful source is a set of materials designed by Old Sturbridge Village. Two student booklets, *The Small Town Sourcebook*, Parts I and II, are handsomely illustrated collections of photographs and other primary materials. Through these works, students can examine the social history of New England's people from the period of the 1820s to the present. Family, work, and community are topics described, and data on these topics are presented, along with questions suggestive of projects for students to undertake. In addition to the students' materials, the museum has developed a highly useful teacher's manual, *Guide to the Small Town Sourcebook.* This guide provides additional documents, a finding guide for more information on specific topics, background essays for teachers, and a very complete section of teaching activities. Although much of the material is clearly designed for elementary students, it would be a simple matter to adapt the ideas for use by secondary or older students. The approach used in these materials could also be appropriately adapted for teachers outside the New England area. Old Sturbridge Village also has a museum bookstore from which one can order other student and teacher materials, including curriculum kits, historical reprints, background papers, posters, study prints, slides, and reproduction artifacts for classroom use. A catalogue is available from the Museum Education Department, Old Sturbridge Village, Sturbridge, Massachusetts 01566.

To find some of these curriculum guides as well as citations to articles about local history that have appeared in education journals, teachers with access to ERIC collections will want to check the ERIC printed indexes, *Resources in Education* and *Current Index to Journals in Education*. The guides and some articles have been placed on microfiche, and they are available for use at any library that has the ERIC Clearinghouse for Social Studies/ Social Science Education collection.

Research and writing manuals. Another category of how-to-do-it manuals concentrates on the techniques of research and writing. Although not concerned with classroom strategies, these guides written for the layman will be useful to teachers and students. Thomas E. Felt's *Researching, Writing, and Publishing Local History* (Nashville: American Association for State and Local History 1976) is one recently published manual. In addition to explaining how and where to do research, and how to construct footnotes and bibliographies, Felt's book has a section on do-it-yourself publishing that could be valuable to a local history class. Donald Dean Parker's *Local History: How to Gather It, Write It, and Publish It* (New York: Social Science Research Council, 1944) is dated, but still valuable. Marcia Muth Miller's *Collecting and Using Local History* (Santa Fe: New Mexico Research Library of the Southwest, 1971) is another brief (31 pages) but useful guide. Jacques Barzun and Henry F. Graff's *The Modern Researcher*, revised edition (New York: Harcourt Brace and World, 1970), has an excellent section on writing. However, the most useful writing manual is still William Strunk, Jr., and E. B. White's *The Elements of Style* (New York: Macmillan, 1959).

Selection of Books and Articles on Topics of Local History

There are now a number of useful articles and books on the various topics of local history. Some have been cited as end notes to the chapters in this book. The following list is not inclusive; it contains only those works that we have personally used. There are many other useful items available to those who have the time to search them out. We have organized our list into the categories most commonly used for courses or units in local history. Materials available on microfiche have the ERIC retrieval number listed.

Architecture

Ackerman, James S., "Listening to Architecture," *Harvard Educational Review* 39 (Fall 1969): 4–10. Ackerman describes what he calls the "language" of architecture as he discusses scale, materials, and site.

Bicknell, A. J., and Williams Comstock, *Victorian Architecture: Two Pattern Books*, Athenaeum of Philadelphia and the American Life Foundation, 1976. First published in 1873 and 1881, these two pattern books were among the most popular books that builders used.

Blumenson, John J.-G., *Identifying American Architecture* (Nashville: The American Association for State and Local History, 1977). This identification guide will help students determine styles and identify architectural terms through a comparison of buildings they examine with photographs from the book. All major styles of American architecture from the Spanish colonial to Art Moderne are included.

Clark, Clifford, E., "Domestic Architecture as an Index to Social History: The Romantic Revival and the Cult of Domesticity in America, 1840–1870," *Journal of Interdisciplinary History* (Summer 1976). Clark presents a psychological interpretation of the interrelationships between architecture and life style.

Cohen, Lizabeth, "Reading a Room: A Primer to the Parsonage Parlor," *Rural Visitor*, Museum Education Department, Old Sturbridge Village, Sturbridge, Massachusetts.

Methods of reading the artifacts within a room and how to make sense of them are described.

Cohen, Ruth Schwartz, "A Case of Technology and Change: The Washing Machine and the Working Wife," in *Clio's Consciousness Raised: New Perspectives on the History of Women*, edited by Mary Hartman and Lois Banner (New York: Harper and Row, 1974). This is a useful example of the literature that describes how social roles have changed as a result of technology and how these changes are reflected in the use of space within households.

Danzer, Gerald, "Buildings as Sources: Architecture and the Social Studies," *High School Journal* 57, no. 5 (February 1974): 204–213. This article describes the ways architecture can be used in social studies courses and provides a guide for looking at buildings.

Downing, Andrew Jackson, *The Architecture of Country Houses* (1850; reprint ed., New York: Dover Publications, 1969). This is a reprint of the D. Appleton and Company edition of 1850. Downing's designs for Gothic cottages and villas had an enormous influence on Victorian architecture, and the results of his designs can still be seen around the country.

Lohmann, Mary, *A New Look at History* (Old Lyme, Connecticut: Old Lyme Bicentennial Commission, 1975). ED 116992. This work includes a number of exercises that will help students learn to identify architectural terms and styles. Lohmann also includes material on home furnishings.

Noble, Allen G., "Evolution and Classification of Nineteenth-Century Housing in Ohio," *Journal of Geography* 74, no. 5 (May 1975): 285–302. Using Ohio as the basis for study, Noble describes settlement patterns and architectural styles. He describes the evolution of house styles from their European models.

O'Dowd, Angela, "Exploring Staten Island through Its Architecture," *Instructor* 82 (August/September 1972): 137–140. This is an excellent model of a walking tour that teaches elements of architecture as well as concepts involved in historic preservation.

Rabinowitz, Richard, "The Crisis in the Classroom: Architecture and Education," *History of Education Quarterly* 14 (Spring 1974). The article describes a number of uses of architecture in the teaching of history.

Swank, Scott, "Room Study Checklist," Education Division, Winterthur Museum. Although the checklist is only four pages long, it guides students through five categories of ways to study rooms in historic houses. The categories include: spatial characteristics, utilitarian purposes, formal characteristics, furnishings, and history of functional characteristics. The ideas can be adapted to any historic house.

Whiffen, Marcus, *American Architecture Since 1780: A Guide to the Styles* (Cambridge, Mass.: Massachusetts Institute of Technology Press, 1969). Although this work has been largely supplanted by the Blumenson work cited earler, Whiffen's work is still useful.

Cemeteries

Davoren, John F. X., *Procedures Manual for an Inventory of the Historic Assets of the Commonwealth, Part III—Burial Grounds* (Boston: Massachusetts Historic Commission, 1968). This comprehensive guide is adaptable to any of the older regions of the nation.

Journal for the Gloucester Experiment: A School-Community Partnership Project (Gloucester, Mass.: Gloucester Community Development Corporation, 1975). This publication describes the methods used to develop the high school course described in Chapter 3.

"Making Tombstone Rubbings a Work of Art," *Southern Living*, July 1976, pp. 64–65.

Matthews, Bruce, and Joseph Smith, *The Cemetery: An Outdoor Education Unit* (Cortland, N.Y.: Cortland-Madison Board of Cooperative Educational Services, 1975). ED 160 283. This resource packet is multidisciplinary and is designed to be used with students of different ages. Included in the guide are pretrip activities, sample survey forms, sample tally sheets, and post-trip suggestions.

Weitzman, David, *Underfoot: An Everyday Guide to Exploring the American Past* (New York: Charles Scribner's Sons, 1976). Weitzman suggests a number of exercises that can be adapted for class use. The book is useful for a number of other topics in local history.

Family History

Boylan, Anne M., "Family History Questionnaires: Two Examples," *The History Teacher* 10 (February 1977): 211–220. This article describes two alternatives to the typical family history. The basic methods used, family history questionnaires, generated data that could be used in an American history class and in courses on social history. One example illustrates the changing conditions of women in the areas of child-bearing ages, education level, and work patterns. The other provides information on social class and social mobility.

Brown, Richard D., and Tamara Hareven, *Writing the Social History of One's Family: Revised Guidelines for Faculty Members and Students* (Worcester, Mass.: Department of History, Clark University, 1973). ED 099 245, 1975. These guidelines were developed as part of the Anonymous Family History Project, and they can be adapted to any individual or class project on the topic.

Culbert, David H., "Undergraduates as Historians: Family History Projects Add Meaning to an Introductory Survey," *The History Teacher* 7 (November 1973): 7–17. This article describes the assignment Culbert gave to his class at Louisiana State University. He provides a format for researching a family history as well as suggestions on ways to present a finished project.

Doane, Gilbert Harry, *Searching for Your Ancestors* (New York: Bantam Books, 1974). Doane's work has long been a standard source in the field.

Fredrich, Barbara E., "Family Migration History: A Project in Introductory Cultural Geography," *Journal of Geography* 76 (November 1977): 215–224. This article describes a project in which students develop maps tracing the origin of their families and write a paper on their family history. Four case studies are described.

Jeffrey, Kirk. "Family Biography: A Guide to Resources," in *Access to History*, edited by Richard H. Brown (Chicago: The Newberry Library, 1976), ED 129 678. A useful guide to sources that can be used to plan a family history project as part of a general history course.

Jeffrey, Kirk. "Write a History of Your Own Family: Further Observations and Suggestions," *The History Teacher* 7 (May 1974): 365–373. Some welcome caveats are described by Kirk. Pitfalls can be all too common in student projects unless teachers clearly point out the problems that might occur.

Kyvig, David E., and Myron Marty, *Your Family History: A Handbook for Research and Writing* (Arlington Heights, Ill.: AHM Publishing Corporation, 1978). The authors provide a detailed method for producing a complete family history.

Miller, Carolynne L., *Genealogical Research: A Basic Guide*, American Association for State and Local History, Technical Leaflet no. 14, *History News* 24, no. 3 (March 1969). This leaflet includes information on how to use family data, public records, and library research to construct a family history. Sample lineage charts are included.

Myrick, Shelby, "Glossary of Legal Terminology: An Aid to Genealogists," American Association for State and Local History, Technical Leaflet no. 55, *History News* 25, no. 7 (July 1970). The special vocabulary needed to research in early documents and records is explained in this pamphlet.

Penna, Anthony, "Discovering Roots: The Family in History," *Social Education* 41 (October 1977): 478–481. Penna provides a genealogical chart and a series of questions students might ask about their family origins.

Steel, D. J., and L. Taylor, "Family History in Schools: The Development of a New Approach to the Teaching of History," *The History and Social Science Teacher* 10 (Winter 1974): 17–26. The authors present a persuasive argument for the inclusion of family history in the social studies curriculum.

Oral History

Baum, Willa, *Oral History for the Local Historical Society* and *Transcribing and Editing Oral History* (Nashville: American Association for State and Local History, 1971 and 1977). Both of these booklets are brief but comprehensive. They are the most useful short works in the field.

Cutler, William, et al., "Oral History as a Teaching Tool," *The Oral History Review* 1 (1973): 29–47. The broad uses of oral history are well described in this work.

Ebner, Michael, "Students as Oral Historians," *The History Teacher* 9 (February 1976): 196–201. Ebner describes a course in oral and community history that he taught at Lake Forest College. The principal objective was to determine how the residents of that affluent suburb were affected by the Great Depression. The article is useful in suggesting how oral history can be integrated into an American history course.

Garner, Van Hastings, *Oral History: A New Experience in Learning* (Dayton, Oh.: Pflaum Publishing Co., 1975). This booklet provides simple, direct suggestions on oral history techniques and examples of interviews conducted by Garner's students.

Henderson, Joyce, "Oral History Goes to School," *Social Studies Review* 15 (Fall 1975): 10–12, 41. EJ 140 280. Henderson describes a number of school projects in oral history that are adaptable to any community.

Martin, Lois, "Oral History—How to Mesh the Process and the Substance in U.S. History," *The Social Studies* 63 (December 1972): 322–336. This short article is as practical as the title suggests.

Mehaffey, George, and Thad Sitton, "Oral History as a Classroom Tool," *Social Education* 41 (May 1977): 378–381. This is a brief introduction to the utility of using oral history and a short description of how to do it.

Mehaffey, George, and Thad Sitton, "Oral History in the Classroom," series 2, no. 8, *How-To-Do-It Series* (Washington, D.C.: The National Council for the Social Studies, 1979). This is the best short introduction to the topic for secondary teachers. The authors suggest a number of ways oral history might be used in local history projects.

Pennsylvania Department of Education, "Oral History: What? Why? When?" Division of Art and Humanities, Bureau of Curriculum Services, Department of Education, 1975. ED 117 014. This paper suggests nine different uses of oral history in the curriculum for secondary schools, as well as useful hints for setting up a program and for interviewing.

Tyrrell, William G., "Tape-Recording Local History," American Association for State and Local History, Technical Leaflet no. 35, *History News* 21, no. 5 (May 1966; revised 1973). Tyrrell provides a brief summary of the most important issues involved in conducting oral history projects.

Wolkerstorfer, Sister John Christine, "Oral History—A New Look at Local History," *Catholic Library World* 47 (October 1975): 104–107. The article describes a college oral history project. Emphasis is on what makes a quality program, the mechanics of setting up a program, and the benefits of a program for the college and the local community.

Photographs

Eakle, Arlene, *Photograph Analysis* (Salt Lake City: Family History World, 1976). The emphasis in this book is on family history. It is a manual and workbook produced for teachers.

Basic Art Techniques for Slide Production, Pamphlet VI–27 (Rochester, N.Y.: Kodak Publication, 1978). This technical publication provides information on how to label slides, make slides and filmstrip frames, and how to produce other slide art.

Basic Copying, Pamphlet VI–28 (Rochester, N.Y.: Kodak Publication, 1977). The substance of this technical leaflet is how to make copies of photographs.

Bowditch, George, *Cataloging Photographs*: *A Procedure for Small Collections*, American Association for State and Local History, Technical Leaflet no. 57, *History News* 26, no. 11 (November 1971; revised 1975). Although this publication was meant for the small historical society, the information is useful for the teacher who plans to continue using local history for some time.

Freidman, Renee, "Historic Photographs," *History News* 32 (February 1977): 42, 51–52. This article deals with the different types of historical photographs.

Gore, Gary, "Historic Photographs," *History News* 32 (October 1977): 284–286. This article deals with methods of reproduction of historic photographs.

Noren, Catherine Hanf, *The Camera of My Family* (New York: Alfred A. Knopf, 1976). An excellent example of the use of photographs in reconstructing the history of one family.

Steele, Steve, "Historic Photographs," *History News* 33 (February 1978): 38–39. The various uses of historic photographs are discussed.

Vanderbilt, Paul, "Filing Your Photographs: Some Basic Procedures," American Association for State and Local History, Technical Leaflet no. 36, *History News* 21, no. 6 (June 1966). Methods for keeping track of photographs and preserving the collection are described.

Weitzman, David, *My Backyard History Book* (Boston: Little Brown and Company, 1975). The author presents simple guides for taking photographs, doing copy work, and caring for photographs.

Weitzman, David, *Underfoot: An Everyday Guide to Exploring the American Past* (New York: Charles Scribner's Sons, 1976). Weitzman presents some of the same information as in the previous book, but in a considerably more sophisticated manner. He provides many useful ideas.

Quantitative Studies

Dollar, Charles M., and Richard Jensen, *Historian's Guide to Statistics: Quantitative Analysis and Historical Research* (New York: Holt, Rinehart and Winston, Inc., 1971). One of the early works in the field, it is still useful as an introduction.

Griffen, Clyde, "Occupational Mobility in Nineteenth-Century America: Problems and Possibilities," *Jornal of Social History* 5 (Spring 1972): 310–330. This article points out the problems that can be encountered in the use of quantitative data.

Swierenga, Robert P., "Computers and American History: The Impact of the 'New' Generation," *Journal of American History* 40 (March 1974): 1045–1070. Swierenga argues for methods courses in computer technology at the college level and describes the types of materials that can be quantified.

Warner, Sam Bass, Jr., "Appendix A: A Local Historian's Guide to Social Statistics," in *Streetcar Suburbs* (Cambridge, Mass.: Harvard University Press, 1962). Warner is probably the most useful source for the secondary teacher who wishes both to understand the techniques of quantification and the uses to which it might be put.

General

Benedict, Paul L., "Historic Site Interpretation," American Association for State and Local History, Technical Leaflet no. 19, *History News* 26, no. 3 (March 1971). Benedict suggests techniques to make a field trip to a historic site worthwhile. While the pamphlet describes the use of the field trip for younger students, the ideas can be adapted to any age level.

Diem, Richard A., "Field-Based History," *The Social Studies* 67 (November/December 1976): 238–241. Diem describes how one might study a particular neighborhood through field trips, the use of newspapers, titles and deeds to land, and church records.

Douch, Robert, "Local History," in *New Movements in the Study and Teaching of History*, edited by Martin Ballard (London: Temple Smith, 1971). This chapter provides a comprehensive rationale for the teaching of local history.

Estus, Charles et al., "An Interdisciplinary Approach to Community Studies," *The History Teacher* 13 (November 1979): 37–48. This is a description of an undergraduate course offered at Assumption College. It is a good companion piece to the Gerber article.

Friedberger, Mark, and Janice Reiff Webster, "Social Structure and State and Local History," *Western Historical Quarterly* 9 (July 1978): 297–314. The authors argue for social structure as the unifying theme in local history courses.

Gerber, David A., "Local and Community History: Some Cautionary Remarks on an Idea Whose Time Has Returned," *The History Teacher* 13 (November 1979): 7–30. This is an important article on the uses and abuses of local history. Gerber describes both the benefits and the serious problems that can be a part of such a study. He also presents a short history of the local history movement, putting it into historical perspective. The article should be read by anyone planning extensive use of local history materials.

Hale, Richard W., Jr., "Methods of Research for the Amateur Historian," American Association for State and Local History, Technical Leaflet no. 21, *History News* 24, no. 9 (September 1969). Hale offers the beginning researcher a number of tips for first encounters with the materials of local history.

Penna, Anthony B., "Schools as Archives," *The History Teacher* 9

(November 1975): 19–28. Penna suggests a number of uses students might make of the routine records generated in schools.

Russo, David J., *Families and Communities: A New View of American History* (Nashville: American Association for State and Local History, 1974). Russo suggests that the most productive study of American history should begin with the smallest unit, the family, and proceed to the national story. The book provides an excellent conceptual framework for local history studies.

Williams, Catherine M., *The Community as Textbook* (Bloomington, Ind.: Phi Delta Kappa Educational Publication, 1975). ED 112 481. Williams provides suggestions on how community resources can be organized and utilized.

Williams, James C., "So You've Got Some Old Ruins—Now What?" *AHA Newsletter* 18 (January 1980): 6–10. Williams reports on his work in the new Public Historical Studies Program at the University of California, Santa Barbara, and the use he made of the studies of historical preservation in his community college courses at Gavilan College.

Agencies as Sources

Agencies such as state, regional, and local museums and historical societies, as well as public libraries, community-sponsored youth groups, and some individuals, have developed local history projects. Some of these groups welcome collaboration with school or college classes. Although it would be impossible to cite all of the excellent projects we have heard of, it might be useful to describe a few to suggest some of the possibilities available.

Perhaps the best-known living history museum is Old Sturbridge Village, Massachusetts, where the museum education staff has designed materials that have been used by countless visitors and are also used around the country from the elementary grades through college. For example, Professor Robert Wheeler of Cleveland State University uses the Sturbridge family history materials developed for the Colonial and early National period in one of his courses. He has his students analyze those materials and then examine Ohio census data to reconstitute families from specific time periods in the Cleveland area. A similar activity using that materials packet is part of the fifth-grade social studies curriculum in the schools of Aurora, Colorado. Other curriculum kits available from Old Sturbridge Village include materials on work and on community. The museum is also a source for a number of background papers, teaching notes, reproduction artifacts, audio-visual materials, and other supplementary materials.[1]

A second example of ways in which museum-developed materials are being used in the classroom is the special-interest kit that may be borrowed by teachers from the local historical society or from the larger museums. The Colorado State Historical Society has put together a number of such kits for elementary school use dealing with the history of that state. Using authentic artifacts, each kit is designed to replicate as nearly as possible the types of material items a person typical of a group might have in his possession. The miner's kit would contain maps of the mining region, gold pans and picks, and samples of ore. The trapper's kit would include a Green River knife, buckskins, and a beaver trap. All of these occupation-based kits contain readings and a number of activities teachers can use with students in the classroom. The Society has also developed a number of "Grandmother's Trunks." Each of these is an actual trunk, manufactured about 1900. Each has been lined with paper made in the time period, and each is filled with the type of mementos, including family photographs, that an actual grandmother might have saved. Each of the trunks has been designed to represent the grandmother of a particular ethnic group, such as Cheyenne, Anglo-American, black, Mexican-American, or Italian. These trunks were designed for elementary students, but they have been used with great success in secondary classrooms as well.

A number of other museums across the country are providing such materials for teachers to borrow and use in their schools. Some other museums and societies are doing much more. They are co-operating with the schools in developing programs that are part of the school curriculum. A superb example of such co-operation is the Allen House project in Newton, Massachusetts.

Here the co-operating agencies include the Allen House Preservation Corporation, the Newton Public Schools, the Bay State Historical League, the Educational Collaborative for Boston, and the University of Massachusetts Graduate School of Education. In addition, the Museum Education Department of Old Sturbridge Village is acting in an advisory capacity. Basically, the Allen House project revolves around the rich resource of the house of Nathaniel T. Allen, a noted educator of the 1840s and 1850s. Allen used his home to house the Horace Mann Model School and, later, his own West Newton English and Classical School. Both schools were far ahead of their time and were somewhat controversial in nature. Their founder was also an activist in other concerns of his time. He backed women's rights, was a pacifist, believed in education for blacks, and maintained a station of the underground railroad. The manuscript collection that is part of the archives housed at the Allen home includes, among other things, material on the peace movement of the time, abolition issues, and the Free Soil party. The historic house curators will help students utilize these resources as they undertake projects in a high school local history course called, "The Allen House." Students will also be involved in the restoration project the Allen House staff is currently undertaking.

Another interesting project that suggests the possibilities of school-museum co-operation is the Museum-in-the-School project of the Portland Museum/Roosevelt Community School located in Louisville, Kentucky. The combination museum/school project serves the 500 students of Roosevelt public school as well as the whole area of Portland, a community of Louisville with about 20,000 residents. The Museum-in-the-School program teaches the students local history through the use of such activities as oral history, photography, film, and so on. The program is an integral part of the school program and is considered an important part of the basic skills-building focus of elementary education.

The Sonoran Heritage project of the Tucson, Arizona, Public Library is a program sponsored by the National Endowment for the Humanities. The project has developed a number of packets of materials that can be used both for group and individual study. The packets "are meant to stimulate reading and research, thinking, writing, collecting, and organizing projects and activities in neighborhoods, families, clubs, or alone." [2] Topics that have been developed include *Shelter, Food, Work, Clothing, Play, Family, Power, Destiny*, and *Genius*. One may note that these materials were not expressly designed for use in classrooms, but a number of them are being utilized by Tucson area teachers in that manner. Some of the packets have been useful to students who have been doing individual projects of a local nature that have been entered into the National History Day contests in Arizona. All of these packets include a rich variety of activities and useful bibliographies. They include a great number of primary sources, including census data, old maps, and first-hand accounts.

Two other NEH-funded projects that could be excellent resources for teachers in particular areas include the Minnesota Social History Project at St. Mary's College, Winona, Minnesota 55987, which is under the direction of Dr. William L. Crozier, and the Mid-South Humanities Project, Middle Tennessee State University, Murfreesboro, Tennessee 37132, under the direction of Dr. James K. Huhta and Dr. Francis R. Ginanni. The Minnesota Project is cited a number of times in this book because the use the project made of census materials can be appropriate in any area. The Mid-South Humanities Project has developed demonstration centers staffed by participant teams who attended an institute at Middle Tennesse State University. The focus of this project has been to revitalize student interest in literature and history in the Mid-South through the use of local and regional heritage sources. Both of these projects have developed exciting materials that can be used in those particular regions and can also be adapted to any locality in the nation.

The Chicago Metro History Fair, organized by David Ruchman and Arthur Anderson and housed at the Newberry Library in Chicago, is an example of another co-operative project between the schools and a community institution. Students in the Chicago area schools develop local history projects that are entered into a regional competition. The fair staff conducts in-service workshops for teachers who help prepare their students for the contest, and the staff also works directly with students as they develop their projects.

Other examples of collaborative projects include the Newark

Public Radio station, which is developing radio programs featuring Newark public high school students interviewing Newark senior citizens for an oral history project; the Cobb-Marietta Girls Club of Marietta, Georgia, which involved girls interviewing older women to discover the changing roles and life styles of women in the historical development of Cobb County; and the development of walking tours, Grandmas' trunks, and other materials by Maureen Della Maggiora, a volunteer at the Petaluma, California, Historical Library Association. Clearly, work in local history is being done by great numbers of people around the nation. A phone call to the various agencies within a particular region is apt to turn up similar projects that might be useful.

But programs such as these described are still all too rare. More often, the school and the local historical agencies work independently and often duplicate efforts. There are a number of barriers that seem to keep the two types of institutions apart. Museums and historical societies serve a much wider audience than school students. They need to set up exhibits and procedures to serve that wider audience. When they are geared to serve students, they must contend with limited staff time and limited budgets. They cannot be expected to develop kits on individual lessons for the hundreds of thousands of school children who could be served by loaned materials or who troop through their halls each year. There are teachers who treat a field trip to a museum as a personal holiday for themselves. They arrive early or late, do not keep their students under control, and some even cancel trips without letting the museum know. Administrative and organizational problems often stand in the way of teachers who would like to undertake co-operative educational ventures. But it does not really seem to be overworked museum professionals and school administrative blocks that have set up the barriers between the two types of educational institutions.

The real problem seems to be that neither group really knows enough about the resources of the other to co-operate effectively in the educational process with which both are concerned. Sometimes there is simply not a realization on the part of museum people that students want to give as well as receive. Many students, especially those in secondary schools and colleges, have a great deal to offer. They can help to collect the oral history materials a museum would like to preserve. They can transcribe these materials, file them, and advertise their availability. They can scrub and apply wallpaper and paint and do carpentry work in restoration projects. They can catalogue manuscripts and other documentary materials, and they can do any number of other chores that are part of museum work. For experience of that sort, students should receive academic credit. On the other hand, the museum people can be more receptive to the needs of the students. They can make available the primary documents and the artifacts that will provide students with a particularly evocative experience. The museum will gain a clientele that understands that such resources are being preserved for them and their children, and they will appreciate the usefulness of the museum's efforts. It is vital that they do. Without the preservation efforts of the museums and historical societies, students might never understand their own heritage.

Teachers and agency staff people who would like to set up a collaborative program might wish to examine the brochure developed by Alberta Sebolt, Director of Museum Education, at Old Sturbridge Village. *Building Collaborative Programs: Museums and Schools* describes the steps one might wish to consider in such an undertaking:

A Beginning: Guidelines for Building Relationships
1. Begin where you are.
   —recognize your resources, your position, your strengths and weaknesses
   —recognize where others are
2. Begin slowly and realistically. Be careful not to build barriers.
   —recognize your limitations
   —be candid and realistic
3. Involve and include others who need to be 'in on' the planning. Build and strengthen team planning.
4. Establish clear time and program guidelines.
   —you can not plan forever
   —go ahead and try a program
5. Build from your strengths and successes.

—put together the strongest elements first

—take advantage of the moment

Help each other to do better what both have agreed they want to do!

From this point, Sebolt also describes, step by step, the process of building a program. Planning, development, implementation, revision, and planning for the future are points that need consideration. Co-operation is the key. As Sebolt says, "Building any program contains many elements. Building a collaborative program between institutions increases the number of elements necessary for success. The program becomes a group possession, which results from many compromises. Truly, group 'ownership' is important if you are to sustain the program over time." [3]

3

Using Material Culture as Local History Sources

MOST United States history books devote at least a few pages to the art, architecture, and other forms of material culture that characterized an age. Some textbooks provide photographs or other illustrations of broadsides, campaign posters, and campaign buttons, early American agricultural tools, and perhaps examples of early American crafts. But no photograph in a textbook can substitute for the experience of handling an object or viewing it three-dimensionally.

Tangible artifacts can help students to understand the material culture of a time period and the idea, assumptions and attitudes of the people who fabricated them. As James Deetz has persuasively argued:

> . . . artifacts reflect cognitions. Material culture systems represent the minds of the people who put them together. As we study particular artifacts in their real contexts, we can plug into an overall scheme that examines the whole sweep of change in material culture. For instance, one can see changes in worldview in the transition from sprawling, haphazard timberframe houses to symmetrical Georgian mansion, on the coming of standardized individual place settings for meals, or in the change from spontaneous string band to tightly organized bluegrass music.[1]

Deetz makes a further important point: that written records represent only the elite of the past—only the top 5 percent of the population, he asserts—and so we must rely on methods other than those of a traditional history study if we wish to understand the ideas, assumptions, and attitudes of the other 95 percent of the people of the past. Methods that can be used to do that come from folklore studies, cultural geography, historical and industrial archaeology, environmental and social psychology, and, of course, museum studies.

The list of items of material and popular culture one could study is nearly endless. One could examine song lyrics, greeting card styles, house or business furnishings, changing types of agricultural implements, styles of baby clothes, or even different types of writing implements—and some people do spend their lives working with such items—but for the purposes of this chapter, we will focus upon the items that seem to produce the most useful data for students: the city or town itself, as a whole; buildings; public art; artifacts that might be classified as keepsakes or mementos; and cemeteries.

The Physical City

Most students, like most adults, pay little attention to the form of the city or town in which they live. They may be able to name the tallest building, largest department store, and the main streets, but most have seldom stopped to consider that an urban setting includes such other things as open spaces, boundaries, and street furnishings. Most people have never been trained to notice the textures produced by a variety of building materials or the patterns that occur as buildings are reflected in the glass facades of other buildings.

Buildings are always a part of the larger environment, and they reflect that environment.

> In older sections of the city they stand tightly against one another, forming a fence around the street upon which all the structures focus their attention. In the newer suburban areas, by contrast, the buildings are detached from one another, withdrawn from the street, and set in the frame of a landscape. The street is no longer the focus of neighborhood life and, with its disappearance a new order of life activities emerges. The very appearance of the buildings in the suburban scene is softer, simpler, and less cosmo-

Plate 3.1. Textures and patterns of the physical city.

politan. The street and its bustle dissolves into a moat of greenery and driveways. The street as an area also disappears in the high-rise residential areas. Here the buildings are too high to define the street or connect the residents with their avenue. The street is abandoned to the automobile and becomes a no man's land between residential islands.[2]

But to see buildings set into such patterns as Gerald Danzer describes is to see also the individual structures that make up that pattern. One appropriate way to help students to observe rather than to "just look" is to take them on a walking tour and ask them to examine carefully some of these elements of the cityscape.

Gerald Danzer has developed a plan for such a walk. He asks students to look around carefully as they walk and to consider:

1. *Space* (How does the absence of buildings create urban form and provide room for transportation and other amenities?)
2. *Scale* (What is it in relationship to a person, to the total

environment, to nature, and what role does it play in producing a sense of the intimate or the monumental?)

3. *Color and light* (How does the city look in daylight and at night? How do seasonal changes affect the appearance of the city?)

4. *Choreography* (What is the form and flow of movement? Where are the nodes of activity?)

5. *Boundaries* (How do curbs, levels, lawns and plantings, fences and walls, steps, platforms, and ramps define areas?)

6. *Street furniture* (Are there lighting fixtures, benches, signs, kiosks, bus shelters, telephone booths, drinking fountains, clocks, waste baskets, formal art and sculpture, traffic indicators, safety islands, mailboxes, manholes, grates, drains, and utility covers?)

7. *Buildings* (How do facades, entrances, and windows affect their appearance? How do they affect you?)

8. *Texture* (What are the materials used for the structures of the city? Are they coarse-grained or fine? Are these textures uniform?)[3]

Such a walking tour will help students to sharpen their powers of observation. One might follow up such a walk by showing a few slides of the local city, reinforcing the ideas developed on the walk. Photographs help students to think in new modes.

A second general approach to looking at the city is offered by David C. Goldfield in his superb article, "Living History: The Physical City as Artifact and Teaching Tool." [4] One might, he suggests, examine such questions as the way cities and then suburbs have led to segregation, ask how the concerns of the progressives for "humane housing" affected housing patterns, how traffic congestion was caused by the gridiron plan; how the plan led to frequent intersections, shallow blocks, and the rise of skyscrapers; and how all these elements led to the modern concept of the pedestrian mall. One might also study the practice of building cemeteries in the city because "City fathers deemed the clean air and quietude of the cemetery and the exercise of walking to be excellent preventatives of disease." [5] When cemeteries could no longer take the crush of the crowds that used them, the city park became the next outdoor area to serve as a solution to the problem of disease in the crowded city. Students might research to see

Plate 3.2. Contrasting shapes contribute to the visual excitement of the Tucson Civic Center.

whether these were the motives for the development of parks in their city. Beyond streets and open spaces, Goldfield suggests that students study buildings as the third component of the physical city. To analyze buildings, he suggests four factors to consider:

> First, what is the function of the building and how has it changed over time? For example, did it begin as a warehouse near the railroad tracks and is it now a restaurant? Second, what is the form of the building? In this analysis architectural style—the exterior facade and interior design—is most important. What, for example does a low concrete-block structure with rooms that partition equally state about community development as opposed to a rambling Victorian house replete with turrets and circular rooms with curlicues on the ceiling? Third, what is the physical context of the structure? What other types of buildings surround

Plate 3.3. Glass, concrete, and brick provide contrasts in textures.

it—then and now? Was the local church with presumptious Gothic architecture designed to demonstrate a rededication to God or express a community's self-importance? What is the significance of the church's location in the center of town, surrounded by commercial establishments, rather than in a quiet residential community? Finally, what implications can the student derive from the study of buildings? What insights into a better urban community can the student gain from analyzing this aspect of the physical city?[6]

Goldfield follows up this list of questions with an example of ways in which such a study might be used in a specific course. His model for the study is the two-story row house that has been such a ubiquitous feature of American cities and towns. The same methodological framework, the questioning of form, function, context, and implications might be used for any type of building anywhere, or for the study of the role of open spaces and of streets within the city.

Plate 3.4. Urban form is also created by open space.

The Neighborhood Study

One could confine a study of the type described by Goldfield to a small neighborhood that adjoins or is fairly near the school or campus. One such study was designed by Catherine Taylor, to introduce students to two old neighborhoods in Boulder,

Colorado. Entitled "Local History Reflected in Two Boulder Neighborhoods," [7] the study focused on the oldest residential area in the city and a contiguous early "suburb." The residential area contains the oldest house in town and has many houses dating from the 1870s and 1880s. The "suburb," the Mapleton Hill neighborhood, has many large, expensive houses built during the 1890s and early 1900s.

Research for the teaching materials uncovered many early photographs, maps including a "bird's-eye view," sketches, architectural plans, and other documents that, together, created a lively sense of the area's past. For example, the first church in Boulder was built on the dividing line between the two neighborhoods. "What a help it would be," said the first minister, "for the county seat to have a substantial church on the hillside whose tower would be visible for miles down the valley." This first minister documented the construction of the church he so longed for, and there are two versions of his recollections available. The manuscript version was written while he served the church, from 1865 to 1875. It is full of insights into the daily life of the pioneers of the region. Miners, down from the mountains to buy supplies, often donated a day's work to the building of the church; one local businessman, owner of one of the earliest stores in the town, could always be counted upon to donate another fifty dollars or so for materials. The published version is less interesting, but both documents in edited form were given to the students to read before they examined the neighborhoods.

Taylor designed a walking tour to present a chronological history of the neighborhoods (see Appendix C). Emphasis was placed on changes in the landscape, from bare mesa lands to tree-lined streets containing comfortable Queen Anne and shingle-style houses. Not only did the students have an opportunity to see the first permanent houses built in their town, but they also saw several examples of adaptive use of older buildings and were introduced to the concept of historic preservation. The walking tour was supplemented by several follow-up activities.

A slide-show provided visual and verbal information difficult to incorporate into the tour-guide directions. Several individual and group activities were used to help students learn to use other local history sources. In one inquiry exercise, "The Historian as Cartographer," students viewed slides made from Sanborn Insurance maps for one of the neighborhoods over four different time periods. The students used data from the slides to answer a series of questions about why the neighborhood might have developed the way it did. In a second exercise, students used old plat maps to try to determine why, way out in the West, where vacant land stretched to the horizon, the building lots were only twenty-five feet wide. Both the plat maps and the Sanborn maps, as well as a large collection of photographs and business directories, were used by one group of students who built a scale model of one particular block as it appeared in 1883.

Taylor designed this particular program to be a springboard for other student projects. Items she suggested included:

—Study one house and describe how it has changed over time.
—Study one family that has lived in one of the neighborhoods since it was built. [Several families do, and Taylor provided students with a list of those who were willing to be interviewed by students.]
—Study one architectural style, comparing several homes built in that style.
—Interview people who have restored old homes and find out what is involved.
—Relate this neighborhood to the rest of Boulder. Study old city directories, newspapers, etc., to find out where residents shopped, went to school, went to church, and where they went for recreation and pleasure.
—Study one kind of architectural detail, perhaps relating it to advertisements in catalogs and newspapers if it was mass-produced, or to the carpenter's or stonemason's techniques if it is handcrafted. Reproduce original examples of the trim yourself.
—Research old photographs of the neighborhood. Develop a photo-display.
—Study the process by which a building becomes a landmark and is protected by local and federal laws.[8]

Another example of a way walking tours can be used to interest students in an older neighborhood was developed by Angela

O'Dowd in Tompkinsville, New York, an old community on the north shore of Staten Island. The community, like so many others in the nation, was in a transitional period. Students in the schools were a mixture of non-English-speaking newcomers from Santo Domingo, Colombia, Cuba, and India, and the sons and daughters of business and professional people, the civic leaders of Tomkinsville. The buildings in the community reflected that. Old, established businesses remained in the shopping area, but they were being joined by ethnic businesses meant to serve the newer residents, and on every block were empty stores—the sure sign of a deteriorating neighborhood. "While driving to work," O'Dowd says, "I became fascinated and haunted by the evidences of proud traditions combined with past pressures of the seventies. What about the future? What attitudes would assure perpetuation of a thriving community? What could the schools do to help?" [9]

In response to that question, O'Dowd developed curriculum materials designed to enhance students' environmental awareness and to develop their civic pride and their concern for the future of their town. The architecture of the city was the original focus. Students took a number of walking tours to see the different neighborhoods of the city. As they toured, the students began to learn the terms of architecture and began to appreciate and to support efforts then under way for the restoration of some of the important houses in the community as well as the restoration of a three-block area of attached duplex homes that had deteriorated badly. One particular house—the Pritchard house—helped the students to understand how thoroughly houses might change in appearance. Built in 1845, the Pritchard house had originally combined Greek Revival and Italian Palazzo with quoin corners. Somewhere along the way, it had also gained modified carpenter's lace. The house had been "kept up to date," in an attempt to make it fit into a changing neighborhood.

This knowledge of the ways houses of the past reflect their owner's concerns about the community helped some students to understand why their parents were concerned about a high-rise apartment building proposed for their neighborhood. The proposed building would not only cast a shadow over their street, but would also change the flavor of the neighborhood. The students were also beginning to understand that, in their community, there were deeper studies to be made about the causes of poor housing, the economic plight of certain residents, and the racial prejudices encountered by some families. Students learn to see more than buildings on walking tours; they can also develop sociological insights.

Buildings as Structures

In using buildings as sources for local history, one is not necessarily or continually considering the architectural style of the structure. Buildings can be examined from many points of view, with a number of motives in mind. Buildings are always a part of the larger environment, and they reflect that environment. As Gerald Danzer states, "Social function, technological development, aesthetic taste, and economic factors are all revealed in a building." [10] Examining a building closely to consider all these elements can be a rewarding experience. Danzer supplies a format for doing so. Students might wish to start with their own school building and then examine other buildings in the community. Danzer's guide, which appears below, was developed to cover as many areas of concern as possible. Students should answer only those questions applicable to the particular building they are examining.

A GUIDE TO LOOKING AT A BUILDING

I. Identifying the building
   A. What is its name?
   B. Where is it located?
   C. When was it built?
   D. Who was the architect?
   E. For what purpose was the structure built?
II. The building's historical dimensions
   A. What features make the building unique?
   B. What elements make the structure one of a group? What gives the building its commonality?
   C. Does the building reflect change?
      1. Has the building changed to keep up with engineering developments?

    2. Has the building been remodeled to keep it in style?

    3. Has it been altered to meet different functions?

III. Classifying the building

  A. Does the building reflect high culture or vernacular culture?

  B. Is this a monumental building?

  C. Is this building distinguished by its special function?

IV. The site

  A. Note the physical geography of the building's location.

  B. What is the relationship of the building to transportation facilities?

  C. How does the building fit into its immediate surroundings? Especially note its relationship to other buildings.

  D. How is the building situated on its lot?

V. Technical aspects

  A. How is the building supported?

  B. How has the architect provided for lighting, heating, access, and sanitation?

  C. Are the materials used in the building noteworthy?

    1. Are they native or imported?

    2. Is there any relationship of the materials to technical aspects or special problems of the structure or location?

    3. Were the materials chosen for aesthetic purposes?

VI. Function: the use of the building

  A. How well did the building fulfill its original use? Were there any serious problems in using the building?

  B. Current function: What changes had to be made to accommodate any new functions? Does the structure still serve a satisfactory purpose?

  C. Were there any intermediate uses between its original use and its current function?

  D. Discuss the relationship between function and location.

VII. Economic aspects

  A. How was the building financed? Who paid for the construction? How did this influence things like design, use, materials, location, etc.?

  B. Note the allocation of space in the building to various functions.

VIII. Legal aspects

  A. Does the building reflect a zoning code?

B. Does the building reflect a tax structure?
C. How is the property described in legal terms?
  1. The land
  2. The building
D. List the governmental units to which the property is subjected.

IX. Aesthetic aspects
A. Discuss the relationship between the building's form and function.
B. Note the building's proportions. Are they pleasing?
C. What is the architectural style of the building? Is it historical or innovative? Is it appropriate? Does it have charm?
D. Note the decoration of the building. Discuss the building as an art form.
E. Is the site of the building appropriately landscaped?
F. What does the building represent? Does it advertise something?

X. The building and people
A. What mood or emotional climate does the building give to the people who occupy it and those who visit it?
B. How does the building manage people?
  1. Does it bring people together or separate them?
  2. Are there any elements of confusion or disorientation about the building?
C. Does the building reflect the class, status, or role of the people using it?[11]

Some of Danzer's questions will require historical research, and students who find the historical aspect of the guide interesting may wish to use it as a start toward researching the history of a particular public building, business building, or interesting house. They may choose a building important in their own family's history, that of a family prominent in the community, or they may choose to study a house that simply intrigues them by its beauty or distinctive qualities.

Whatever type of building is chosen, students should first obtain permission from the owner of the building to do the research. One can, of course, do the study without such permission, but doing so can be considered an invasion of privacy and will make the search more difficult. If the present owner of the property holds the property abstract or gives one permission to examine it at the mortgage holder's office, the first step of the research can go very quickly. The property abstract will list all references to deeds, wills, mortgages, probate records, court litigation, and tax sales affecting the property. If the abstract is not available, then all that information can be obtained from the several offices at the county courthouse. To obtain the information needed, one must know the township, subdivision, block, and lot number, plus the location on a specific lot—that is, north or south half, east or west half. The county clerk and recorder can help students with that task.

If the courthouse is distant from the school or if students cannot work there, they may still find interesting information about the house. Real estate maps, such as the Sanborn maps, will provide much of the data needed. County plat or township maps can be used. The building may appear in an old bird's-eye view of the city. There may be prints of lithographs of the early city, showing the structure in question. Photographs of streetscapes may be available. The local newspaper may have articles about the construction of the building or of social affairs held there. City directories will list the building's street address, its occupants at any given time, and the purpose for which it was used. Manuscript collections may provide both personal and business papers of some of the families who owned the structure. Often, notes about the payment of bills for contractors, architects, remodeling, and so on will be found. Finally, it might be possible for students to interview the building's former owners and tenants. A good guide for doing that type of research is Linda Ellsworth's "The History of a House." [12] Although the citations Ellsworth lists are to materials in Pensacola, Florida, the types of information she describes are available in most communities in the United States and Canada.

As an example of the way a series of photographs of a building can provide clues to research in other forms, see plates 3.5 and 3.6. Note that the photographs are also useful for pointing out to students how remolding can change the appearance of a building.

Plates 3.5 and 3.6. *What visual evidence indicates that the buildings pictured here are the same?*—Boulder Historical Society. Plate 3.6 from the L. Paddock Collection, Boulder Historical Society. Both reprinted by permission.

Building as Architecture

While it is true that buildings reflect the history of the community and of the people who lived there, buildings can obviously be studied also for their architectural value. The visual appreciation of architecture is seldom taught in schools, but it should be. Constructing a building is not just a craft, but an art form, as well. A knowledge of the styles of architecture to be found in the local area and an appreciation for their forms can add much pleasure to one's everyday life. Every local community will have sufficient diversity of building styles that students can learn a vocabulary of architecture and an understanding of the qualities that make good style. At the same time, of course, one is noting the particular styles popular in a region and the reasons for their popularity.

The use of slides or the walking tour are the most effective methods of teaching vernacular architecture, the type of architecture one is usually most interested in using for local history. There are a number of useful sources to help students and teachers begin such a study. *The Old-House Journal* has published an inexpensive guide to the kinds of houses typically found in America.[13] A more complete guide is John J.-G. Blumenson's *Identifying American Architecture*,[14] which covers thirty-nine styles built in America from 1600 to 1945. Blumenson's book includes well-labeled photographs of these styles, as well as a pictorial glossary of terms. Most states now have architectural description guides for the use of people who are developing nominations for state or federal national registries of historic landmarks. These guides provide sketches of all important architectural terms. Teachers may also develop their own guides for students, using examples found near the school.

An introduction to the topic might include a simple walking-tour guide. Figure 3.1 is illustrative of examples one might use.

For students who like competitive activities, one might develop an architectural treasure hunt. A class can be divided into three or four teams, with each team examining the same square block, but looking for different architectural details. One member of each team should record the addresses where the item was found and the information should be checked when the students return to the classroom. As the papers are checked, one might have a member of the team draw the detail on the chalkboard and label it by the proper term. One could also use an opaque projector for this activity. Typical details one might include on the treasure hunt are sketched in figure 3.2. For teachers who cannot manage even simple sketches (and there are a lot of us around), one can usually find students who enjoy that task; or one can take photographs and trace from the print.

Once students have begun to note and name the characteristic details of a variety of architectural styles, they will become interested in the classifications used to denote each of the styles and the time periods in which styles were popular. That interest can then be developed to help students to understand the cultural aspirations and perceptions of beauty that influenced architects or builders in the local community at a given time in history. A number of suggestions for exercises that may be used to integrate local architecture into the American history curriculum may be found in Richard Rabinowitz's "The Crisis of the Classroom." [15]

Using Architecture to Understand Local Social History

A number of approaches can be taken to help students understand that much in our daily life, manners, and modes of behavior is conditioned by the ways in which we occupy the interior space of our dwellings. In most homes, there has been a front and a back area of the house—a public and a private sector. The behavior of the occupants and their guests has been affected by these areas. The use of floor plans can make that evident. Mary Lohmann, for example, has developed an activity in which students copy a typical floor plan from a Colonial-style house and then draw a floor plan of their own house, to the same scale.[16] After careful comparison of the two different plans, students write a paper discussing the probable differences in daily life, comfort, and privacy that their own families would have experienced through the influence of the house-space itself. One might also ask students studying interior-space concepts to consider a number of questions developed by Thomas J. Schlereth:

> How do homes reflect changing attitudes toward family, religion, community, and work? To what extent are family roles expressed

1. Find one building that has windows like this: ▶
Address of building_____

_____

Federal Style window. In Boulder, dates from 1870s.

2. Find at least three buildings that have tall, narrow windows like these. Record the address of each ▶ building and sketch in the kind of *lintel*, or trim, around the top of each window. Also record the building material the lintel is made of.

a. Address_____

_____

Lintel is made of_____

_____

b. Address_____

_____

Lintel is made of_____

_____

c. Address_____

_____

Lintel is made of_____

Fig. 3.1.   Example of an effective walking-tour guide to introduce students to types of architecture in the vicinity of the school.—Drawings by Warren L. Kirbo. Text based on classroom materials assembled by Catherine Taylor, Boulder Valley (Colorado) Schools, 1977. Used by permission.

3. Find at least one building that shows details like these—*Romanesque,* or round top arches, and other forms influenced by the architecture of H. H. Richardson. Look for buildings built with rough stone trim around arched doorways and windows. Also look for towers and turrets, rows of small, arched windows, and carved sandstone trim.

Address of building_____

_____

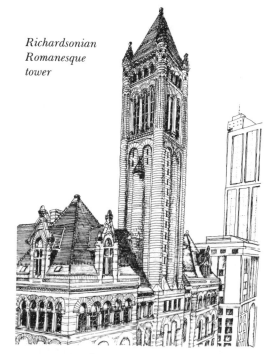

Richardsonian Romanesque tower

Richardsonian Romanesque

4. Find at least one building that has cast-iron *tie-rod anchors* on the outside in a star pattern.

Address of the building_____

_____

Fig. 3.2. Shown here on facing pages are typical architectural details that could be included for classes on an architectural treasure hunt—Drawings by Warren L. Kirbo.

within a house (men versus women versus children)? What are the expected behaviors of individuals within the various home spaces (the taboos, rituals, social conventions)? Which living spaces are more flexible? Most specialized? How is the house divided into public and private, ceremonial and utilitarian spaces? What role do real, symbolic, or psychological barriers—doors, lower ceilings, front and back hallways, side doors, or changes in wall or floor materials and finishes—tell us about the social history (and stratification) of the residents? [17]

A simple but illuminating approach to start students thinking about ways a house affects individual lives might be to have the students draw their own houses from memory. Even young adults will be able to come up with thoughts such as those expressed by Nancy Hoober in the "memory" expressed in figure 3.3.

Another good introduction to the study of houses as a source of social history is the historic house museum. Specific historic house museums can be studied in a number of ways. Frequently, the curators will have developed activities for students who visit. In some instances, the teacher in charge of students visiting the museum will want to work with the museum staff to develop productive activities for study. If that approach is taken, one might wish to study Thomas J. Schlereth's brilliant description of seven strategies that might be used. For each strategy, Schlereth suggests an inquiry focus, describes a number of student projects that might be conducted, and lists useful bibliographic references. Each strategy is related to specific disciplines:

1. House Forms and Types (cultural anthropology and folklife)
2. Interior Space Concepts (environmental and social psychology)
3. Furnishings and Household Artifacts (decorative arts and social history)
4. Geographic and Ecological Relationships (cultural and historical geography)
5. Literary and Symbolic Interpretations (American studies and literary history)
6. Architectural Features and Styles (architectural history)
7. Museum Interpretation and Analysis (museum studies).[18]

Each focus has great potential for the classroom.

KITCHEN: Very small; a lot of time was spent here, talking to Mom. If Mom had something important to say to you, she would position herself between you and the door.

DINING ROOM: Some of my fondest memories are centered in this room. The family lingers for hours after a meal, talking and laughing.

MY BEDROOM: Was on the second floor. I loved listening to the rain on the roof and the squirrels running along the ridge. There was a house rule that you were not to be disturbed when you were in your room, so my bedroom was a wonderful retreat.—Nancy Hoober

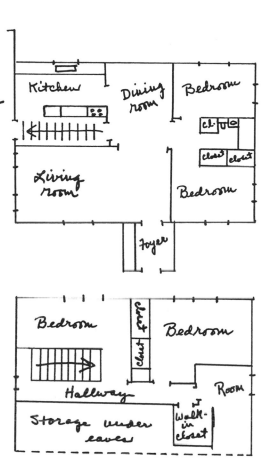

Fig. 3.3. Student Nancy Hoober's sketches and comment on the house where she grew up, from "Memories of Rooms," in Making Connections: A Family History Workbook, *edited by Karen Dahood (Tucson, Ariz.: Tucson Public Library, 1979), p. 55. The book resulted from work done for the Tucson Public Library's Sonoran Heritage Project, a National Endowment for the Humanities Learning Library at the Tucson Public Library, 1979.*—Reprinted by permission.

Fine Art

The role of architecture and the role of folk crafts in local history studies have been well established for some time. The other arts have not been used as extensively as they might. Some secondary students have done competent studies of poets or other writers of a local area and have shown how local color can add verisimilitude to written works. The symbolic dimension of cultural experience has been used with good effect in American studies courses at the college level, through the works of Henry Nash Smith, Leo Marx, and others. Alan Trachtenberg's *The Brooklyn Bridge: Fact and Symbol*, showed how a "monument became both a historical fact and a cultural symbol to the local New York community and to Americans at large." [19] Most communities, however, have no particular examples of this type. Still, there is bound to be some public art in all but the very smallest towns. One might examine the war memorials in the city park or in front of the courthouse or city hall.

In a park in New Hampshire, for example, monuments commemorating three wars are built of three different materials— granite for the Civil War, iron for World War I, and wood for World War II. Only those who died are listed on the Civil War monument; all who served are listed on the World War I monument. The number of names is greater for the Civil War. Facts like these suggest such questions as: How wealthy was the town at different periods? What proportion of the town's people participated in each of the wars? Students who find answers to such questions will learn a great deal about the history of the town and the values of the people living during a particular time period.[20]

Sculpture, and a community's reaction to it, can develop into a larger study of values, past and present. One thinks immediately of Chicago and the controversy there over the pieces by Picasso and Calder; but other cities, too, have had problems convincing the public that some works *are* art. "Workmen in Oakland, California, dismantled a controversial statue, 'Mother Peace' . . . after the work created a furor. Public pressure to remove the art work was so great that City Council members voted $2,400 to take it down from in front of the county courthouse. . . ." [21] Thus the

Plate 3.7. Art echoing the vertical lines of architecture.

history of public sculpture can also reflect value conflicts within a community.

Students who feel strongly about one side or the other in such a conflict can use the controversy as the genesis of a local history project. Simple questionnaires administered to freinds, neigh-

Plate 3.8. A visual surprise within an urban setting.

bors, and people on the street may be tabulated according to sex, age, ethnic identification, and perceived social and economic class. Newspaper stories and editorials can provide additional information. A recent incident can then be compared with one that took place in the community's past—and one can be almost certain that

Plate 3.9. Modern art as a complement to modern architecture.

there was such an incident. Perhaps it concerned a memorial or decoration for a public building, rather than a piece of sculpture. One period that is often fruitful for such incidents is the Depression. Public structures were welcomed for the economic benefit they brought to a town, but nearly everyone had comments to make on the quality of the work.

Sculpture added to Boulder High School in Boulder, Colorado, is an interesting example. *Minnie* and *Jake* are rotund figures meant to represent Strength and Wisdom. They were commissioned as part of the Federal Artists Program, and the school board as well as the city council were delighted with the idea that "real" sculpture would decorate the fine educational complex happily built with federal funds. The unveiling was a disaster, however, and for a time it appeared that public indignation would force the removal of these statues in the same way that *Mother Peace* was destroyed in Oakland. Cool heads finally prevailed, but the storm of protest is renewed during every football season, when cross-town rivals paint the statues red (their school color); and, just as regularly, funds must be found to sandblast *Minnie* and *Jake* to remove the stain of the Fairview Knights. The school newspaper annually produces a story on *Minnie* and *Jake*, and the local newspaper often reviews the old controversy. Students studying these responses over forty years can discover changes in popular taste. Other documents that could be used in the project include school board minutes, federal records, and oral interviews.

Rhode Island has prepared an extensive set of activities for studying state history, many of which are applicable for local study, as well. After students investigate monuments, statues, and sculptural forms, they are asked to relate examples of sculpture to people and events in the community's history. They are to do this by finding the answer to such questions as: "Who made it? What or whom, if anything or anybody, does it represent? Why was it made, and who were the people responsible?" [22]

Obviously, public art can be examined on as many levels as architecture can. Much depends on the interest and maturity level of the students, the interest and knowledge of the teacher, and, of course, the availability of the resources in a particular community.

Using Artifacts in Local History Research

Heirlooms, *keepsakes*, *souvenirs*, *mementos*, and *memorabilia* are some of the terms we use to describe the belongings all kinds of people have seemed to save throughout the past. These possessions are kinds of things that can be found in "Grandma's trunk," in the back of a dresser drawer, or in an attic or basement storeroom. They may be pulled out, on occasion, when someone wants to "do something with all these old things"; but chances are, most such items simply are rearranged until their owners can get to them some other time. The families of students might well donate some of these artifacts for classroom activities. Other families will lend materials for special displays. Artifacts of this type may also be donated to the class by the local museum, especially when the museum has a very large collection of similar items with little monetary worth. Museums will also lend kits of artifacts that can be used to help students develop a sense of society in a time past.

Ways students can analyze these artifacts were described in chapter 1. Here, it is important to suggest that, if one does decide to maintain a collection of artifacts, there is a responsibility that should be met. A hodgepodge of "things" is of little use unless they can be catalogued and classified in some manner. Most artifacts can be labeled by using a small dot of correction fluid and marking that with a pen, using India ink. Objects that cannnot be marked in that manner might be kept in a plastic envelope or a plastic box that is labeled. The label should record the number of the object, and the date of acquisition. The catalogue card, which bears the same label, should include the location where the artifact is stored, a brief description of the object, and the name of the donor. A sample card is shown in figure 3.4.[23]

Types of activities that can be used to good effect with artifacts will vary according to the maturity of the students involved and

	ARTIFACT
Number	Date
Identity	Location
Description	

Fig. 3.4.   A sample card for cataloguing and classifying artifacts collected as a classroom activity.

the relationship the artifacts have to the local area. Teachers will find useful ideas in publications written for museum education curators. One such leaflet, "School Loan Exhibits," by Frances A. Brayton, of Elmira, New York, describes the contents of typical kits developed for use by school students in Chemung County, New York.[24] Any teacher will find this leaflet helpful for ideas about the logistics involved in using traveling kits of artifacts. As most such exhibits have been planned for elementary students, many teachers at the secondary or college level do not realize that the same or similar exhibits are equally useful for older students. One simply changes the sophistication of the presentation or has an older student imagine what a younger student can learn from the materials. Many older students will then develop kits as a project. The Chemung County exhibits and kits cover such topics as household items of pioneer days, tools and implements, early transportation, the local canal, children's toys and school items, the Iroquois Indians, the Civil War, folk art, nineteenth-century architecture, migrations, and Mark Twain's life in Elmira. Every local area has almost limitless possibilities for similar kits that will interest students.

Cemeteries as Sources of Data

Cemeteries can be used as additional sources of information for a variety of local history projects, or they may be used as the focus of certain specialized studies. If one is, for instance, concerned with the ethnic identification of the earliest settlers and there is scanty information about that in the available written sources, a trip to the earliest cemetery in the community to read the names on the headstones would help one to draw some conclusions—tentatively, at least. If, on the other hand, one's local history project is a study of the "Civil War Graveyard of _____," then the cemetery itself and its internal evidence will become the focus of the study. In either case, however, other types of sources should be used in conjunction with the cemetery itself. A third type of project that draws on data from cemeteries is the study of the rate of cultural change in a particular region and the diffusion of such change. Archaeologists and social historians are finding that changes in motifs used for tombstone symbology, types of stone used for headstones, and the style of epitaphs over a period of years tends to reflect changes in religious beliefs and the influences of social class. Because this type of study requires evidence from a number of graveyards within a region, it is not practical for many school students to undertake. It is, however, a project that might be used by a teacher over a number of years.

No matter what type of study one is going to conduct in a cemetery, it is important to obtain permission before field study is begun. In some areas, cemeteries have become overrun with student tours, with casual visitors, and even with vandals. Some cemetery associations have had to close their grounds to the casual visitor. Most will welcome students, if arrangements have been made ahead of time, and in some instances, cemetery authorities will even send representatives to help students with their research.

Frequently, a teacher will want to have the whole class make one short study of a representative cemetery. Although all students will probably not wish to choose a topic related to the field trip, the experience can be useful in providing them with a sense of the type of data one can obtain. The following set of questions might be used for such an introductory visit:

The Cemetery as Data Source: The Field Trip
General Information

1. How many graves are there in the burial ground? What is the oldest? Most recent?
2. How many markers bear the same last name?
3. Can you identify family plots? How?
4. How many generations do the names on the markers represent?
5. What is the average age of death for each decade of the cemetery's use? Use copies of the following chart to help you in your tabulations: [25]

Decade: 1860–1869

AGE	No. Females	No. Males	AGE	No. Females	No. Males
0– 6			51–55		
6–10			56–60		
11–15			61–65		
16–20			66–70		
21–25			71–75		
26–30			76–80		
31–35			81–85		
36–40			85–90		
41–45			91–95		
46–50			96–100		

6. What is the ratio of graves of men to those of women?
7. Has the number of children who died when they were under age five changed over the decades? What does this tell you?
8. Is there an age period of life when the ratio of deaths of men far exceeds that of women? Why might that be so?

Ethnic Identification
1. Do many tombstones name the country of birth? If so, list several of these.
2. Does the style of headstone or grave marker differ by ethnic group? Explain and describe.
3. How many different ethnic groups can you identify by the types of names found? (Any good book on the origin of names will provide a reference for this question.)
4. Is there a definite time span during which particular ethnic group members were buried in the cemetery? How do you account for this?
5. Where and of what denominations are the nearest churches? Has this been influential in determining who was buried in the cemetery? Do these churches have a particular ethnic membership?

6. Are there now, or have there ever been, any ethnic or religious restrictions on who may be buried in any of the cemeteries in your area? Check cemetery records.

Symbology and Inscriptions

1. Do the types of carvings on the tombstones differ according to the age of the persons buried? Are you more likely to find lambs or flowers, for instance, on a child's stone than on a marker for an adult? Describe the differences you find.
2. Are there differences in style between the carvings on the headstones of men and women?
3. Are there carvings or brass plates that indicate that the person buried had been a member of a fraternal organization? Is that group still active in your community?
4. Have the symbols on the headstones changed in style, over the years? Are they more decorative now than formerly, or less so?
5. What can the inscriptions on the headstones tell you about the people buried there? Are there any that describe a person as a "good mother," "loving husband," "pioneer settler," or the like? Have these kinds of descriptions changed, over the years?

Compiling the information developed through such a study requires that students organize charts and graphs for reporting the statistical data gathered. They must make cross-tabulations and frequency distributions. These data must be tabulated and coded, along with the statistics generated. Visual data may be brought back to the classroom in the form of rubbings and photographs, sketches, and site maps. The final report, usually a group effort, provides answers to students' own questions, as well as a straightforward factual history of the cemetery.

Projects

Cemeteries can be used as the basis of a great number of different local history projects. Some students studying the occupations of early settlers will want to find out which craftsman became responsible for making headstones. Not all communities had stonecutters, in the early days. Harriette Merrifield Forbes[26] points out that many early New England headstone-cutters were printers, engravers, woodcarvers, or bricklayers, and they made headstones only as a side line. In the absence of birth and mortality records for a given community, at some time in the past, the cemetery may be the only source from which one can draw general conclusions. The wealth of particular families or segments of a population in an older community might also be inferred from a cemetery study. Students will think of many more ways one might apply such data.

Projects centering on the cemetery itself can be interesting for some students. In Carmel, New York, for example, a class studied the local Revolutionary War Graveyard.[27] Students did statistical studies such as those suggested in the cemetery-as-data-source worksheet above, but they also examined the types of stone used for the headstones and footstones. Audrey E. Wilson has developed a number of interdisciplinary projects to be done at a local cemetery, and among these, she has students examine the types of stone available for grave marking, discover whether these

Plate 3.10.   New England churchyard.—From *Early Man.* Reprinted by permission.

Plate 3.11.   Papago Indian Cemetery, Tucson, Arizona.

stones were from local outcroppings, study the transportation difficulties in obtaining the stones, and, finally, study the stones for legibility as related to stone type.[28]

Perhaps the most popular studies of cemeteries for students is the collection of rubbings or photographs of interesting headstones. Rubbings may be made with any paper and crayons or soft pencils, but lightweight rice paper and graphite sticks or charcoal crayons produce the best results. A spray fixative applied to the finished rubbing before it is removed from the stone will help to protect it against smudging. Rubbings may be affixed to poster board, and they do make interesting displays for projects. A more important use of rubbings is that they provide a copy of headstone information that can be carried back to the classroom as data for additional studies. The same is true of photographs.

Good photographs of tombstones are technically quite difficult. Mary-Ellen Jones, "Photographing Tombstones: Equipment and Techniques," describes both the problems and solutions.[29] Although she gives directions for making rubbings and for transcribing, Jones thinks that, in most instances, photography is a technique far superior to rubbings. As anyone who has worked with rubbings knows, they are bulky to store, and they will not always pick up three-dimensional motifs. Although transcribing is important and must always be done in conjunction with other methods, a photograph can record, with less effort and with less chance of error, both the motif and the shape of the stone, as well as the lettering.

With so many of our cemeteries being destroyed by weathering and vandalism, photographs can provide a permanent record for researchers in the future. Jones believes that every cemetery study should include data on the cemetery itself, as well as on each tombstone. An index card for the cemetery should include state, county, city or nearest town, directions to the location, descriptive data about the condition, and information on whether or not a key is needed to enter. Tombstone data should include all names and dates; the name of the stonecutter, if it is visible; the nature of the epitaph, if there is one; and the symbology used. Photographs and negatives should be keyed to these data and stored with them.

Students who wish to record data from a small family burial plot or who work as part of a larger community effort to record and perhaps restore a cemetery will find John J. Newman's leaflet, "Cemetery Transcribing: Preparations and Procedures," [30] essential. Newman describes ways to map the graveyard, tools needed for the study, methods used for transcribing the inscriptions on headstones, approaches to developing both legal and simple descriptions of the cemetery plat, and procedures for making a sample transcription of a cemetery.

Such instructions would be valuable for a class or large group project concerned with the restoration of a local graveyard. The Gloucester, Massachusetts, Community Development Corporation has done such a restoration and has published a set of notes for the use of other communities wishing to do a similar project. Both technical and legal information are included in the Gloucester publication. In addition, Elsa Martz has written a useful monograph, entitled "Cemetery Restoration as a High School Course." [31]

A superb example of the way in which such studies may be both a contribution to a town and a useful experience in learning methods of historical research is the project developed by Richard J. Riley for the Quincy, Massachusetts, Public Schools. In this instance, students work during the summer to restore existing tombstones and search for those that are missing from the 340-year-old Hancock Cemetery. For each grave site within the cemetery, students fill out a data sheet that includes information on the material used in the headstone, the condition of the stone, the condition of the inscription, the shape of the headstone, and other bits of information. Riley provides each student with instructions for recording this information and charts to use in determining the shapes and designs of the gravestones. A copy of these materials is included in the appendix. The study goes beyond mere restoration activities, however; Riley uses the cemetery as the focus for a study of the history of Quincy as a whole. Some students may study the history of a family whose burial plot is located in the cemetery; some do research on the ethnicity of early settlers, the life expectancy of Quincy citizens as compared to that of citizens of other New England towns, or investigate changes in land ownership or land use during the time the cemetery has been in existence. Riley also has students compare tombstone art with styles popular in other areas of material culture at a particular time: wig styles, lacework, broadsides, and architecture. Students study the techniques and tools used in tombstone-carving, as well as tombstone symbology. Questions students are asked to consider include:

1. Why are there different types of symbolism?
2. How does the symbolism reflect the religious ideology of Puritans and other groups?
3. How does the seriation of styles in Hancock Cemetery compare with other cemeteries? What does comparison of several seriation patterns tell us about cultural change?
4. Does the symbolism used correlate with the economic and social status of the person buried? [32]

A very detailed study focusing on questions similar to those Riley asks of his students is being conducted by James Deetz and

Plates 3.12 and 3.13.   One of the major components of the Hancock Cemetery Restoration Project was to remove heavy vegetation that was damaging the gravestones. Trees were cut down, gravestones removed, and root systems dug out. Stones were then reset using modern techniques.—Richard J. Riley. Reprinted by permission.

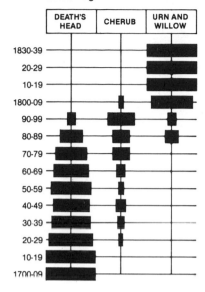

Cambridge

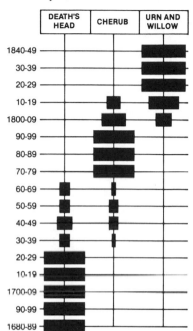

Plymouth

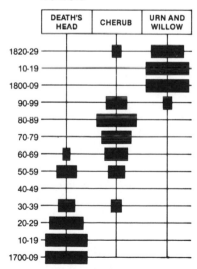

Concord

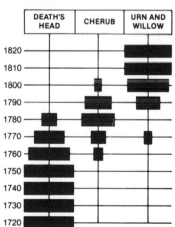

Stoneham

Fig. 3.5. Growth and decline in popularity of New England gravestone designs are revealed in "battleship-shaped" curves on graphs plotted by archaeologists James Deetz and Edwin Dethlefsen, in a study of archaeological dating methods based on increasing and decreasing popularity of different types of artifacts.—Reprinted, with permission, from "Death-Heads, Cherubs, and Shaded Urns," by Felicia A. Holton, in *Early Man*, Autumn 1979, p. 7.

Fig. 3.6.   Drawings from photographs of New England gravestones studied by James Deetz and Edwin Dethlefsen show changes in gravestone design from death's-head to cherub.—Reprinted, with permission, from "Death-heads, Cherubs, and Shaded Urns," by Felicia A. Holton, in *Early Man*, Autumn 1979, p. 8.

Edwin Dethlefsen. Anthropologists Deetz and Dethlefsen study the rate of cultural change and cultural diffusion in colonial New England through an examination of the changing popularity of certain designs carved on headstones. Figure 3.5 displays the "battleship-shaped curves" that show the seriation of the change from death's-head to cherub to urn and willow symbols as styles for headstone decoration. Using that data and historical records, the two investigators have suggested that, when death's-heads were popular, orthodox Puritanism was universal in New England. By the early eighteenth century, religious rules were less strictly enforced, and New Englanders of that time held a more

Plate 3.14. Headstone decorations changed, over time.—Reprinted, with permission, from "Death-Heads, Cherubs, and Shaded Urns," by Felicia A. Holton, in *Early Man,* Autumn 1979, p. 6.

optimistic outlook. The cherubs on headstones reflect this more cheerful outlook. The rise of the urn and willow, the two men suggest, was a reflection of the more intellectual religions (Unitarianism, for example) popular at the beginning of the nineteenth century.[33]

For students living in New England, the data printed in figure 3.5 might be used to see how well their community follows the general trend of the region. Students in other areas of the country might use the method to see whether there are similar kinds of changes made, over time, in the type of symbology used.[34]

Students will find that, in most eighteenth- and nineteenth-century cemeteries, the motifs can be classified into five main categories: classical revival, flowers, hands, animals, and angels. Epitaphs range from brief statements—"Loving Wife," "Pioneer Settler," "A Friend to All," to four-line poems. Some are witty, in the John Dryden mode:

> Here lies my wife:
> Here let her lie!
>
> Now she's at rest—
> and so am I.[35]

Others are wistful and sad:

> Here lies my wife
> My joy, my pleasure
> Here waits for me
> My wife, my life.[36]

In combination with other materials from the time, the cemetery study can reveal the public face the people of the community showed toward the loss of loved ones. Epitaphs, religious symbolism, folk art, styles in carving and lettering, and trends in cemetery furniture—all are useful primary source material that may be helpful in doing demographic, genealogical, and social history studies.

Part 2
Content and Concepts

4

Teaching about Families
with Local History Sources

FAMILY history is receiving increasing attention in history and
social studies classrooms. Although the study of the family as a
social institution and agency of acculturation has been common
enough in sociology and anthropology courses, the study of family history in history courses is relatively new. The colonial family
or the family in industrial America may have been lecture topics
in social history courses in some universities; but prior to the
1970s, the family was seldom mentioned in history survey courses.
Early in that decade, reports began to appear in educational journals from teachers who were assigning family history projects to
students as optional work in American history courses.[1] The students usually compiled personal family histories, based on
genealogical research. The publication in late 1976 of Alex
Haley's *Roots: The Saga of An American Family* and the subsequent
television mini-series added greatly to the popularity of that kind
of family history. Family history in school and college classrooms
still primarily means involving students in a search for the roots of
their own families.[2]

Personal family history projects can be useful teaching tools,
but they also have serious limitations. Their principal value, as
best one can judge from the limited literature on the use of such
projects, is to stimulate a student's interest in the past. As Kirk
Jeffrey has put it, they "enliven the study of history."[3] Yet one
suspects that the students' newly found interest in the past is
focused mainly on themselves and their families, rather than on

history in the broader sense. As Davis Bitton has described the response of his students, "There was a sense of delight in human characters within their families; there was gratification at what the family had accomplished; there was obvious sense on the part of the authors [of family history papers] that these people, their own families, were solid stock, the salt of the earth." [4] Bitton suggests that the temptation for a student to seek solace and reassurance in the history of his own family may be so strong that the result is a form of emotional therapy that is imcompatible with critical historical scholarship. By relating the history of their own families to some broader historical context, students should ideally come away with a deeper understanding of the past than would otherwise be possible. Professor Jeffrey, for example, insists "that the student relate the history of his family in some way to larger social trends and that he not present me with either a barebones genealogy or an autobiography." [5] One wonders, however, whether most students who do family history projects really do see them primarily as the means toward such an end rather than as ends sufficient in themselves.

Investigating the History of Local Families

Some difficulties inherent in personal family history projects can be avoided by having students investigate the history of other people's families. "In fact," says Davis Bitton, "if one of the purposes of historical study in general is to develop the ability to examine a subject with a certain sense of distance, the study of other families might achieve this purpose better than the study of one's own." [6] By being able to view the family studied in the same emotionally detached way that he would view any other aspect of the past, the student may also find it easier to relate that family to other historical developments. The principal disadvantage of selecting a family other than one's own is that sources will likely be more difficult to find.

Sufficient source materials will probably exist in most communities, however, for the history of any business or white-collar-class family that lived there for more than one generation. The dates of births, marriages, divorces, and deaths in the family will be available in public records. Property transfers, wills, and estate records will be available in the county clerk's office. The local newspaper probably published obituaries for various members of the family. Members of the family who still live in the community may also be available as oral history sources. Such sources will be available for middle-class families, as well as for wealthy and prominent families. While the sources will probably be more abundant for the wealthy and prominent, still, local family history projects do not have to be limited to the elite.

Teachers involved with Project Probe in New York state developed a set of materials with accompanying activities based on the family of a local tailor. J. Y. Brown, the tailor, had lived in Windsor, New York, during the 1840s and 1850s. The basic sources of information were portions of Brown's diary and diaries of his two wives. Using these sources, the teachers developed activities suitable for junior high school students. Among them were map exercises based on the movements of people mentioned in the diaries and genealogical assignments that clarified the family relationships of those people. The teachers also taped an interview with an elderly resident of Windsor who had known one of the tailor's sons. Other activities focused on churches and graveyards mentioned in Brown's diary.[7]

Writing the history of a local family can also help to illuminate the history of the community. Finding out how one family carved a niche for itself in the local community can reveal a good deal about the texture of everday life in the town. Family history can also help to relate local history to broader historical developments. A family that prospered and became one of the town's prominent families may serve as an example of successful and upwardly mobile families everywhere, even though it may not be representative of most local families. The migration route that brought the family to the community may also be suggestive of larger patterns of population movement. Figures 4.1 and 4.2 and plates 4.1 through 4.5 suggest both the kinds of sources available for local family history and some of the ways that local family history can be linked to larger historical developments.

SOME SOURCES FOR A HISTORY
OF
THE HENRY D. FONDA FAMILY

The Fonda Family

1880 Federal Census:

Fonda, Henry D.	66/?	New York/NY/NY	Surveyor
Catherine	55/?	Penn./Va/Pa	Wife
Edward	16	Ill.	
DeWitt	11	Ill.	

Fonda, Giles	32/?	Ill.	Druggist
Edna	24/?	Ohio/NY/Conn.	Wife
Gracie	5	Colo.	
Edna L.	3	Colo.	
Ethel P.	1	Colo.	

| Fonda, George | 21/m21 | Ill. | Apothecary |
| Mary | 20/m20 | Michigan/Vt/NY | Wife |

1900 Federal Census:

Fonda, Dewitt	31/m23	Ill.	Soda pop manufacturer,
Ida	30/m22	Kansas/Ger/Ger	rents house at 1017
Louis	1	Colo.	Pine
Fonda, George	41/m21	Ill.	Druggist, owns home at
Mary	40/m20	Mich.	827 Pine; had two
Katherine	10	Colo.	children, both living
Blenda	23	Sweden/Swe/Swe	Servant, immigrated to
Swanson			U.S. in 1890

Other Fondas: Henry's widow lived in Denver in 1900; Giles and his daughter
Edna were also renting rooms in Denver.

Fig. 4.1. Example of federal census information available for family histories.

Deaths and Funerals

George F. Fonda, Pioneer Boulder Resident, Dies

For Nearly Seventy Years Was a Leading Citizen of this City

George F. Fonda, resident of Boulder since May 6, 1874, died this morning at 2:30 at the Community Hospital, where he was taken last Thursday. In failing health for some time, he became seriously ill the first of the week.

No man had played a more interesting or important part in the development of Boulder than Mr. Fonda, who, since being named a member of the governor's staff by the late James H. Peabody in 1903, has been known as "Colonel."

Mr. Fonda served the city of Boulder as an alderman, as foreman and chief of its volunteer fire department, as chief of the paid department that he was instrumental in establishing, as tuba player in the Boulder Band, as a member of its horse-racing and baseball teams, as a member of civic committees in promoting streetcar lines, industries, hotel construction, and everything else designed to improve the city and vicinity.

Col. Fonda was born in Augusta, Ill., Nov. 6, 1858, and moved with his parents to Soloman City, Kans., from which place he came to Boulder to join his brother, Giles, who had established a drug and stationery business in the late 1860s.

A biography of Mr. Fonda says he worked his way to Denver on a train as a peanut boy and arrived in Boulder over the Boulder Valley Railroad, which had its depot at 24th and Pearl. He worked for his brother at $10 per month and board, while sleeping on the floor of the drugstore, which was located at 1216–18 Pearl. When his brother decided to move to Leadville, Mr. Fonda, then but eighteen, was sold the business on time. He developed the store, disposing of the stationery stock but keeping a wallpaper and paint division for many years. He constructed the modern brick building which is now Pullen Store and in which Mr. Fonda continued his drug business until retiring in 1919.

He was married to Mary E. Jones, Nov. 24, 1879, at Nederland. They came to Boulder after the wedding and in 1901 built the fine home at 2135 8th, ... the scene of some of the finest parties in Boulder's history. Mrs. Fonda is one of Boulder's most popular women.

Mr. Fonda is survived by his wife and a daughter, Elizabeth H. Adams, wife of Attorney Ethelbert Adams of Grand Junction. ... Another daughter, Catherine, wife of Montgomery East, died in 1924. Other survivors are three grandchildren and a brother. ... D. C. Fonda, retired head of the Fonda Bottling Works. Eben G. Fine is a brother-in-law and Hal S. Coulson, photographer, is a nephew.

Fig. 4.2. Boulder Daily Camera *news story on the death of pioneer resident George F. Fonda illustrates ways family and community history coexist.*

Plate 4.1.   Pearl Street, Boulder, Colorado, in 1885, with the Fonda drug-store on the left.—Western History Department, Denver Public Library. Reprinted by permission.

Whether it is used for personal family history or for investigating local families, the genealogical approach itself has limitations. Concentration on a single family tends to illuminate what is unique about it. Any family's particular configuration of individual lives makes it one of a kind. Compiling the genealogies of arbitrarily chosen families is not a fruitful method for examining broader aspects of the historical development of the family as a social institution. One cannot generalize about families in American history on the basis of such studies. To find out what families have had in common requires a different approach, one that will yield frequency distributions of characteristics of large numbers of families. Even if it were possible to assemble a large number of personal family histories, one would never know how representative they were, so long as they were selected arbitrarily. To go beyond genealogy to the broader study of the family in American history requires an approach much different from those described thus far.

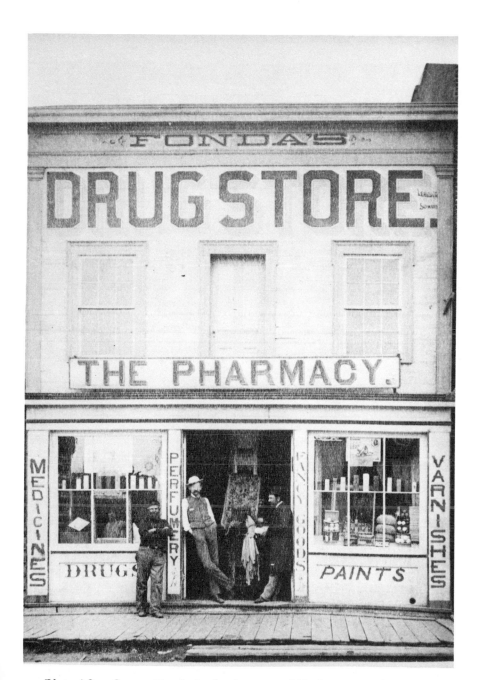

Plate 4.2.   George Fonda in the doorway of his drugstore, about 1885.—
Western History Department, Denver Public Library. Reprinted by permission.

Plate 4.3. The interior of the Fonda drugstore.—Western History Department, Denver Public Library. Reprinted by permission.

Using Local Sources to Investigate the Family in American History

If family history is to make a significant contribution to history and social studies education, it must transcend family genealogy and engage students in the study of the family in history. It must bring students into contact with that emerging body of historical knowledge that has resulted from the investigation of various aspects of the family in historical time. Inspired by the work of Louis Henry and other French historical demographers in the 1950s, historians of the family in Western Europe, Great Britain, and the United States have created an essentially new field of historical research. Like other areas of the "new social history," this newly emerging tradition of family history emphasizes the experiences of ordinary people, rather than of an elite and is concerned with groups, rather than individuals. Instead of the unique experiences of individual families, this new history is concerned about the impact of large-scale social changes upon fami-

Plate 4.4. During their early years in Boulder, George Fonda and his family lived in this unimposing frame house.

lies in general. To make projects dealing with large numbers of families manageable, historians have found it expedient to limit the size of the geographical area included in their research. Most of the family history studies done so far have focused on individual communities.[8]

The case-study approach used by historians of the family has obvious implications for the teaching of family history. By utilizing local sources of data and by adapting the methods used by historians of the family, teachers can involve students in similar family history investigations.[9] They can investigate family size and household structure, ages at which people married, the spacing of children, and aspects of the family life cycle. By using local data, they can find out what characteristics families in their community shared with those in similar communities that have been ex-

*Plate 4.5. As the drugstore business prospered, the upwardly mobile Fondas
built this more substantial house.*

amined by historians. Students in New England communities who
use local sources to investigate the colonial family, for example,
can compare their findings about family size and age at marriage
with those of John Demos in his study of Plymouth.[10] Even where
no comparable scholarly study exists, students can develop tentative hypotheses about the size and structure of the American
family during various time periods on the basis of locally available
data.

Much of the scholarly interest in the history of the family has
focused on questions of family structure. The idea that the size
and structure of the family changed substantially during the
nineteenth century as a result of industrialization and urbanization has loomed rather large in modern sociological theory. It has
been widely assumed that the nuclear family is of rather recent
origin, having evolved from an extended form of family organization that was presumably the dominant type of family of preindustrial times. By focusing on the question of family structure,

historians have discovered that the nuclear *household*, at least, has been the basic living arrangement for the past two hundred years. Households of the twentieth century are smaller than those of colonial America, but they are not radically different in structure.[11]

The simplest way to introduce students to the preindustrial family of early nineteenth-century America is to use the packet of family-history materials developed by the museum staff at Old Sturbridge Village.[12] The packet consists of a set of "reconstituted" family cards and a set of household cards. The family cards contain information about a representative sample of seventy-three Sturbridge, Massachusetts, families for the period 1790 to 1840. Included in this data are names of husband, wife, and children; dates of birth, marriage, and death, when known; and information about occupation and property holdings of the head of the household, taken from the 1824 Sturbridge tax list. By using a subset of thirty-five cards representative of the larger sample, students can compute the average family size, marriage age, number of "early babies" (those born within eight months of the wedding), intervals between births, infant mortality rates, the rate of childbirth-related maternal mortality, and average landholdings. The household cards, which are based on the United States census for 1820, list the name and age of each person then living in the household. (A household includes all the persons living at an address whether or not they were members of the family.) The Sturbridge packet can be used to introduce students to the data and methods of family history, to explore characteristics of the preindustrial, early-nineteenth-century American family, or as a basis for comparing data about household structure of the industrial era taken from the students' own community.

Comparable data on household structure for the industrial era for any community can be found in the federal manuscript census returns. The manuscript returns are the enumeration sheets that the census takers carried with them from door to door, and they are available on microfilm through the census of 1900 (except for the 1890 returns). Not all the manuscript censuses are equally useful. The censuses from 1790 through 1850 list the number of persons in each household, but not the names and ages of indi-

---

THE PLINY FREEMAN FAMILY

FREEMAN FAMILY [Pliny]

Husband:	Pliny	b. 9/24/1780	d. 10/10/1855 in Webster, Mass.
Wife:	Delia	b. 4/21/1781	d. 3/20/1839
Married:	10/5/1802		
Children:	*Silas Marsh*	b. 8/7/1803	m. 3/27/1831 to Maria R. Upham of Sutton, Mass. d. 11/4/1880 in Millbury, Mass.
	Pliny	b. 4/14/1806	m. 9/8/1835 in Cleveland, Ohio d. 11/2/1894 in Geneseo, Illinois
	Beulah	b. 12/6/1807	m. 4/1/1832 to Walter S. Rosenbrooks d. 7/5/1835 in Oxford, Mass.
	Delia	b. 4/4/1810	m. 4/4/1833 to John S. W. May of Leicester, Mass. d. 11/2/1864 in Webster, Mass.
	Florella	b. 5/26/1812	m. 12/11/1833 to Bradford Baylis Southbridge, Mass. d. 11/27/1876 in Bristol, Penna.
	Augusta	b. 12/25/1815	m. 3/30/1841 to Holowell A. Perrin
	Dwight	b. 1/15/1819	m. 6/14/1852 in Webster, Mass.
2nd Wife:	Mrs. Mary Pease Widow	b. 8/7/1784 Boston, Mass.	d. 2/3/1850
Married:	7/1/1840		
Children:	None		

Fig. 4.3.   A reconstituted family card from the "Households and Families" packet prepared by Old Sturbridge Village, Sturbridge, Massachusetts.—Reprinted with permission.

viduals, except for the household head. The censuses of 1860 and 1870 do provide that information, but do not identify the relationship of each person to the household head. The censuses beginning in 1880 do list that useful information. Each of the censuses from 1850 lists the place of birth of each person; beginning in 1880 they also include the birthplace of the mother and father of each individual. That makes it relatively easy to establish the ethnic origins of families. Any census from 1850 on can easily be used to investigate family and household structure. Data from two or more census periods will show change over time.[13]

To make the federal censuses usable for classroom activities, the data must be transcribed from the microfilm reel and reduced to manageable size. Household data even for a community as small as 10,000 people in 1880, for example, would be overwhelming to both teacher and students. With a household of average size—about 5 persons, in 1880—a population of 10,000 would represent approximately 2,000 households. To save time and to reduce the number of household data cards to be worked with in the classroom, the teacher should take a sample of these households. A statistical manual commonly used by historians indicates that a sample of 250 would ensure an adequate degree of randomness (80 out of 100 different random samples of that size would have an error of less than 4 percentage points).[14] Thus the teacher would need to copy only the information for approximately every eighth family. If the stack of 250 data cards in the sample still seems to be too unwieldy for classroom use, it can be further reduced by selecting representative cards from the sample. For example, if 30 percent of the systematically sampled households were extended in form, so must be 30 percent of the final sample. If ethnicity is one of the variables to be considered in the classroom activity and 25 percent of the household heads in the systematic sample were of Irish origin, so must be an equal proportion of the cards finally selected.

With a set of household data cards representing their own community, students can explore several dimensions of nineteenth-century family and household life. They can investigate some rather basic questions about the relations between generations. Did elderly parents tend to live in their children's households, or did they live separately? Did married daughters and sons continue to live in their parents' households? Did unmarried young adults continue to live with their parents? The students will probably find that the nuclear family was the most common form of family organization and that relatively few young adults in their mid-twenties were still living at home. They will very likely discover many young, unmarried adults boarding in households other than their parents'. Boarding out was a common transitional stage between living at home and establishing a separate household. The observation that boarding was a far more common living arrangement in the nineteenth century than it is today can lead to other questions. What was the average age of boarders in the community? Was it common to the life style of young people? What percentage of young, unmarried adults lived in single-person households of their own? Which was more common, boarding or living alone? The students will also discover that servants who "lived in" were more common then than now. What kinds of families employed live-in servants? Who were the servants? Were some ethnic groups more heavily represented than others in the servant group? Was being a servant a lifetime occupation, or was the job largely restricted to a certain age group? With the teacher's assistance, students can also compare data from their community with that of other communities for which historical studies exist, to determine how representative were the families in their community.[15]

Still another dimension can be added to this historical inquiry into family size and household structure by having students compare the past with the present. Of course, it is not possible to examine individual families in more recent census years, as the manuscript returns after 1900 are not open to the public. The published volumes for the decennial censuses and other published reports are available in any library that is a repository of federal government documents and will provide an abundance of general information about families and households. With such data, students can plot the continuing decline in the birth rate and in the size of the American family. The frequent surveys conducted by the Bureau of the Census between decennial census years also provide timely information about current trends. The most rapidly growing type of household in the United States, by the end of the 1970s, for example, was the household consisting of a single individual. Single persons setting up households of their own stand in sharp contrast to the nineteenth-century pattern of single individuals living as boarders in other households. Current census data about single-person households can serve as a springboard for considering a variety of social and cultural changes that have taken place in the United States during the twentieth century.

While much of the scholarly historical interest in the family has been focused on questions of family size and structure, changes in the roles of family members are no less important. The roles ascribed to various members of the family today were not necessarily the roles they performed in the past. Adult members of the family in colonial America performed a variety of roles that would later be delegated to outside agencies—including the major responsibility for educating the young and for vocational training. In both rural families and urban working-class families of a century ago, women and children contributed in a much more direct way to the economic survival of the family than they do in most families today. An investigation of changing family roles based on such local history sources as contemporary newspaper items, published reports concerning child and female labor, or oral history interviews can provide the basis for a wide-ranging consideration of economic and social changes.

Investigating Family Cycles with Local Historical Sources

Although the nuclear family has been a remarkably stable institution for at least two hundred years, that is not necessarily true for individual families. Children marry and leave home, husbands and wives obtain divorces, elderly parents die, and elderly grandparents temporarily move in. Dynamic elements of family life tend to become obscured when one concentrates on family structure at a single point in time. To conclude that most American families have been nuclear in structure may be correct, but it does not tell the whole story. An individual family may have been organized quite differently at various times. Some knowledge of the typical cycles that families have passed through is essential to an understanding of the family in American history.

Studying the cycles of individual families over time requires an approach somewhat different from the cross-sectional analysis used for studying family structure. It has to be an approach, as Tamara K. Hareven has suggested, that "treats the family as a process over time rather than as a static unit at certain points in time. It assumes that individuals live through a variety of patterns of family structure and household organization during different stages of their life cycle." [16] Ideally, it would mean combining the information available on state or federal census returns about age, occupation, ethnicity, and value of property with all the other local data needed to reconstitute individual families. In addition, city directory data should be combed to find out when relatives, servants, and boarders moved in or out of a household. "If one studies the cycle of individual families over time," Professor Hareven concluded,

> one would find that household organization and family structure are correlated to the age of the household head and the ages of various family members. . . . The points of transition from one family type to another and the nature of transition do differ, however, in different ethnic and social-economic groups. Viewed from this perspective, race, ethnicity, and occupation become crucial variables in determining longitudinal changes in the family cycle.[17]

While a systematic analysis of local family cycles in the past requires more extensive research than most teachers have time for, examples of family cycles can be demonstrated without much difficulty by the use of selected local history data. Tracing individual families through two or three census periods will provide at least a series of snapshots of that family, rather than just one view. The directors of the Minnesota Social History Project assembled data on two Winona, Minnesota, families as an example of what teachers can do with such longitudinal data taken from census returns. While not designed solely as a demonstration of family cycles, the material can be used for that purpose. Data in figure 4.4 on the family of Addison B. Youmans provides an example of one kind of family cycle. A perusal of census returns for any community would uncover other variations. While an arbitrary selection would not produce examples that were necessarily representative of the families in the community, they would adequately demonstrate the concept of family cycles.

Using Local History to Investigate the Impact of Larger Events upon the Family

Although the nuclear family has been described as isolated and detached, it is nonetheless integrated into the larger society in many ways. Changes in land tenure and in the geographic location of economic opportunity uprooted hundreds of thousands of families in the nineteenth century and affected them in countless ways. The stresses within families caused by new technological developments making traditional skills obsolete are immeasurable, but must have been deeply felt. Some of the ways in which larger societal events have left their imprint upon the American family have received more scholarly attention than others. More attention has been given to such obviously traumatic events as immigration, wars, and economic depression than to more subtle shifts in the cultural and intellectual climate.

The impact of the Great Depression of the 1930s on the family in the United States has been extensively documented. Social scientists and social workers conducted numerous surveys during and immediately after the depression to determine its affect on family life.[18] The published results indicate, as one might suspect, that the depression did not affect all families alike. Those in which the breadwinner remained employed, for example, often fared rather well. Some families closed ranks in the face of adversity; others found family bonds seriously weakened. Unemployment of the husband and father often meant that the wife or older children had to find work. This, in turn, affected status and power relationships within the family, with unemployed fathers commonly losing a measure of control over their children. Unemployment of the father or his taking a less prestigious job also often meant a loss of social status for the whole family. The effects of that were felt by children in their social relationships, as well as by the adults. The effects of the depression on the family were varied

146

Household Number/ Family Number	Surname	First Name	Occupation
356/358	Youmans	A. B.	Lumber Merchant
		Mary	
		Frank	
		Frederick	
	McLure	Fedora	Servant
	Youmans	Vincent	
		Catherine	

Source: 1860 Federal Manuscript Census, Winona, Minn.

183/173	Youmans	Vincent	Retired
		Catherine	Keeps House
188/179	Youmans	Addison B	Sawmill & Lumber Dealer
		Mary J	Keeps House
		Frank M	Attending School
		Harry	
	Travers	Eliza	Domestic
	Morey	M. B.	School Teacher
	Cutter	Edgar	Works in Grocery Store
	Tuttle	Jane	Keeps House
	Tuttle	John H	Teamster

Source: 1870 Federal Manuscript Census, Winona, MN.

441/479	Youmans	Addison	Lumber Manufacturer
		Mary J	Wife/keeps house
		Frank	Son/Machinist
		Harry	Son/at school
	Anderson	Hannah	Servant/single
	Olson	Annie L	Servant/single
	Stubsted	Louis	Servant/married
		Laura	Wife

Source: 1880 Federal Manuscript Census, Winona, MN.

Ward - 1	Youmans	Addison	Retired
#4		Mary J	Wife
P 98	Foley	Mary	Domestic
	Laabs	Adella A. W.	Domestic
	Aulenbacker	John	Laborer

*(Years in District/Years in State)

Fig. 4.4.   Minnesota state census figures for 1905, collected 13 June 1905 at Winona, Minnesota—Reprinted from their newsletter MISHAP, by permission of the Minnesota Social History Project, Saint Mary's College, Winona, Minnesota.

Birthplace FBP & MBP	Age/Sex	$Real Property/ $Personal Prop.	Address
N.Y.	29/M	$10,000/$15,000	1st Ward
N.Y.	28/F		
Minn.	2/M		
Minn.	4/12/M		
N.Y.	23/F		
N.Y.	66/M		
N.Y.	62/F		
N.Y.	75/M	————/$5,000	1st Ward
N.Y.	71/F		
N.Y.	40/M	$23,000/$17,000	1st Ward
N.Y.	36/F		
Minn.	12/M		
Minn.	1/M		
Ireland	25/F		
N.Y.	12/F		
Mass.	16/M		
Conn.	58/F		
N.J.	23/M		
N.Y./N.Y./N.Y.	50/M		Wilson
N.Y./N.Y./N.Y.	49/F		
Minn./N.Y./N.Y.	22/M		
Minn./N.Y./N.Y.	11/M		
Sweden/S/S	21/F		
Norway/N/N	29/F		
Norway/N/N	29/M		
Norway/N/N	25/F		
N.Y./N.Y./N.Y.	75/M	(YD-48/YS-48)*	215 Wilson
N.Y./N.Y./N.Y.	73/F	(YD-48/YS-48)*	
Tenn./Ire/Ire	35/F	(YD-34/YS-10)*	
Maine/Ger/Ger	17/F	(YD-17/YS-17)*	
Wisc./Ger/Ger	31/M	(YD-8/YS-6)*	

and far-reaching.[19] It is also an aspect of family history that lends itself easily to local historical research.

How was family life affected by the depression in your community? Although data was collected for many communities during the 1930s, the chances are remote that yours was one of them. However, some of the same kind of information can still be retrieved through oral history research. Many of the nuances of feelings that the social surveys of the 1930s were able to record will long since have been forgotten. Still, useful information about relationships within and beyond the family can still be retrieved, as the following segment of an interview conducted by one of the authors will demonstrate.

MEMORIES OF A DEPRESSION CHILDHOOD

An Interview with Celeste Woodley

Q. You mentioned that your husband, Joe, as a child could only get a hand-made toy for Christmas. What did the corresponding salary of your father mean for your ability to have things as a child during the depression?

A. It seemed to me that we were never wanting. . . . We weren't really a toy-oriented family, but I would say we were sort of a candy-oriented family, as I recall.

The big sign of prestige at school—and by this time, I must have been in the first or second grade, probably the first—was to be able to buy penny candy at the little store across the street; and anybody who could get a hold of a couple of pennies and maybe a nickel, once in a while, was really big stuff at school; and there was competition, I guess you would say, among some of us to see who could buy the most candy, and then we always gave it to our friends. But it was definitely a status symbol to be able to go over and come back from the store with a small sack of penny candy . . . and come back and distribute it among your friends, because in a way that sort of bought you prestige.

Q. In terms of relationships between children and parents, what was the effect of the depression on those families that were really in need?

A. From what I can gather from what my husband has told me and from a friend of mine in Boulder who was also very poor during the depression, the effect on the family was to bring them much closer together, to bring them to an awareness of how much they meant to one another and how much they depended on one another for succor and for encouragement and for life itself. In our family, I would say that the depression had a unifying effect on us, too, but in a different way. . . . In my own family, the theme was challenge. I learned to work—or, at least, to *think* work, during the depression. Nobody in my family was ever still a minute. Everybody was always out there looking for work, working twice as hard as they normally would, driven perhaps by the idea that, if they didn't work, there wouldn't be any and that pressure, that drive to continue to work, no matter what time it was, no matter what day it was, stayed with me for the rest of my life.

Q. So, being, so to speak, a child of the depression was a lasting influence?

A. It was for me. . . . I could guess, and I am going to, that other people had such bad experiences during the depression, experiences of defeat, that they never recovered from it.[20]

Local residents who were either adults or children during the depression will still be able to recall many aspects of family life during those years. They will probably remember whether the head of the family was unemployed, whether other members of the family had to find work to help make ends meet, or whether one or another member of the family had to leave the community to find work elsewhere. Those who were children then may remember whether their family had enough money to buy presents at Christmas or other special occasions and whether they felt more or less poor than other children of their age.

5
Teaching Economic History with Local History Sources

THE local community is a rich resource for the teaching of economic history. Local history is quite often thought of in terms of the economic milestones in a community's development. Local historians over the years have tended to select such events as the founding of the first bank or gristmill, the coming of the railroad, the building of the textile mill or refinery, or the closing of the coal mines as the benchmarks of a community's development. They have done so for good reason. To a large extent, the local pattern of economic growth and change provides towns and cities with their individual identities. Much of the early character of a community probably was determined by the economic resources available and by the way the first settlers set out to exploit them. The texture of life was very distinctive in a frontier garrison town, an agricultural village, a whaling port, or a mining town. Much of a community's eventual social and political history was probably closely entwined with its continued economic evolution. This ever-present and probably best-documented dimension of local history can be put to a variety of uses in the history classroom.

The Local Community as a Case Study in Economic History

The most straightforward way to use local sources for teaching economic history is to focus either on the community's economic growth (or economic decline) or on a particular local industry or economic event. In either instance, the object will be to use the local pattern as an example of some larger development. It is not necessary for the local economy to be a microcosm of the regional or national economy for a teacher to be able to follow that procedure. That is expecting too much of any locality, although some communities may be more representative or typical than others. The local historical experience can still be used selectively to illustrate one or another aspect of economic development. That can be done in a community dominated by a single industry or in a rural community caught in the backwaters of industrial development. Even suburban bedroom communities participated in the economic growth or decline of adjacent urban centers. Every community will provide some opportunities for students to learn about economic change in American history through the use of local sources and information.

Even if a community's economic history appears to be distinctly atypical, it will still share a great deal in common with other communities. The technological and economic changes that have transformed American society over the past century and a half had little respect for local boundaries. New manufacturing processes, methods of distribution, or forms of economic organization were rapidly disseminated throughout the country. Industrialization tended to make traditional crafts and skills obsolete with little local or regional variation. The differences were largely in timing and in degree. Within that area of large-scale or structural changes in the American economy, locally generated data will be most reflective of broader patterns of development.

Many newspapers either have a regular local history column or sporadically carry local historical items heavily weighted with the economic events of the past. A newspaper item about the town's long-since-departed flour mills brought to class and read by the teacher may be all that is needed to demonstrate the impact of mass production and national marketing on once-prosperous local manufacturers. A clipping file of such historical items will be a useful resource. That is not to say that the teacher should rely exclusively on secondary accounts of this kind. While they are a source of information that should not be overlooked, they do not

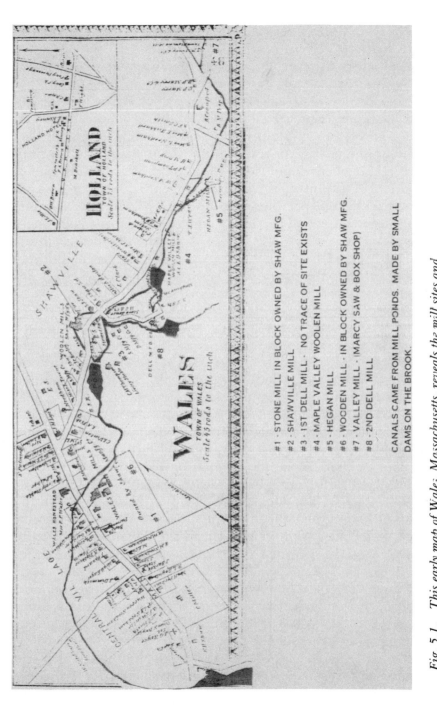

Fig. 5.1. This early map of Wales, Massachusetts, reveals the mill sites and the mill ponds made by small dams on the brook. —Albert J. George, Old Sturbridge Village, Sturbridge, Massachusetts. Reprinted by permission.

#1 - STONE MILL IN BLOCK OWNED BY SHAW MFG.

#2 - SHAWVILLE MILL

#3 - 1ST DELL MILL - NO TRACE OF SITE EXISTS

#4 - MAPLE VALLEY WOOLEN MILL

#5 - HEGAN MILL

#6 - WOODEN MILL - IN BLOCK OWNED BY SHAW MFG.

#7 - VALLEY MILL - (MARCY SAW & BOX SHOP)

#8 - 2ND DELL MILL

CANALS CAME FROM MILL PONDS. MADE BY SMALL DAMS ON THE BROOK.

provide the opportunity for student involvement that primary historical sources can.

Two social studies teachers in Sturbridge, Massachusetts, developed a local economic history unit involving both teachers and students in research, using primary source materials. The project focused on the nearby town of Wales, which is now a small summer recreational community of a thousand population. Initial investigation of the town uncovered the earlier existence of an extensive textile mill complex. Summing it up later, the two investigators commented, "This was a surprise and provoked many questions on our part. . . . *What happened?* Why did these mills die when all around us we have communities in which industry thrived well into the twentieth century?" [1] In the local history project they developed, their students searched for answers to those questions.

The disappearance of the textile mills at Wales, Massachusetts, became the focus for a wide-ranging, multidisciplinary investigation. To identify geographical features and land-use patterns that might have affected the local economy, the students examined road maps, topographical maps, and land-use maps. On-site field studies led them through the woods and beyond the mill pond to the canals, sluiceways, and ruins of the old water-powered mills. Using gazetteers and nineteenth-century industrial statistics, they were able to chart economic trends for that area over several decades. Archival research by the teachers produced a notice of bankruptcy proceedings against one of the principal mills in the town, which indicated that the mills had closed for economic reasons. A telltale stationery letterhead for one of the mills gave Wales as the address for the mill, but the nearby town of Palmer as the freight office address. The railroad ran through Palmer, not through Wales. After weighing the evidence, the students concluded that the lack of a local railroad must have been a significant factor in the closing of the mills.

Students can gain as much insight into economic development and change from the history of failure as they can from local economic success stories. The students who investigated the disappearance of the mills at Wales, Massachusetts, learned in a very concrete way about the role of transportation in industrial de-

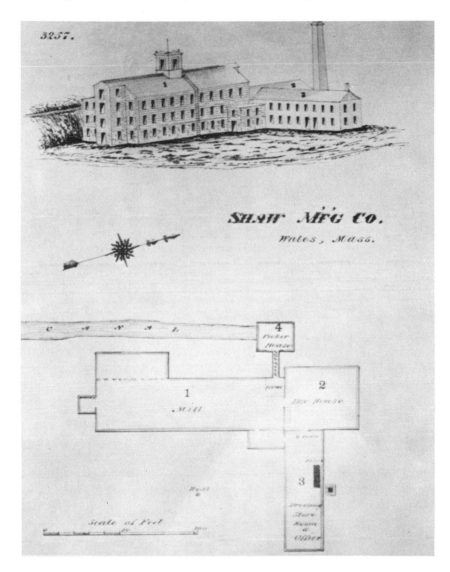

Fig. 5.2.   The woolen mill of the Shaw Manufacturing Company.—Merrimack Valley Textile Museum, North Andover, Massachusetts. Reprinted by permission.

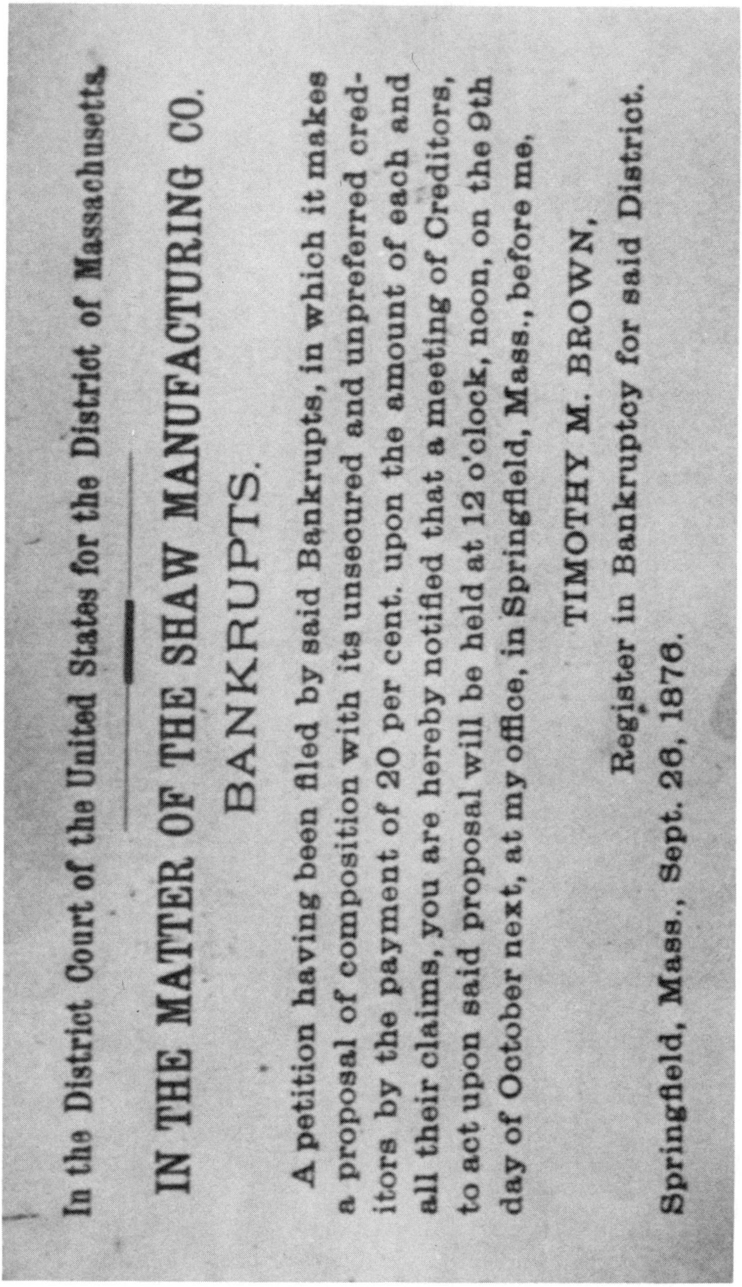

In the District Court of the United States for the District of Massachusetts.

IN THE MATTER OF THE SHAW MANUFACTURING CO.

BANKRUPTS.

A petition having been filed by said Bankrupts, in which it makes a proposal of composition with its unsecured and unpreferred creditors by the payment of 20 per cent. upon the amount of each and all their claims, you are hereby notified that a meeting of Creditors, to act upon said proposal will be held at 12 o'clock, noon, on the 9th day of October next, at my office, in Springfield, Mass., before me,

TIMOTHY M. BROWN,

Register in Bankruptcy for said District.

Springfield, Mass., Sept. 26, 1876.

Fig. 5.3. Archival evidence concerning the Shaw Manufacturing Company.—Albert J. George, Old Sturbridge Village, Sturbridge, Massachusetts. Reprinted by permission.

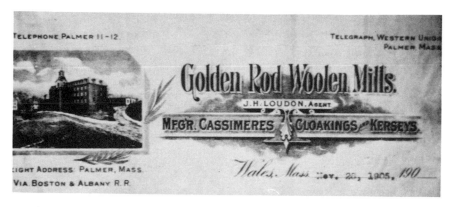

Fig. 5.4.   Letterhead of one of the Wales mills.—Albert J. George, Old Sturbridge Village, Sturbridge, Massachusetts. Reprinted by permission.

velopment. Every section of the country has such nonsuccess stories. The exhausted coal mines and oil fields of the midwest and the abandoned gold and silver mines of the Rocky Mountain states are object lessons about the fate of nonrenewable natural resources. Several dimensions of economic change can be illustrated or investigated by focusing on the transition from the use of one resource to another. Gene E. Rooze developed a local history unit about an abandoned farm community. Although the farms were abandoned because of low productivity, the area was not depopulated or unutilized. Some towns in the area survived as manufacturing centers, being able to attract factories because of the surplus labor force. Other people used the area on a commuting basis. Incorporated into the national forest system, "the marginal farms . . . now serve as recreational areas for metropolitan centers once inaccessible because of existing modes of transportation and communication."[2] The abandoned farms that at first glance were evidence of economic decline were only a reflection of a larger pattern of change in economic development and land use.

Investigation of a community's economic growth does not necessarily require elaborate projects with field trips and visits to local history archives. A simple activity can be constructed with data the teacher brings to class, permitting the students to compare the local economy at two different time periods. The most convenient source for such data probably will be the published volumes of either the federal or the state census. Although the kind of information may vary from census to census, typical data for towns and counties will indicate the number of acres of improved land, acreage planted in various crops, value of farm property and farm products, number of various kinds of live-stock, and number and kinds of manufacturing establishments. That information can be organized in tabular form and prepared as handouts for the students, as in the following example.

To show teachers how to use local history sources to develop a "community depth study," the New York State Education Department has developed a sample project including economic history data taken from two New York state censuses.[3] The data on manufacturing establishments, a portion of which is reproduced in tables 5.1 and 5.2, are only a small part of the information collected for the town of Cazenovia and for Madison County, New York. The sample materials, which teachers could replicate for their own town and county, also included data concerning agricultural production, climate, and population; newspaper clippings about local economic activity and advertisements from local merchants; and maps and selected government documents. A set of questions accompanies the materials, to help teachers exploit the data as fully as possible. Among them are the following:

Q. What industries were most numerous in Cazenovia and in Madison County?

Q. Which 1855 industries were also found in 1825? Which period had the greater variety of industries?

Q. In 1825 industries were almost all farm-related. Did this same pattern hold true in 1855? Comparing the town and county in which area did the local industries tend to be more closely related to the farm?

Q. Which industries depended on local materials for their manufacture?

Q. Which industries required specialized training on the part of those engaged in them?

Q. To what extent was industry specialized in 1855 as compared with 1825?

Q. In which period was industry more self-sufficient?

TABLE 5.1

Statistics on Manufacturing, 1820s

Manufactories	Town of Cazenovia	Madison County
	Number	
Grist Mills	9	54
Saw mills	14	152
Oil mills	2	7
Fulling mills	7	36
Carding machines	10	41
Cotton factories	0	2
Woolen factories	1	12
Cotton & Woolen factories	0	1
Iron works	0	4
Trip hammers	1	8
Distilleries	8	37
Asheries	4	67

SOURCE: New York State Census of 1825, in *Assembly Journal 1826; Teaching the Age of Homespun: Guide for Seventh-Grade Social Studies* (Albany: New York State Education Department, 1965), p. 29.

Other questions were designed to help the teachers use other kinds of data included in the study.

Maps and photographs can also be valuable historical sources for documenting the economic growth or decline of a community. The growth of a town reflected in the platting of new additions can be traced in local plat books, real estate atlases, and insurance maps. Historical photographs of the same commercial buildings and streets taken several years apart can show stages of economic growth as store fronts changed and as one type of land use replaced another. Changes in land use reflecting basic economic changes in a community can also be documented by successive editions of insurance maps, which identify the purpose for which each structure on the map was used. The physical expansion of a community in more recent years can also be impressively demonstrated by the use of aerial photographs. A great many areas of the United States have been photographed from the air several times during the past three or four decades. A sequence of such photographs taken ten years or so apart can be used quite effectively to demonstrate recent growth of an area. The most extensive collec-

TABLE 5.2

Statistics on Manufacturing, 1850s

Manufacturing & Processing Establishments	Town of Cazenovia	Madison County
	Number	
Grist Mills	4	22
Distilleries	2	9
Breweries	1	1
Cider Mills	0	1
Oil Mills	1	1
Chandleriers and soap manufactories	2	6
Wool cloth and yarn manufactories	1	6
Carding and cloth dressing, establishments	0	1
Tanneries	4	22
Harness, saddle and truck manufactories	4	16
Boot and shoe shops	6	30
Bakeries	0	1
Saw Mills	7	75
Shingle factories	0	1
Lath factories	1	2
Cabinet manufacturing shops	3	12
Chair factories	0	3
Turners' establishments	0	2
Joiners' establishments	1	1
Asheries	0	2
Saleratus manufactories	1	1
Sash and blind manufactories	1	4
Paper Mills	1	2
Stone quarries	0	4
Lime manufactories	0	2
Water lime manufactories	0	1
Marble manufactories	0	3
Plaster mills	0	4
Coopers	1	9
Box manufactories	0	2
Cheese box manufactories	0	3
Paper box manufactories	0	1
Coach and wagon manufactories	5	21
Boat building shops	0	1
Fork factories	0	1
Hoe factories	0	1

SOURCE: New York State Census of 1855, Franklin B. Hough, Albany, 1857; *Teaching the Age of Homespun: A Guide for Seventh-Grade Social Studies* (Albany: New York State Education Department, 1965), pp. 40–41.

tion of aerial photographs available to most teachers is that of the
U.S. Geological Survey of the Department of the Interior. Information about the numbers and dates of photographs available
for a particular area can be obtained by writing or calling the
nearest National Cartographic Information Center. Addresses of
the several NCIC offices in the United States are listed below.

U.S. Geological Survey
National Cartographic
 Information Center
507 National Center
Reston, Virginia 22092

U.S. Geological Survey
Rocky Mountain Mapping Center
National Cartographic
 Information Center
Stop 504, Denver Federal Center
Denver, Colorado 80225

U.S. Geological Survey
Eastern Mapping Center
National Cartographic
 Information Center
536 National Center
Reston, Virginia 22092

U.S. Geological Survey
Western Mapping Center
National Cartographic
 Information Center
345 Middlefield Road
Menlo, Park, California 94025

U.S. Geological Survey
Mid-Continent Mapping Center
National Cartographic
 Information Center
1400 Independence Road
Rolla, Missouri 65401

U.S. Geological Survey
National Cartographic
 Information Center
National Space Technology
 Laboratories
NSTL Station, Mississippi 39529

Teaching Economic History with Local Occupational Data

Investigating the kinds of occupations at which Americans
have worked in the past is another useful approach to economic
history. It will give students a better understanding of the working lives of previous generations of Americans. The most important economic reality in the lives of most people is the job by which
they make a living. The kind of job they have largely determines
their income, their standard of living, their sense of economic
security, and the degree of satisfaction they derive from work. A
list of occupations represented in an eighteenth-century town can
effectively demonstrate the importance of skilled crafts in a preindustrial economy. A similar list for an industrial town of the late
nineteenth century will help students understand the impact of

machine technology and industrial organization on the working lives of Americans. As virtually every structural change in the economy was sooner or later translated into occupational changes, the analysis of occupations at different periods is a useful device for teaching about economic change.

It also provides another opportunity to exploit local historical resources. Both city directories and manuscript census returns provide information about the occupations of local residents. The census information is the more complete, as several decennial censuses list the occupations of each member of a household. Although city directories also at times list occupations, they are less consistent than the censuses. Some entries may list only the occupation for the household head. The census returns may be the only source of information for small towns and rural areas that did not publish city or county directories. However, directories do have the advantage of being easier to use and of being available for the period beyond 1900, which is the last date for which federal manuscript census returns are available. The choice of one source or the other should depend upon the time period in question and the purpose to be served. Neither kind of source exists for the colonial period. To collect occupational data for the period prior to 1790, historians have had to rely chiefly upon local public records. Because of the special problems involved in assembling occupational information for preindustrial America, we shall limit our consideration here to industrial America of the nineteenth century.

Several dimensions of that complex set of changes that we call the Industrial Revolution can be investigated by using occupational information from local city directories. An essential ingredient in the process of industrialization was the transition from production of goods by hand to machine production. It was a gradual revolution affecting different industries at different times. The occupations listed in a nineteenth-century city directory will both reflect the unevennness with which that transformation was taking place and suggest how far it had progressed locally by the date the directory was published. For any community in which the factory system had made any inroad at all, the directory will list both machine operators and skilled craftsmen whose trades were not yet mechanized. Even directories for communities that had no factory workers will list skilled craftsmen whose skills would in time become obsolete because of industrialization. The expanding scale of economic organization is another aspect of industrial development that is reflected indirectly in listings of occupations. The occupations related to railroads—stationmaster, baggage clerk, section hand, car repairman, conductor, engineer—reflect the presence of a large corporation. Most communities by the end of the nineteenth century probably also included a resident agent or "canvasser" for a major national manufacturing company such as the Singer Manufacturing Company or an agricultural implement company. Even in communities that lacked factories, the larger and more disciplined groups associated with industrial America may still have been represented by the local residents who listed their occupation as coal miner, stonecutter, brewery worker, or cigar-maker.

A simple classroom activity can be developed using the occupational information contained in a city directory from virtually any time during the nineteenth century. Its purpose is to give students an opportunity to apply to a concrete situation the general historical knowledge that they have presumably learned in previous class periods about industrialization in nineteenth-century America. The teacher needs only to locate a directory and have the pages (or a systematically taken sample of pages) photocopied for use as a classroom handout. An example of a directory page of 1896 is illustrated in figure 5-5. Each student should receive one or more pages and have a chance to examine the material carefully. Either the students or the teacher should have a dictionary close at hand. What kind of work did a kalsominer do? What is the difference between a shoemaker and a cobbler, a seamstress and a dressmaker, a tinker and a tinsmith, a millwright and a miller?

When it is certain that the students understand what kind of work is involved in the occupations they have before them, the teacher should initiate a discussion to help the students interpret this information in terms of the knowledge they already have about industrialization. Questions similar to the following will facilitate the process:

Which occupations were presumably performed in a factory or in a large work group (ten to twelve persons or more)?
Which occupations involved working with or near machines?

Boulder City Directory.
(COUNTY SEAT OF BOULDER COUNTY.)

ABBREVIATIONS USED IN THIS BOOK.—a, acres; ab, above; agt, agent; av, avenue; bds, boards; bel, below; bet, between; B & M R R R, Burlington & Missouri River Railroad; bldg, building; clk, clerk; com, commission; Co, Company; cor, corner; dlr, dealer; do, ditto; E, east; est, estate; ex, express; ft, foot; hd, head; imp, improvement; ins, insurance; lab, laborer; mfr, manufacturer; N, north; N E, northeast; nr, near; N S, north side; N W, northwest; opp, opposite; p o, post office; propr, proprietor; r, range; res, residence; rd, road; R R, railroad; S, south; S E, southeast; sec, section; secy, secretary; S P Co, Southern Pacific Company; tp, township; S W, southwest; U P R'y, Union Pacific Railway; W, west; W S, west side.

ACADEMIES,
see Appendix.

Adams & Adams (Geo S Adams, Guy A Adams), lawyers and notaries, 1245 Pearl.

Adams, Cora Mrs, first cook Silver Dollar restaurant, res do.

Adams, Geo S (Adams & Adams) res 2244 13th st.

Adams, Guy A (Adams & Adams), res 2244 13th st.

Adams, Howard (gardener Mrs L A Streamer) bds do.

Adams, M L, res 1024 Portland Plce.

Addy, Frances B Mrs, res 2245 18th st.

Albee, M A Mrs, res S A Giffin,

Albert, John Jacob Rev, pastor Trinity Lutheran church, res 1235 Spruce st.

Allen chapel, A M E church, Rev Geo H Byas pastor, cor 18th & Pearl st.

Allen, Cora M Mrs, res 2104 Water st

Allen, H S, diamond drill prospector, res 2405 Hill st.

Allen, H W, A M, M D, physician and surgeon, office upstairs NE cor 14th and Pearl, telephone 47, res 1730 Water st.

Allen, John, miner, res ½ mile E of city limits, S of Pearl st.

Allgire, John, miner, rms 1333 Pine st. st.

Allison, Frank, carpenter, 2153 13th st, res 1112 Bluff.

ALLISON, W H,
mgr Boulder Milling & Elevator Co, res 1602 Mapleton ave.

Alpert, Alfred, umbrella menders, res 2341 Hill st.

Alexander, H F, millhand, res 1120 Pearl st.

Alexander, V C Mrs, res 1816 Spruce st.

Ambrook, Charles, physician and surgeon, office and res 1313 Spruce st.

Ambrook, Mary L, physician and surgeon, office and res 1319 Spruce st.

American Volunteers (The), headquarters 1931 12th st.

ANDERSON & BERG,
(Aug L Anderson F A Berg) contractors and builders, 1935 Grove st.

Anderson, Alfred, Lostler Omnibus stables, res 1421 Walnut st.

Anderson, Andrew, lab, res 5th & University ave.

ANDERSON, AUG L,
(Anderson & Berg) res 1935 Grove st.

Anderson, Bertha Miss, domestic (Chas Davis).

Anderson, Carrie Mrs, res 804 Bluff st.

Anderson, Chas, lab, bds 1908 Pearl st.

Anderson, Chas B, carpenter, res 1902 Grove st.

Anderson, F L, barber shop 1910 12th st, res 1822 Pine, cor 20th.

Anderson, Frank, teamster, bds Belvidere hotel.

5

Fig. 5.5.   A page from the city directory for Boulder, Colorado, 1896.

> Which occupations suggest that the worker was probably on the payroll of a large company or corporation?
>
> What skilled occupations are represented that would later become obsolete because of continued industrialization?
>
> What occupations would no longer be found in the community in later years, even though they would still exist in other places?

While most of these questions are related to the extent to which work had become transformed and the scale of organization altered because of industrialization, the final question points to a third aspect of industrialization that should not be wholly neglected. Not only was the process and scale of production changed; it was also centralized to a greater extent than before. Relatively small communities in the nineteenth century provided local employment for brewers, creamerymen, millers, candymakers, cigar-makers, shoemakers, and workers in other crafts for which industrialization would mean centralization of production as well as mechanization. The flight of such occupations from the towns to remote centers of manufacturing is another piece of concrete evidence of the changes in production, transportation, and marketing that have taken place during the past century or so.

Local Occupational Data on the Economic Status of Women

Local historical data about occupations can also be used to document some aspects of the economic role and status of women in the past. The best sources of information for occupations held by women during the nineteenth century are federal and state manuscript census returns. While the census materials are silent about many aspects of women's economic contributions, especially work performed without compensation in the home, they do provide data for answering some important questions. Did women participate significantly in the work force in nineteenth-century America, or was a woman's place really in the home? How did the economic status of women compare to that of men? Did the status of women as reflected in the occupations that they held improve significantly during the nineteenth century?

These were a few of the questions that the directors of the Minnesota Social History Project were interested in when they developed a classroom activity based on state and federal census returns for the town of Winona, Minnesota.[4] They tabulated information about the occupations listed for both men and women in the federal manuscript census of 1880 and the state manuscript census of 1905, as well as data about ethnic background. From that data they were able to determine the extent of women's participation in the work force, the extent to which their rate of participation increased during that time period, the improvement—or lack of it—in women's status relative to that of men, and the extent to which women's occupational status was related to their ethnic background (see tables 5.3 and 5.4). They discovered that, although women made up nearly one-third of the local work force in 1880, when Winona was a small lumbering and farm-marketing town, two-thirds of them were employed in low-status and surely low-paying jobs. Twenty-five years later, when the town had developed into a thriving commercial and cultural center, women's occupational status had substantially improved. Women had also improved their occupational status relative to that of men. However, there were significant ethnic variations. The model developed by the Minnesota Social History Project is a most useful one, as the same kind of information can be compiled for most American communities.

Data from the manuscript census about women's occupations can become the basis for a classroom activity exploring several dimensions of the status of women in nineteenth-century America. Figures such as those reproduced here for Winona, Minnesota, should be prepared for the local community and reproduced as handouts for the students. After the teacher has made sure that the students understand the information, the class can proceed to analyze and interpret the data. The activity should be organized around a series of questions such as the following:

To what extent did women participate in the work force in 1880?
How did the occupational status of women compare to that of men in 1880?
What do the occupations held by women in 1880 suggest about the society's attitude toward the role of women?

TABLE 5.3

Occupational Ranking of the Work Force of Winona, Minnesota, 1880 and 1905. Number and Percent by Sex

	1880				1905				
	Male	Percent	Female	Percent	Male	Percent	Female	Percent	Female Percentage Increase
Professional, High White-Collar	85	98.8	01	0.1	207	97.6	05	0.2	400
Proprietor, Low White-Collar	676	86.1	109	12.7	1258	64.9	682	27.5	525
Skilled	947	86.0	160	18.7	1775	80.0	458	18.4	186
Specified, Unskilled	565	48.9	585	68.3	880	40.6	1130	45.5	93
Unspecified, Unskilled	741	99.7	02	0.2	1848	89.9	208	8.4	1030
Work force Total	3014	77.9	857	22.1	5978	70.7	2483	29.3	190

SOURCE: *Manuscript of the Tenth Census of the United States, 1880; Population of the United States; Manuscript of the Fifth Decennial Census of Minnesota, 1905.* Reprinted by permission from *MISHAP*, newsletter of the Minnesota Social History Project, December 1978, p. 14.

TABLE 5.4

Occupational Rankings of the Work Force of Winona, Minnesota, 1880–1905 by Selected Places of Birth, Percent by Sex

1880

	Native		German		Polish		Irish		Norwegian		English	
	%M	%F	%M	%F	%M	%F	%M	%F	%M	%F	%M	%F
Professional, High White-Collar	4.0	0.2	1.4	0.0	0.0	0.0	1.3	0.0	0.0	0.0	3.6	0.0
Proprietor, Low White-Collar	30.9	17.5	17.0	8.4	8.9	4.2	11.6	10.3	13.1	1.4	25.3	13.3
Skilled	33.3	22.9	33.8	7.6	19.4	8.3	21.0	15.4	32.1	5.4	43.4	6.6
Specified, Unskilled	19.8	59.2	16.0	83.9	15.4	87.5	25.2	74.4	20.2	93.2	20.5	80.0
Unspecified, Unskilled	12.0	0.2	31.9	0.0	56.3	0.0	40.5	0.0	34.5	0.0	7.2	0.0
N =	1397	485	631	118	279	48	147	39	84	74	83	15

1905

	Native		German		Polish		Irish		Norwegian		English	
	%M	%F	%M	%F	%M	%F	%M	%F	%M	%F	%M	%F
Professional, High White-Collar	3.7	0.1	3.7	0.6	1.7	1.3	3.0	0.0	1.0	0.0	5.5	0.0
Proprietor, Low White-Collar	24.0	26.3	18.8	17.4	6.0	34.6	23.9	25.9	10.0	17.2	34.5	66.6
Skilled	30.7	17.0	32.2	21.5	13.0	5.1	30.0	0.0	49.0	17.2	30.9	0.0
Specified, Unskilled	15.6	48.8	14.9	50.6	8.1	52.6	17.9	59.3	14.5	48.3	16.4	33.3
Unspecified, Unskilled	25.9	7.8	30.4	9.9	71.0	6.4	25.4	14.8	24.5	17.2	12.7	0.0
N =	3285	2245	930	172	630	78	67	27	110	29	55	6

SOURCE: Manuscript of the Tenth Census of the United States, 1880; Population of the United States; Manuscript of the Fifth Decennial Census of Minnesota, 1905.

Reprinted by permission from MISHAP Newsletter of the Minnesota Social History Project, December 1978, p. 16.

Did women improve their occupational status relative to men between 1880 and 1905?

Did women from certain ethnic groups improve their status more than those from other groups?

To what extent does the occupational status of women in 1905 suggest a change in attitudes about the role of women?

Does the occupational data for 1905 indicate that women had achieved equality with men in the work force?

Does the data presented here suggest a relationship between economic growth and the improvement of women's occupational status?

What hypotheses are suggested by these data about the relationship between economic growth in nineteenth-century America and the progress made by women by 1905 toward equal legal and political rights?

Information about a single community does not provide an adequate basis for making statements about the status of women or attitudes toward women generally in American society. It will give students an opportunity to examine some aspects of change and to raise broader questions about the role and status of women. The analysis of data such as this will also provide the teacher with the opportunity to incorporate at least some aspects of women's history into an American history course.

Local Historical Sources in Teaching About Consumer Culture

The new technology and new forms of economic organization that made possible the mass production of goods in nineteenth-century America also prepared the way for the consumer culture of the twentieth century. The role once played in the sustaining of economic growth by the railroads, mills, factories, and other purchasers of producers' goods would eventually be assumed by a different kind of customer. After the turn of the century economic growth and prosperity would increasingly come to depend on the purchasers of consumer goods. The application of the assembly line and other techniques of mass production cheapened the cost of a wide range of consumer items. The expansion of consumer credit and the emergence of the modern advertising indus-

Plate 5.1. Photograph collections in libraries and historical societies are important sources of information about occupational opportunities for women.—Colorado Historical Society. Reprinted by permission.

Plate 5.2. Photographs also illustrate sexual differences in occupational opportunities.—Western History Department, Denver Public Library. Reprinted by permission.

try further expanded the size of the consumer goods market. Goods ranging from automobiles to tennis rackets that had once been symbols of upper-class affluence would become part of the everyday material culture of middle-class and even working-class Americans. The extraordinary growth of the consumer goods industries was a cultural as well as an economic phenomenon that deserves more attention than it customarily receives in American history courses.

The potential of the consumer goods industries in the United States to create and to satisfy needs on an unprecedented scale was beginning to be realized during the decade of the 1920s. That period was a time of unparalleled prosperity for the urban majority, with real wages reaching substantially higher levels than ever before. The increased levels of spending on consumer goods and services that the higher salaries and wages made possible produced a new middle-class life style that reached well into the ranks of blue-collar workers. The automobile, once a plaything of the rich, had become a necessity of life for all but the poorest of

Plate 5.3. Advertisements in local newspapers can provide students with an abundance of historical evidence related to the growing demand for consumer goods.—Boulder Daily Camera, January 1, 1924.

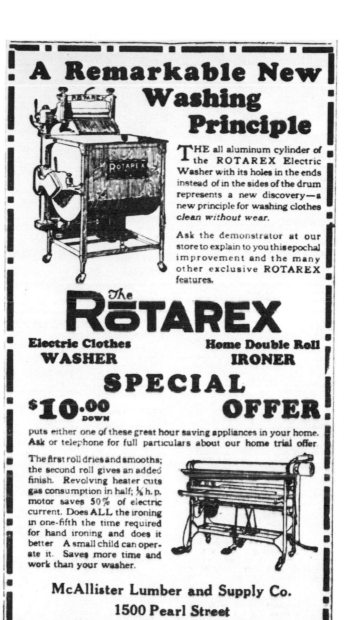

*Plate 5.4. Advertisements for time-saving household appliances were also **common during the 1920s**.—Boulder Daily Camera,* February 25, 1924.

Americans by the end of the 1920s. Hardly less important in this emerging culture of material abundance were the new amenities made possible by the expanding household appliance industries. Electric washing machines, refrigerators, radios, and gramophones were becoming permanent fixtures in the American middle-class way of life. Higher levels of disposable income also meant more money available for vacations, movies, and for sending children to high school and college in greater numbers than ever before. Indeed, much of what Americans have collectively chosen to remember about the 1920s—the flappers, the jazz bands, the sporty roadsters with rumble seats—are images of the emerging consumer culture of that decade.

The growth of the consumer goods industries during the 1920s can be documented both as a cultural and as an economic phenomenon with local historical sources. Local newspaper files are rich sources of evidence, especially for advertisements for new automobiles and for household appliances that appeared almost daily even in small-town newspapers. Newspapers also contain an abundance of news stories and local items in which the automobile is the center of attention. Photographs of family automobiles and of traffic-congested streets are rather common. State and local historical society libraries may also have collections of picture postcards of street scenes vividly documenting the presence of the automobile during that period. Remnants of the material culture of the twenties can also be found in antique shops, junk stores, and local history museums. Such items as radios and Victrolas that may be too expensive to purchase and not available on loan can be photographed and presented to the class through slides. Information about the gadgets and appliances to be found in middle-class homes of the period also can be retrieved through interviews with local residents who still remember what life was like then. Local city directories and business directories will document some aspects of the local economic implications, especially the emergence of new occupations and businesses concerned with the sales and repair of such durable consumer goods as automobiles and radios. The use of several kinds of sources will be demonstrated in the following activity, which is focused on the economic and cultural impact of the automobile on American life during the 1920s.

Perhaps no other single item of consumption during the de-

Plate 5.5.   The roadster: symbol of a new life-style.—Photograph by Charles M. Hiller. Western History Department, Denver Public Library. Reprinted by permission.

cade of the twenties had such a pervasive influence on the way Americans lived as the automobile. It determined the way a substantial number of Americans spent a major portion of their income and what they did with much of their leisure time. It is an appropriate focal point for a classroom activity designed to explore the nature and consequences of consumer spending during the twenties. The influence of the automobile was so pervasive that it is also possible to examine its impact in virtually any community in the United States. Consequently, it is an ideal topic for a local history investigation.

A local history investigation of the impact of the automobile could be integrated into a unit on the 1920s in a United States survey course. It would require a day or two of the unit, with the students working individually or in small groups. The initial class periods of the unit should be devoted to the broader historical developments of the decade, including the emergence of the automobile industry as an aspect of the industrial growth of the

United States at that time. Most United States history textbooks include at least a passing reference to Henry Ford and to the extraordinary growth of the automobile industry during the twenties. A convenient bridge between such a general treatment and the local history investigation that will conclude the unit can be constructed with material on the automobile that Robert Lynd and Helen Lynd included in *Middletown: A Study in Modern Culture*, their classic 1924 study of Muncie, Indiana.[5]

The Lynds discovered that the automobile had made a major impact on the lives of Muncie's residents, affecting both their economic and social behavior in a variety of ways. Half the working-class families they interviewed in 1924 had already bought a car (the percentage was even higher for the business class), and many had either mortgaged their homes or had delayed buying a home to be able to do so. Local merchants were convinced that people in Muncie bought cars even at the expense of clothing, which the following statements made by working-class wives seemed to bear out:

> "We'd rather do without clothes than give up the car," said one mother of nine children. "We used to go to his sister's to visit, but by the time we'd get the children shoed and dressed there wasn't any money left for carfare. Now no matter how they look, we just poke 'em in the car and take 'em along."
>
> "We don't have no fancy clothes when we have the car to pay for," said another. "The car is the only pleasure we have."
>
> "I'll go without food before I'll see us give up the car," said one woman emphatically, and several who were out of work were apparently making precisely this adjustment.[6]

Through interviews with Muncie residents, the Lynds were able to document other changes caused by the automobile, including people's church-going habits and the way they used their leisure time. It had far-reaching cultural as well as social repercussions.

Did the automobile affect other communities in the 1920s in comparable ways? After examining the impact of the automobile on Muncie, the teacher can pose that question and introduce the following local history project. Each student or small group of two or three students should be given the task of examining issues of the local newspaper for one month during the period from 1924

Plate 5.6.   A typical Main Street of the 1920s.—Colorado Historical Society. Reprinted by permission.

to 1925 and of copying news items, advertisements, and editorials related to the automobile. To expedite this research, the teacher should borrow or purchase a microfilm copy of the newspaper for that period, make the film and a microfilm reader easily accessible to the students, and prepare a sign-up sheet so that the roll of microfilm can be efficiently used. The teacher should also explain that the kind of information that the newspaper or any other historical source will yield will not be exactly comparable to the data the Lynds used. It is unlikely that local newspaper reporters asked local residents the same questions that the Lynds asked the people of Muncie. However, the newspaper will provide other kinds of information equally useful for the purpose. The activity can be concluded with a class period spent discussing the various kinds of evidence that the students found in the local newspaper.

The local daily newspaper for Boulder, Colorado, for example, yielded the following materials, among others, for a single month during the year 1924.

1. Almost daily automobile advertisements, many with illustrations, with the automobiles ranging in price from a seven-passenger Studebaker sedan selling for $2,685 to a Ford touring

car, "A Striking Value—at $295." The Ford ad extolled the virtues of "larger-scale production."

2. A news item about the incidence of automobile ownership in the county, which was circumstantial evidence of the effectiveness of the automobile ads:

"One out of every four persons in Boulder county owns an automobile, according to statistics released today at the courthouse. The population of the county is approximately 32,000 and there are 7,800 automobiles. . . . Our one-to-four ration (*sic*) is higher than the United States record of one automobile to every 7.2 persons, according to figures of the automobile industries. . . ."

3. News items that provided evidence of the impact the automobile was having on the health and safety of residents:

"Emma L. Fische and Hildina Jackson are named defendants in a suit for $8,001 filed in district court here today by William Kroulik. . . . Kroulik alleged that an automobile driven thirty-five miles an hour by the defendants ran into his team on the highway three miles north of Longmont, November 17, 1923, and rendered him unconscious. He alleges he suffered cuts and bruises on the face, head and body, that the ligaments in his right leg were torn loose, which will cause him permanent injury. . . . He declared in the complaint that the horses and wagon were separated by sixty-five feet in the accident, and that he was hurled violently to the ground."

"Katheryn Henry, a schoolteacher at Niwot, suffered a broken nose yesterday in an automobile accident on a bridge a mile and a half south of Niwot. . . ."

4. An Associated Press item about a motorized jewelry store robbery in Denver, with the headlines:

Woman Boss of Bandits
Who Robbed Jewelry Store
at Denver Last Evening

She Kept the Auto Running Outside the Store
While They Stuck Up Clerk With $20,000 Worth of
Diamonds in His Keeping—Clean Get-Away

5. A filler at the top of a column suggesting the impact of the automobile on American humor:

The Main Bearing

"Are you sure you have shown me
all the principal parts of this car?"
asked the fair prospective purchaser.

"Yes, madam, all the main ones,"
replied the dealer.

"Well, then, where is the depre-
ciation? Tom told me that was one
of the biggest things about a car."

While the Boulder newspaper did not yield the same kind of evidence that the Lynds had gathered in Muncie, the ads and news stories left no doubt that the automobile had made a major imprint upon the minds and lives of local residents.

6

Teaching Social History with Local History Sources

THE source materials of local history have a wide range of applicability in the teaching of social history. This is true both because the term *social history* itself encompasses such broad areas of human activity and because local activities and associations are central concerns of social history. History survey courses have traditionally included such social history topics as immigration, the growth of cities, and social reform. Textbooks usually define the term still more broadly and include such diverse content as revivalism and religion, public education, sports and recreation, and changing tastes in art and architecture in chapters on social history. The emergence of the "new social history" in recent years has added still other dimensions of meaning, bringing questions of social structure and social processes more sharply into focus. While local history sources are applicable to many of these areas of social history, they do lend themselves more readily to some than to others.

Among the areas included in the more traditional social history, institutional developments are perhaps the easiest to investigate at the local level. The histories of schools and churches are perhaps the most obvious possibilities, but other less formal institutions may qualify as well. Organizations that sponsored sporting events, theatrical performances, and other forms of popular entertainment usually created their share of primary source materials. So did labor organizations, reform organizations, lodges, and other benevolent institutions. That kind of social history does have its restrictions, however. The available evidence tends to document the role of the prominent individuals involved. Newspaper stories, minutes of board meetings, and other archival evidence are usually not broadly representative of a community. As is true of much traditional social history, institutional history is largely an account of the elite.[1]

During the past decade or so, a much different approach to social history—one more concerned with the masses of "anonymous American"—has gained in popularity. This new social history—or "history from the bottom up," as it is sometimes called—represents both a methodological and philosophical break from traditional historiography. It is a deliberate attempt to shift the focus of historical investigation from the influential elite to the ordinary Americans who did not "make history" in the traditional sense. The new approach has been able to bring these faceless Americans into sharper perspective by utilizing masses of quantifiable data. Instead of letters, diaries, and the memoirs of public leaders, which told us a lot about the few, the sources of the new social history are lists and numbers that say a little about a great many individuals.[2]

The new social history lends itself especially well to local history investigations. Much scholarly research in the field has focused on individual communities. Stephen Thernstrom's pioneering study of social mobility among blue-collar workers, for example, was restricted to the town of Newburyport, Massachusetts. Most of the ethnic history studies that have used quantitative methods, such as Kathleen Neils Conzen's *Immigrant Milwaukee, 1836–1860: Accommodation and Community in a Frontier City*; Virginia Yans-McLaughlin's *Family and Community: Italian Immigrants in Buffalo, 1830–1870*; and Josef J. Barton's *Peasants and Strangers: Italians, Rumanians and Slovaks in an American City, 1890–1950*, have focused on ethnic groups in a single city.[3] In most instances, the large numbers of individuals included in most of these studies and the huge quantity of data involved have made it essential for historians to limit the geographical scope of their research. But there are other reasons, as well, for the focus on individual communities. Much of the work in the new social history reflects a serious interest in local communities and the ways they function.

Consequently, these studies provide a variety of models for approaches to local history that can be adapted by teachers.

Several kinds of projects and classroom activities suitable for secondary school and college students follow, showing ways in which local history sources can be used to investigate larger dimensions of American social history. Some are based on new social history approaches using census returns, city directories, and other quantifiable data. Others are more traditional in approach and rely upon more customary sources.

The School as a Source of Social History

The public school is one of the most ubiquitous and enduring of American social institutions. It can be investigated as a social phenomenon worth studying for its own sake, or it can be approached as a source of evidence to document other aspects of social history. Taken together with its curriculum, its standards of discipline, its interior furniture and architecture, and its budgets, the school is highly useful historical evidence. It has, over the course of time, reflected with considerable accuracy the values, aspirations, and fears of the society in which it has existed. Enrollment lists and attendance records of any particular school also reflect ethnic and social changes taking place in its more immediate environment. The school is a sensitive barometer of social change.

This sensitivity of the public school to social change can make it a valuable point of departure for studying the ethnic and social history of a neighborhood. That fact was demonstrated impressively in Pittsburgh, by a curriculum development project using records from a local school to examine the social history of a neighborhood. Packets of student materials were created from information taken from the permanent pupil record cards of the school for the years 1890 and 1920. From the cards came information about the age, sex, grade level, place of birth, and address of the students, as well as the size of their families and the occupations of their parents. That information was accompanied in the packets by maps and photographs of the neighborhood, statistical data about the local population, and miscellaneous items

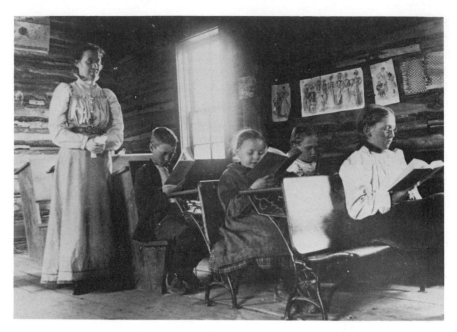

Plate 6.1.   Even pioneer communities provided at least a one-room school.—
Photograph by Charles Redmond. Western History Department, Denver Public Library.
Reprinted by permission.

from school yearbooks and other unofficial school records. By
comparing information for the two years selected, students using
the packets could identify various ethnic and social changes that
had taken place in the neighborhood.[4]

A teacher of a fourth-year German class in a high school in
San Antonio, Texas, used the history of a school in a somewhat
different way to introduce students to the ethnic history of the
community. This school was a German-English-language school
that had existed from 1858 to 1898 in San Antonio. The students'
initial assignment was to translate the minutes of the school's
board of directors, as an exercise in learning to read pre-Satterlin
German script. That assignment, in turn, became a springboard
to a larger ethnic history project. The students collected information about the history of the school and its instructional routine,
which was modeled after the gymnasium system of the patrons'
native Prussia. By using records in the county courthouse, church

Plate 6.2. Many communities had kindergartens by 1900. Lowell Kindergarten, of Grand Junction, Colorado, is pictured here in 1903.—Colorado Historical Society. Reprinted by permission.

membership rolls, gravestones, and records of German-American organizations, the students compiled biographical information about the school's directors and several of its first pupils. The translation assignment had helped them to uncover an important part of the ethnic history of San Antonio in the nineteenth century. The American Association for State and Local History awarded the teacher a certificate of commendation "for leading students to a rich source of local history." [5]

Even the mundane question of the way a school got its name may be a fruitful entree into the social history of a community. That may be true even for schools with rather obvious names, as the students at Philadelphia's Lincoln High School discovered. They found out that the community did not honor Abraham Lincoln's name only out of patriotic sentiment; what they found, instead, was a history of neighborhood rivalries. "The immediate neighborhood, Mayfair, believed the school would carry its name, while older sections such as Holmesburg would not accept the name *Mayfair* for the school. Thus it was called Lincoln, to no one's satisfaction. Articles found in the local newspaper related background material concerning the histories of local communities, their rivalries and antagonisms." [6] There may also have been some satisfaction in discovering that the site of the school was once the county prison farm.

Social Structure and Social Mobility

The social consequences of economic inequality are among the central concerns of social history. The unequal distribution of wealth has been one of the dominant facts of life throughout American history. It has been estimated that in 1860, for example, the wealthiest 5 percent of the population owned somewhat more than 50 percent of the nation's wealth.[7] A Survey Research Center estimate for 1953 indicated that the wealthiest 9 percent of Americans still owned 46 percent of the nation's private assets.[8] This inequality in the distribution of wealth has had various social consequences. Generally speaking, it has produced a stratified society in which some groups have more prestige, status, and influence than others. Wealth is not the only determinant of social status, but in the United States it has historically been the most important one.

An exposure to the ideas of social structure and social stratification is essential if students in American history classes are to understand the social history of any period of American history. Those who had wealth or owned property had access to political power, to education, and to all the amenities that made the life style of the elite so different from that of the poor. That was as true for the America of Thomas Jefferson as for the industrial society of Andrew Carnegie and John D. Rockefeller. Americans of a century ago were probably even more conscious of social differences than we are today. The visible differences between the life styles of the rich and the poor were very great, indeed. As Michael B. Katz has noted, "Poverty in nineteenth-century cities did not mean the absence of luxuries—simple Spartan living with good home-grown food and sturdy home-sewn clothes. Poverty meant absolute deprivation: hunger, cold, sickness, and misery, with almost no place to turn for relief." [9] The challenge to the teacher is to transform the abstract and impersonal idea of social structure or social stratification into human social reality. Local history sources that enable students to place individuals who lived in their own community within the social structure of a past era is an effective way to accomplish that reality.

Although individuals and families did not leave so public a record of wealth as they did of ethnic origins, marriages, and other vital statistics, sufficient data does exist to rank most of the people in a social hierarchy in a general way and to place some of the people with certainty. The most direct evidence of wealth available for most communities is the listing of property values in the 1870 federal manuscript census. Each head of household was asked to declare the value of his or her real estate and personal estate. Whether the figures they gave the census taker were accurate is another question. Concern that the information might fall into the hands of the tax assessor may have led some people to underestimate the value of their property. Egotism may have tempted others to inflate the value. None of the federal censuses before or after 1870 asked for a declaration of wealth. However, the census of 1900 did identify heads of households who owned their own homes. Home ownership can also be identified from county property tax rolls. While home ownership probably correlates with wealth in a general way, it is not a certain indication of an individual's economic or social status. Some working-class families in nineteenth-century America managed to save enough to buy a home; some upper-class families chose to rent rather than to buy. Another measure of wealth is contained in the federal censuses for 1850 and 1860. Persons at the very bottom of the social structure, paupers who had no means of support except for charity and public poor funds, were identified in both censuses.

Faced with this paucity of information about wealth, historians have attempted to devise indirect indicators of social status. The most commonly used are occupational classifications, which rank occupations on a vertical scale. These scales commonly divide occupations into four or five categories, which presumably represent different levels of income, status, and power, or some com-

Plate 6.3. Interior of a miner's lodging. Photographs of room interiors provide evidence of social status.—Western History Department, Denver Public Library. Reprinted by permission.

Plate 6.4. Tea in a parlor of the Gilded Age.—Western History Department, Denver Public Library. Reprinted by permission.

bination of all three (see the socio-economic ranking scale in the appendix). While such scales are valuable for describing the social structure of a community in a general way, they have to be used carefully when describing individuals. They indicate that, *on the average*, skilled craftsmen had higher incomes than machine operators and lower incomes than professional people, but they do not recognize the substantial variations that must have existed within occupations. Some industrious craftsmen were surely better off than some struggling professionals. An individual's occupation is not *necessarily* an indication of income or wealth.[10] Employment of servants is another indirect indicator of social status. Michael B. Katz found that the presence of servants in the households of Hamilton, Ontario, was one of the best ways to distinguish between working-class and wealthy families. Almost 70 percent of Hamilton's wealthiest families in 1861 had servants living with them; working-class families seldom did.[11] That was probably true also for families living in the United States at that time. Finally, two federal censuses, those for 1880 and for 1900, provide still another partial and indirect measure of wealth: they note the number of months during the preceding year that each working person was unemployed.

While the evidence about social structure is limited, and much of it is indirect, it is sufficient for students to undertake simple investigations. By ranking the occupations present in the community and the number of people employed in them at different times, they can examine general changes in the social structure. For example, what were the implications for the local social structure when a marketing town or predominantly commercial city began to attract industry? Did more or fewer people list their occupation as common laborers? Did industrialization alleviate the problem of poverty in the community or make it worse? The evidence can also be used in a more intensive and more interesting way to examine the consequences of economic inequality for individuals and families.

It will be relatively easier for students to identify the socio-economic status of those individuals or families whose occupation placed them either near the top or close to the bottom of the social structure. A laborer whom the census of 1880 indicated was unemployed during half of the previous year and whose name does not appear on the local tax rolls as a property owner was probably very poor. A lawyer who paid taxes on a downtown business building, owned his home, and had a servant in his household was probably doing very well. It will be much less easy for the students to make such judgments about people in the middle range of occupations. Was the carpenter who rented his house and who was unemployed for two months the previous year leading a comfortable, middle-class existence, or was he living on the edge of poverty? There will be fewer ambiguities at the social extremes. For the lawyer and the laborer, wealth and the absence of it had tangible implications for the life styles of their respective families, which students can also find out about. Research in newspapers, collections of historical photographs and maps, church and other institutional membership records, and school attendance records can add substantially to an understanding of what it was like to be wealthy or poor when the families investigated lived in the community.

To say that a society was stratified, that some individuals and families had more wealth and social status than others, does not necessarily mean that it was a static society. Individuals may still have been able to move upward or downward from one status level to another. Indeed, their own perception of that society may have been influenced as much by an awareness that such mobility was possible as by the fact of inequality itself. That some families had more wealth than others may have seemed to them right and proper, the just reward of a society that permitted families to improve their position over time. At least, that is one hypothesis that might be tested. It is as important for students to understand the idea of social mobility and its implications as it is that they grasp the notion of social stratification. Without some awareness of the implications of both, their understanding of American social history will be incomplete.

During the past decade or so, historians have examined the question of social mobility in a number of industrial towns and major cities of the United States. The pioneering study was a book published in 1964 by Stephan Thernstrom, entitled *Poverty and Progress: Social Mobility in a Nineteenth-Century City*.[12] It was a study of working-class occupational mobility in the textile mill town of Newburyport, Massachusetts. Thernstrom's study, as well as the vast majority of the monographs and articles on social mobility in other communities that followed it, used occupational mobility as the principal evidence of social mobility.[13] Movement from one occupational category to another was assumed to be the equivalent of real upward or downward economic and social mobility. That is not necessarily true. A lawyer who fell out of the high-white-collar category to become a low-white-collar saloonkeeper, would be downwardly mobile, according to most socio-economic ranking scales. However, the struggling lawyer who becomes a prosperous saloonkeeper would in reality have been moving upward in economic status. Occupational change may be a very imperfect measure of change in an individual's economic status, but it is a highly convenient yardstick. Both city directories and manuscript census returns identified individuals by occupation. Using these sources, the rate of social mobility can be computed by tracing individuals through two or more census or directory dates and determining whether or not there was a change upward or downward in the status of that person's occupation.

The substantial amount of research done to date indicates that modest gains in occupational status were quite common for individuals who remained in a community over several decades and that the chances were very good that a man's son would improve upon the father's status. There was probably enough evidence of mobility in industrial America to give manual workers a sense that they did live in a fluid society in which it was possible to improve one's position.

The local history sources used by social historians for mobility studies can also be used in the classroom to explore the meaning of social mobility. It is doubtful that either teachers or students will have the time or the resources to undertake a full-scale mobility study for the community. However, data selected by the teacher from two or more census returns or city directories can be used to help students understand the idea of mobility. For example, data on individuals who were downwardly mobile may help the students to understand that mobility was a two-way street. It may have been a source of anxiety within the society, as well as a reason for confidence and optimism. Information on upwardly mobile individuals can be used to explode the myth that rags-to-riches success was common in industrial America. It was extremely rare. Upward mobility typically meant that an unskilled immigrant could eventually work his way up from a common laborer's job to become a semiskilled machine operator. At most, it meant a rags-to-middle-class-respectability success story. Either of these aspects of mobility could easily be examined in a single class period in which the students could work with a sample of names brought to class by the teacher. In the process, the students would also gain some appreciation for the high rate of population turnover in most American communities throughout their history. Many of the individuals whose names appear in one census or directory had left the community before subsequent listings were made.

Social Geography

Investigating the social geography of a community is another useful way for students to approach social history. Social interaction takes place in space, as well as in time. Having students examine this spatial dimension helps to make abstract ideas about social structure and social organization more concrete. Finding the location of businesses in city directories, locating schools and churches on insurance maps, and plotting the boundaries of residential neighborhoods on outline maps helps to make these social spaces more tangible. Equally important, the various spatial or locational patterns that students will discover in the process can be used to raise important questions about the community's social history.

The location of various social and economic activities within a community is the product of a complex set of variables. Locational patterns and land use in the modern American city, for example, have been largely influenced by the explosive force of the internal-combustion engine. Efficient—and, until recently, inexpensive—automobile and truck transportation enticed manufacturing and wholesaling as well as residential land uses from the central city to less congested suburban locations. Some suburban residential areas had developed along streetcar lines even earlier. Much different locational patterns characterized the preindustrial or feudal city. The primitive stage of urban transportation placed a premium on central location. Consequently, the residences of the wealthy and the powerful, as well as the political and religious institutions with which they were connected, were located in the central and most accessible part of the city.[14] Whether premium space in a community is occupied by banks, cathedrals, or both is partly a reflection of the dominant value system of past generations. What would the locational patterns within their own community at various times in the past tell students about the technology or the social and cultural values of its residents?

Teachers who wish to pursue that question can use as a model the study that Ian Davey and Michael Doucet made of the social geography of Hamilton, Ontario, for the early 1850s.[15] By plotting the locations of various activities on a series of maps, Davey and Doucet found out how space in that commercial city of 14,000 population was used. In the first place, it was used intensively. They found that, although the boundaries of the town included some 3.4 square miles of land, only a single square mile had been intensively developed (see figure 6.1). Despite the abundance of outlying space available for the local coachworks, foundries, and

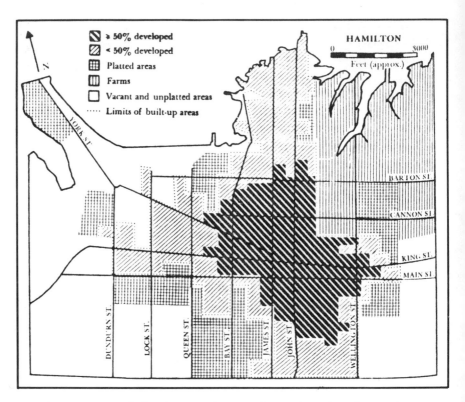

Fig. 6.1. Land development in Hamilton, Ontario, about 1852.—Reprinted, with permission, from "The Social Geography of a Commercial City, Circa 1853," by Ian Davey and Michael Doucet, in *The People of Hamilton, Canada West: Family and Class in a Mid-Nineteenth-Century City*, by Michael B. Katz (Cambridge, Mass.: Harvard University Press, 1975), p. 324.

other small shops, these establishments were clustered near the center of the town (see figure 6.2). So, too, were the city's retail grocery stores (see figure 6.3). Residences were scattered throughout the city, but not randomly distributed according to wealth, occupation or ethnicity. The majority of the wealthiest residents, for example, lived in the core area of the city, as did the poorest of the city's laborers. The laborers who were not so poor tended to live in the peripheral areas of the city. The homes of shoemakers were more evenly distributed throughout the town. Maps of this kind can be constructed for almost any American city

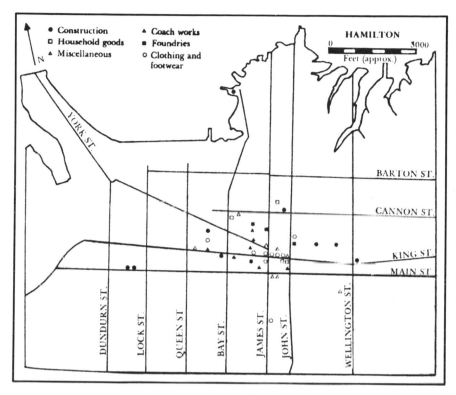

Fig. 6.2. Locations of local foundries, coachworks, and other industries in Hamilton, Ontario, employing more than five workers, about 1852.—Reprinted, with permission, from Davey and Doucet's "Social Geography," in *The People of Hamilton, Canada West*, p. 327.

using data from city and business directories. Whether developed by the teacher or as a student project, the maps can become useful teaching aids for social history.

What can be learned from such maps? The maps for the city of Hamilton, for example, strongly suggest that day-to-day social interaction in the commercial cities of the mid-nineteenth century followed a pattern much different from that followed today. Economic activity of almost every kind was still located in the central area of the city. The core area of the city did not become an island of white-collar workers during the daytime. Rather, a heterogeneous gathering of merchants, clerks, artisans, and laborers

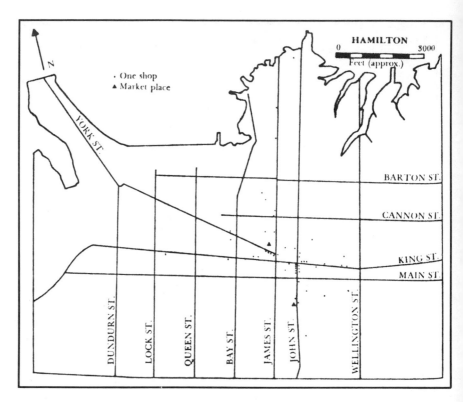

Fig. 6.3. Locations of retail grocery shops in Hamilton, Ontario, about 1852.—Reprinted, with permission, from Davey and Doucet's "Social Geography," in *The People of Hamilton, Canada West*, p. 328.

worked in close proximity to each other. The contrast between the modern city and the preindustrial city is also heightened by the central location of the retail grocery stores. Today their location would more nearly resemble the general distribution of the population, with many stores located in shopping centers adjacent to residential neighborhoods. In Hamilton, in the 1850s, they were clustered along the main access roads near the center of town. The core area of the city was the shopping center. It was centrally located for both the farmers who came into town and for the townspeople who walked downtown to shop. Unlike the downtown areas of modern cities, the central part of Hamilton was not deserted at night. The wealthy merchants had their homes in the core of the city, close to their own business establishments and to the amenities of the central city. That area also housed the inner-city poor, who lived in cheap hotels and boardinghouses. In Hamilton, it was the working class rather than the wealthy that commuted to work. Those who could not afford houses in the core area walked from the outlying residential neighborhoods. The shoemakers whose homes were scattered throughout the city may have worked at home, serving the needs of their own local neighborhood. Making similar maps for their own communities will help students understand that social history has a spatial dimension and that the social geography of a community changes over time.

Ethnic History

Local history sources can also be used to teach more effectively about ethnicity and the history of immigrant groups. Focusing on the history of ethnic groups in a single community makes possible a level of analysis that is indispensable for understanding several aspects of ethnicity. Were new ethnic groups segregated into residential ghettos or residentially integrated into the community? Were the avenues of economic opportunity as open to immigrants and their children as to native-born Americans? Marriage records and other local history sources can be used to examine aspects of immigrant acculturation and assimilation into American society. To what extent did immigrant men marry native-born women? In a variety of ways, local history materials can help students explore significant dimensions of the ethnic experience.

There is a substantial literature that examines the historical experience of immigrants and ethnic groups at the community level. Some studies concentrate on a particular ethnic group, such as the Irish in Boston, the Italians in Chicago, or blacks in New York City. Others examine several ethnic groups within a city and compare their experiences. While some monographs focus on a single dimension of the immigrant experience, such as social mobility, others provide a much fuller analysis. Settlement patterns, the process of migration, institutional development, the political role of immigrants, and the process of assimilation are

Plate 6.5.   Family gatherings helped maintain ethnic consciousness.—Western History Department, Denver Public Library. Reprinted by permission.

some of the areas frequently included. It is an extensive and valuable literature that will provide teachers with a variety of models that can be adapted for classroom use.[16]

Simple classroom activities and student projects that explore aspects of immigration history can be developed using demographic data about your community. The basic source for each of the examples below is the federal manuscript census returns for two of the decennial censuses that provide information about place of birth. The censuses for 1850, 1860, and 1870 list the place of birth of each person enumerated. Those for 1880 and 1900 also list the parents' place of birth, making it possible to identify the ethnic background of those heads of households who were the children of foreign-born parents.

The Immigration Factor in Community Growth

The numerical importance of immigrants in a community can be easily determined by finding the proportion of foreign-born heads of households at any given time. It is important that heads of households be used as the criterion rather than individuals. Otherise the number of native-born children of foreign-born parents will inflate the proportion of native-born residents. That can be illustrated by the following tables adapted from Kathleen Neils Conzen's *Immigrant Milwaukee*.[17] In table 6.1, the percentage of the native-born population was inflated for both census years by the presence of native-born children of immigrant parents. Table 6.2, based on a systematic sample of every fourth household head listed in the census, is a more accurate reflection of the numerical importance of Milwaukee's ethnic population. The first table also suggests that immigration was relatively less important to the city in 1860 than it was ten years before. In fact, as table 6.2 indicates, the percentage of ethnic households had increased.

TABLE 6.1

Size and Origins of Milwaukee's Population, 1850–1860

Year	Total	Nativity	N.	Percent of Total
1850	20,061	Native	7,181	36%
		Foreign	12,782	64%
1860	45,246	Native	22,398	49.5%
		Foreign	22,848	50.5%

SOURCE: Adapted from Kathleen Neils Conzen, *Immigrant Milwaukee, 1836–1860; Accommodation and Community in a Frontier City* (Cambridge, Mass.: Harvard University Press, 1976), p. 14.

TABLE 6.2

Origins of Sample Heads of Household of Milwaukee, 1850–1860

Year	Number in Sample	Nativity	Percentage of Total
1850	1,020	Native	22%
		Foreign	78%
1860	2,266	Native	16%
		Foreign	84%

SOURCE: Adapted from Kathleen Neils Conzen, *Immigrant Milwaukee, 1836–1860: Accommodation and Community in a Frontier City* (Cambridge, Mass.: Harvard University Press, 1976), p. 16.

Some Areas Attracted Specific Immigrant Groups

It is a rather common pattern for one or another immigrant group to be attracted to a city or region in disproportionately large numbers. Trying to account for the relative proportions of immigrants from different countries in your community can lead students into larger aspects of economic and social history. The following suggests some lines of inquiry that might be followed:

1. *Historical Coincidence*:

German immigrants were the largest foreign-born ethnic group in Milwaukee, for example, largely by historical accident. The opening of the farmlands of Wisconsin for settlement happened to coincide with the large influx of German immigration. "The great majority of German immigrants, particularly, came to America in search of land," Kathleen Neils Conzen has noted. "Thus the Milwaukee German settlement was in many respects a consequence of the greater migration to the Wisconsin farmlands." [18]

2. *Occupational Specialization*:

Some immigrant groups settled where they did because the location offered them the opportunity to practice specialized skills that they had brought with them. Welsh coal miners were attracted to the anthracite fields of Pennsylvania; Greek sponge divers, to the Tampa area; Cornish hard-rock miners, to the copper-mining regions of Michigan and to the silver mines of the Rocky Mountain states.

3. *Territorial Proximity*:

Geographical proximity helps to explain why some ethnic groups are concentrated in certain parts of the United States. They settled most densely in the areas easiest to get to, in "the nearest available real estate." [19] That factor largely explains the concentration of French Canadians in New England, Mexican-Americans in the Southwest, and the presence of large European ethnic concentrations in cities along the Atlantic Coast.

4. *Environmental Affinity*:

Cultural geographers also strongly suspect that environmental factors have influenced ethnic locational patterns in the United States.[20] Immigrants may have found certain areas more congenial because the climate, soil, plant cover, or terrain was similar to that which they had left. That would help to explain the settlement of Icelanders and Finns in some of the marginal places of the upper midwest that were ignored by other ethnic groups, or the settlement of Italians and Armenians in sections of California's Central Valley. The German-Russians who emigrated from the semiarid Volga region may have found the western high plains where they settled in the late-nineteenth century more attractive than other places for the same reason.

5. *Chain Migration*:

While some emigrants may have packed up their belongings and headed off into the unknown, a great many others did not. They left for a known destination, with friends or relatives waiting there to greet them. Such chains of migration between a village in Europe and a city in the United States help to account for the growth of many immigrant communities. In his study of immigrant communities in Cleveland, Josef Barton found that more than half the Italians who arrived in that city came in streams of at least twenty persons from the same village. He located the data on village origins in parish marriage registers and in naturalization records.[21]

Activities and projects focusing on the ethnic communities that many immigrant groups established are also effective ways to involve students in the study of ethnic history. Many ethnic groups established institutions, organizations, and predominantly ethnic neighborhoods that provided a supportive environment for traditional values and ways of doing things. Sociologist Milton Gordon has suggested that such communal arrangements performed an especially important function for the newly arrived immigrant. "The self-contained communal life of the immigrant colonies served, then, as a kind of decompression chamber in which the newcomers could, at their own pace, make a reasonable adjustment to the new forces of a society vastly different from that which they had known in the Old World." [22] The extent to which the ethnic community served as a cushion to soften the shock of migration or to preserve the traditional culture must have varied greatly from one immigrant group to another. Some ethnic

Plate 6.6.   In many instances, ethnicity limited one's occupational choices.—
Western History Department, Denver Public Library. Reprinted by permission.

groups hardly maintained a separate identity. Others created cohesive communities that survived for several generations. The object is to have students find out what kind of communal bonds existed within the immigrant groups in their community and how important a role these played in the lives of immigrants.

The following checklist will help guide a local history investigation of ethnic communities. It includes three major ingredients of cultural and social cohesiveness, although it does not claim to be comprehensive. The teacher may wish to add or delete items, depending upon the ethnic groups concerned.

Language

Many but not all immigrant groups spoke a native language different from English. Use of that language in everyday affairs was a great convenience and meant, to some extent, that the immigrant could learn the new language at his own convenience. It also became a badge or symbol of cultural or group loyalty, especially to the older generation. For these and other reasons, the language and the extent to which it was used and perpetuated is important to an understanding of the ethnic community. It would be useful to find answers to the following questions.

1. Did the ethnic community have its own language?
2. Was it used only at home, or was it a "public language," as well?
3. Was it retained beyond the first generation of immigrants?
4. Was it taught in any systematic or institutionalized way to the younger generation? Were there parochial schools in which the language was taught or used?
5. Did the community have foreign-language newspapers?

Neighborhood or Residential Clustering

Residential propinquity also tended to strengthen the bonds of community within immigrant groups. The ability to find help and friendship among neighbors of one's own background lessened the dependence upon outsiders and the need for contact with them. The clustering of ethnic customers also made it possible for ethnic grocery stores, cafes, and specialty shops to be established. In most cities in nineteenth-century America, ethnic concentration could also be translated into political power, with ethnic precincts or wards being able to exchange votes for political influence or jobs in city government.

What is an ethnic neighborhood? The stereotype of solidly segregated neighborhoods reflected in such popular nicknames as "Little Italy," "Germantown," or "Dublin" has been seriously questioned in recent historical scholarship. Few cities seem to have had areas even as large as a voting ward that were exclusively or even primarily occupied by a single ethnic group. In most cities, ethnic neighborhoods probably consisted of areas of only a few square blocks that were probably not the exclusive territory of a single ethnic group. One way to identify such areas of ethnic dominance is to divide the residential areas of a city into cells of about four square blocks each. Assign each student one cell as an out-of-class project. By linking names and information about ethnic background from the manuscript census to names and addresses in the city directory, the students will be able to determine the ethnic background of each resident at the time the census was taken. Any cell in which 60 percent or more of the residents were members of one ethnic group can be considered a residential area dominated by that group.[23] The following questions can be used to help guide a classroom discussion about the results of the research.

1. Were there neighborhoods in the city in which one ethnic group was dominant?
2. Were some ethnic groups more segregated than others?
3. Were immigrants who had white-collar occupations as likely to live in ethnic neighborhoods as those who were manual laborers?
4. For the city at large, was ethnic background or proximity to work most important in determining where immigrants lived?

Ethnic Organizations

Religious, benevolent, and social organizations are also useful indices of ethnic community existence. While the most frequent and probably the most important social contacts were the informal ones maintained in the corner tavern, at the market, or at the town pump, the more formal associations are easier to document. Such formal organizations as church parishes or congregations, mutual-benefit societies, and fraternal lodges did play an important role in binding an ethnic community together. The following questions can be used to direct students toward possible topics for investigation:

1. Did the immigrant group have its own church parish or congregation?
2. Were religious services conducted in the native language of the immigrant group?
3. Did the ethnic group maintain its own parochial schools?
4. Did the group organize mutual assistance societies, such as burial or insurance societies?
5. Did the group establish organizations and societies designed to protect the interests of the ethnic group?
6. Did the immigrants organize their own social or fraternal societies?

Local history sources have been frequently used to teach Afro-American history. Although information about blacks as well as other racial minorities is not as abundant as that for middle-class whites, several kinds of sources do exist. Census data is especially useful. The federal manuscript censuses beginning in 1850 identified individuals by race. City directories occasionally did likewise. The public school district in Madison, Wisconsin, also found sufficient published census data to create several units on local Afro-American history. A unit designed for the eleventh-grade American history course contained census data about black rural-to-urban and South-to-North migration since 1929, which permitted the students to account for the presence of blacks in Madison. A fifth-grade unit developed by that district also included a map showing black residential distribution in Madison, along with recent census information about jobs held by Madison's black workers.[24] Shirla R. McClain and Ambrose A. Clegg, Jr., located a great variety of historical sources for blacks in Akron, Ohio, including church records, census returns and city directories, public records, minutes of meetings of black organizations, and black college yearbooks.[25] Other activities and projects that teachers have developed for teaching about local racial minorities have relied heavily on oral history research.

Oral history research, useful for many kinds of local history investigations, is often indispensable for the history of local racial minorities. As Carlos Cortes has pointed out for Mexican-Americans, "Since the Mexican-American generally has been neglected in local books, newspapers, and other written sources, only the fringe of his experience can be discovered through reading. This study process must be supplemented by oral investigation if students are to develop a true knowledge and understanding of local Mexican-American society, culture, and history."[26] That is perhaps equally true for local studies of Indians, Asian-Americans, and blacks. A teacher in a black history course at the Lima campus of Ohio State University relied heavily on oral history research for his students' local history projects. One of the required assignments in Dominic Candeloro's course was a five-page paper on local black history. A two-hour interview in the classroom with a local black civic leader produced a basic chronology of local black history and a list of possible topics to be explored. From that information the class developed a questionnaire concerning black participation in local politics, religion, and the labor movement, as well as questions asking for each respondent's date of arrival in the city and information about how the person was treated by Akron's white population at various periods of time. The class then assembled a list of persons to be interviewed. When completed the student papers were submitted to an editorial committee, which produced a mimeographed report entitled "The Black History of Lima: A Preliminary Study." Although the instructor reported that the results did not represent outstanding local history, the experience did broaden their intellectual and social horizons. Candeloro says, "The very fact that the project has brought inexperienced white students into contact for the first time with numerous black figures in the community was enough to justify it." [27] Oral history can be a useful method for investigating social history in its broadest sense, which is history at the grass roots—history from the bottom up.

7

Teaching Political History with Local History Sources

IN spite of the fact that political history has been the most frequently taught aspect of American history, it seems also to be the topic of American history that is least remembered by students. Routine polls indicate the public has little knowledge about the functioning of governmental institutions, and less confidence that these institutions are performing adequately. Secondary students have even less knowledge about the government of their local community. National attention was brought to this problem in 1977, when a Gallup Youth Poll showed that fewer than 15 percent of the high school seniors surveyed nationally knew the names of their local government officials, the form of governmental structure, the way it operated, and the types of services it provided.

There has been some change of a positive nature since 1977, chiefly because curriculum committees and a few national textbook publishers have begun to develop strategies, materials, and guidelines addressing the problem. Most of these new approaches utilize local history sources. Firsthand experiences develop interest in the topic and engage the students' interest in the study. There is great variety among these new materials, but they can generally be categorized under four general approaches. One approach has students compare local institutions and local decision-making over a period of time; a second popular strategy has students survey and chart the deployment of resources within a community. This strategy sometimes uses a historical approach. A third method has students use local examples to test generalizations about national political history and political change. The fourth approach has students examine the political role the local area might have played in the larger history of the country.

All of these approaches can provide rich experiences for students, and all of them might be used to develop units or lessons in a local history course, a United States history course, or in a government or political science course.

Local Government Forms and Decision-Making

The study of the history of the development and activities of the local government can be highly interesting to students. They are usually surprised to find that many of the problems of city life we consider to be modern—pollution, poorly devised transportation networks, and perhaps malfeasance on the part of an elected official—were problems for many early communities, as well. The first "suburb" of the city, a residential neighborhood on a hill, may have been built there so that people could escape from the settling of coal soot in the middle of the town. Old newspapers often discuss the townspeople's wanting the city government to do something about such pollution. Sometimes small western towns enacted ordinances stating that horses had to be tethered on side streets, to keep the main thoroughfare free from the confusion that might result from horses breaking free during gunfights. And nearly every community has stories of the mayor or tax collector who absconds with the public treasury. But there are also more basic or important studies that students might undertake. For example, in many eastern communities, the town government and the regular town meetings appear on the surface to be very little different from those that were held in the seventeenth century. When students examine the locus of power in the community, however, they are likely to find that, while the structure might look the same, the decision-making apparatus has undergone numerous changes over the years.

In the western states, much of what has been institutionalized were the rules and regulations developed and administered by the ordinary citizens of the community. In the absence of federal laws, many frontier people took upon themselves such duties as regulating water use, holding trials, convicting and executing wrongdoers such as horse thieves, and, in the mining areas, developing land-use rules and regulations.

Some of the laws written by a motley group of miners in the Gregory District, Kansas Territory are a good example:

> At a meeting of the miners of Gregory Diggings on the North Fork of Clear creek, K.T. on the evening of the 8th inst., [June 8, 1859] Wilk Defrees was elected President and Joseph Casto, Secretary.
>
> 1st. Resolved that this Mining District shall be bounded as follows: Commencing at the mouth of the North Fork of Clear creek, and following the divide between said stream and Rallston Creek running seven miles up the last named stream to a point known as Miners Camp. Thence South West to the Divide between the North Fork of Clear creek and the South Branch of the Same to place of beginning.
> 2nd. Resolved that no miner shall hold more than one claim except by purchase or discovery. . . .
> 4. Resolved that each miner shall be entitled to hold one mountain claim, one gulch claim and one creek claim for the purpose of washing, the first to be used 100 feet long and fifty feet wide, the second 100 feet up and down the river or gulch and extending from bank to bank. . . .
> 9. Resolved that when two parties wishing to use water on the same stream or ravine for quartz mining purposes, no person shall be entitled to the use of more than one half of the water.[1]

Students studying such materials will quickly discover that these codes were based on an assumption that eventually the federal government would do away with the Indian claims to title for much of the land being camped upon. The miners were basing their claims on the pre-emption laws that they thought would soon go into effect. Such laws provided that actual settlers on land of public domain would have first chance to buy their holdings when the land was surveyed and offered for public sale. When the Territory of Colorado was established in 1861, that is precisely what happened, in some instances. In other instances, the men who had signed the Miner's Code had long since departed to find a fortune elsewhere.

County courthouses, municipal courts, and local and state historical societies hold cartons of materials on similar locally developed codes. Many are also discussed in the letters these early settlers sent back home. Often, early newspapers will have printed the codes (in the case of the Gilpin District, the code itself stated that the laws be printed in the *Rocky Mountain News*—the only newspaper in the general area, and that a hundred extra copies be bought for the use of the miners). Just how these codes, and those of such groups as the "peoples' courts," which were in some instances little more than vigilante committees, were later incorporated into territorial and state laws, provides an interesting study. Students may also trace the names of signers of such codes, to see whether they were among the first elected officials of the local and state government.

Surveying and Charting Governmental Resources

A number of teachers have found that, when students do a survey of the local community, they enhance their understanding of the way local government works and the ways other institutions within a community can be influential in determining the quality of life the citizens enjoy. Frequently, when such surveys are completed, students will want to know why and how things came to be this way. They may then wish to do research to find out how institutions developed over time and how decisions about that development were made.

Students in Boulder, Colorado, found through a survey that there seemed to be an inordinate number of parks and other open spaces in the older sections of the town. In researching to find out why this was so, they found that a main focus of local politics during the Progressive period had been a "City Beautiful" movement. In 1890, the Boulder Improvement Society was formed to lobby the city government "to make Boulder more beautiful, more healthful, and in every way more desireable." [2] In 1909 the group hired landscape architect Frederick Olmsted, Jr., to develop a beautification plan for the city. His report[3] was found in the pamphlet files of the municipal library, and the plans for the parks the students were curious about were carefully described. This particular project then went three ways. Some students were still concerned with the parks themselves, and they compared Olmsted's plans with the existing parks. Others became interested in the role of the Olmsteds in the national city park system movement, and that made a nice link with national history. A third group of students researched city records and old newspapers to find out how the lobby had pressured the government and to find out how many of Olmsted's recommendations had actually been financed by the city government. Simple surveys can suggest any number of projects of this type.

There are a number of sources one can use to develop a local survey instrument. The League of Women Voters published a pamphlet, "Know Your Community," in 1972, which is available at any League office or from the national office, which is located at 1730 M. Street, N.W., Washington, D.C. 20036. This publication lists hundreds of questions one can ask about the community background; the structure and functions of local government; the popular control of governments; financing the local government; public protection including fire and police protection, local courts, and jails; municipal services, transportation, and utilities; education; libraries and museums; public health; public welfare; housing and urban renewal; planning and zoning; recreation and parks; and there is even a section that includes tips on publishing a completed survey. This pamphlet is useful for any community, but it is especially helpful if one is doing the local history of a recently developed suburb. These places that at first glance may seem to have little to offer in the way of historical research do have a history of political development, even if it is a short history.

A survey developed by the Chicago Metro History Fair covers many of the same topics, but it is more particularly designed to help students develop enough background on their communities to ensure their having adequate knowledge to choose a history project for entry into the contest that the fair sponsors. This activity is reprinted in full because it is so adaptable to any community.[4] The point is to examine the historical dimension of each of the categories.

INTRODUCTION TO YOUR COMMUNITY

1. Obtain a map of your neighborhood, town or suburb from the agency of government concerned with planning.
2. Trace only the outline of your community's boundaries and major transportation arteries on a ditto. Or using an appropriate scale (to fill an 8½-by-11-inch sheet) draw your community's boundaries and major transportation arteries on a ditto. Run off enough copies for each student to have ten community outlines.
3. Assign groups of students to pinpoint the various community resources by placing symbols on the appropriate places on the map. Each group should be responsible for one category and should share its findings with the group, so that the others can mark their maps and make additions and corrections.
    The categories include the following:
    A. Police and fire stations
    B. Schools and libraries (include colleges and universities)
    C. Places of worship
    D. Shopping centers or areas
    E. Hospitals and/or medical buildings or centers
    F. Entertainment centers (movie theaters, playhouses, amusement centers)
    G. Transportation system (traffic movement into and out of the community, movement within the community. Cars, bicycles, walking, etc.)
    H. Industry or commercial operations (beyond retail under "D")
    I. Parks and recreational facilities
    J. Governmental offices (services including health and mental health facilities)
    K. Financial institutions—banks, savings and loans
    L. Community resources—community newspapers, organizations, landmarks, historical sites
4. As they go into the larger communities beyond their neighborhoods, the students can be asked to list the needs and services for which they and their families go outside the immediate community.
5. With this packet of information, the students either as individuals, or in groups, can now begin to define their specific projects. Essentially, whatever specific form the projects may

take, the students will be learning to see their communities in new and different ways.

The model shown in figure 7.1 is merely a suggested format. Teachers and students should feel free to adapt this project sheet to their own particular needs.

Examining National Political Developments through Local History Sources

Local sources can also be useful for examining the larger developments of political history. The source materials of local history can provide students with an opportunity to examine critically historical generalizations found in textbooks or elsewhere. A survey of the town history to find out where national and local political developments do converge might be a useful project for the teacher or activity for the students: Did the Colonial controversy over taxation have local political repercussions? Were local political factions divided over the ratification of the Constitution? Was there a local suffragette movement? Such possible points of convergence could provide the basis for any number of future student projects, should sufficient local source materials be available.

Local sources can also provide insight into political processes that history textbooks tend to overlook. There is, for example, the process by which people relate their own local and immediate concerns with larger national issues. It is unrealistic to assume that most people identify instinctively with national issues remote from their everyday lives, or that, in a country as large and diverse as the United States, people relate to national issues for the same reasons. The following activity was developed to give students some insight into the way national political issues have been translated into questions of local concern by astute local newspaper editors.

In a United States history survey course, during a class session on the progressive movement, one of the authors asked the students what they thought *progressivism* meant, to the ordinary American of that era. Most textbooks provide adequate accounts of progressive reform movements in the cities and at the state and

Community History Project

Specific topic_____

Qualifications of topic (time, point of view, aspect, or limitations)_____

_____

Community (cities) involved:_____ Precinct:_____ Ward:_____

City_____ Town or village_____ County_____

Metropolitan area_____

Resources to be considered:

Records:

     Censuses_____   Books_____

     Diaries_____   Articles_____

     Newspapers (metropolitan)_____   Letters_____

     Newspapers (local or neighborhood)_____

Graphics: *Buildings:*

     Maps_____   Residences_____

     Sketches or paintings_____   Industrial_____

     Photographs_____   Public_____

                                       Landmarks_____

Artifacts:

     Machines_____   Furniture_____

     Tools_____   Clothing_____

Oral history interviews:

_____

_____

_____

_____

_____

_____

In each instance, indicate the name of the person to be interviewed and indicate what part the interview might play in your investigation.

Final result: Presentation of completed research

     Paper_____

     Dramatization_____

     Photographic display with written or taped explanation_____

_____

     Slide/tape presentation_____

     Movie_____

     Model_____

     Map (plat, topographic, physical)_____

_____

Fig. 7.1. Sample form for student use in class community history projects.

national levels. But what did progressivism mean to Americans who lived in the small towns and the predominantly rural areas of the country? During the Progressive Era, most Americans still lived in such places. How did those Americans relate to problems and issues that, for the most part, had their roots in the industrial cities?

To help students explore this question, the instructor had collected a series of editorials from one of Boulder's local newspapers for the period from 1897 to 1907. Boulder was then a marketing and supply town of fewer than ten thousand people, with virtually no industry. How would the citizens and voters of a small town such as this identify, for example, with the symbols and rhetoric of those progressive politicians then campaigning against the trusts? As the students quickly discovered, the local newspaper editor made it very easy for them to do so. In the *Boulder Daily Camera*, they found, among others, the following editorials:

June 20, 1897
   One of the worst habits is the consumption of iced water and iced tea in the hot days of the summer and we are glad to discover that Boulder people have given it up. For this we are under lasting obligation to the local ice trust which has made the price so high that people can't afford to abuse their stomachs as formerly. The ice trust, is, therefore, a blessing in disguise and we trust people with due humility will regard the great blessings it confers.

The local lumber trust was a little more serious, and it brought more than tongue-in-cheek chiding from the crusading editor:

October 7, 1905
   The Weekly Boulder *Times* joins the *Herald* in telling people that if the lumbermen want to combine that is their business. The former even advocates that the newspapers have an agreement on advertising rates and job work. . . . If the papers charge excessively for advertising, business men would use some other vehicle for exploiting their wares. But lumber and cement and windows and all the materials of interior construction of a home should never be permitted to be made the subject of a combination in restraint of competition any more than your groceries should be. . . . The fact that Boulder lumbermen formed a combination with Denver lumbermen indicates that unless the one Denver house stands out they will have Boulder paying them just what they demand.

June 2, 1906

It [the commercial association] was appealed to for the purpose of having stopped such articles as the Camera published last
night. . . . The lumbermen have but one point on which we are to
be convinced to stop this agitation—THEY MUST SHOW THAT
THEY ARE NOT MEMBERS OF A COMBINE IN RESTRAINT OF
TRADE OR COMPETITION.

And so it went, for several more issues. Students who compared such editorials to the general description about trusts in
their United States history books found that, although the issues
of the local area were hardly of the same magnitude as those
concerning the nation at large, the intent of the local "trusts" and
the ire of the muckraking editor were very much a part of the
national trend. Students who read other editorials found that
national consumer issues also had their local counterparts. The
Boulder water supply, for example, was said to be tainted. The
editor compared it to what one would find in a buffalo wallow;
and in September of that year, he said that the mayor had conceded that tailings from a stamp mill had been run into the local
creek. "That is part of the slimy stuff now constituting our drinking water. It may not be injurious to your health, but it is not an
appetizing mess." By the time the students had finished reading
these representative items from a local newspaper, they under-
stood that national political concerns had their local reflections
even in the small communities of the West.

This type of exercise can be used with equal effect in a local
history class or in a United States history survey. The teacher may
prepare the materials ahead of time for students to use in the
classroom, or students might wish to use the same simple method
to produce a set of materials as a project. Topics that lend themselves to such treatment include the local reaction to the war
effort from 1914 to 1918, the response to WPA construction in a
city, or the location of a CCC camp near the town. Most local
newspapers are now indexed and available on microfilm. They
may be housed at the public library, or in the newspaper office
itself. It is laborious to copy the microfilm and to place the contents into some sort of usable order, but many students become so
involved with the potential results that they will bear with the long
hours it takes.

Using Local Sources to Recreate National-Local Political Events

One belief students seem to bring to a study of United States history is that all the important events of national history either happened somewhere else or in a past so distant that it has little to do with them as individuals in modern society. Using local history as a focus for role-playing activities can help dispel those notions. Using either of the two models below, teachers may find that they can develop exercises using local events to show how people in different communities respond to a political event in different ways.

The first example is a role-playing activity that recreates the election of 1836 in London, Ontario. Designed by teacher Susan Smith Blocker[5] for her course in local history, the activity focuses on issues facing the inhabitants of the struggling young village of London in particular and Upper Canadians in general in the years preceding the 1837 Rebellion. The project asks students to recognize the impact the issues had on individuals and invites debate about why an individual took the position he did. More important, however, it is designed to help students to understand the part played by their community of London in a critical period of their country's past.

Seven important roles are involved in the activity. Each reflects an actual person representative of one of the conflicting viewpoints in the town. The issues were varied and reflected a number of concerns. Important natural harbor locations crucial to water transport for agricultural products could not be used by farmers because these locations had been given to wealthy businessmen by the provinicial government. Farmers also complained of the neglect of the government to set tariffs to protect them from the competition of American wheat farmers. Although the Church of England was not legally the state church, the government of the colony acted as if it were the established church in much the same way it was in England. There was controversy over the control of education. Should it be under the control of the "state" church? Should it be controlled by the state at all? Finally, a new lieutenant-governor, the crown's representative, had dismissed the executive council after it had demanded its right to be consulted on all issues of public business. The lieutenant-governor had felt that the council existed only to "confer dignity upon his proceeding."

The activity itself was a panel discussion in which students represented the seven points of view as they might have been expressed by the seven influential men of the town at that time. Students in small groups had done research from a number of sources that the teacher provided, including a number of histories of the local region. As in any exercise in role-playing, the debriefing was the most important segment. Students were asked to consider whether their motivations in responding to the discussion were the same as those apparently influencing the actual historical characters, and they were to assess the usefulness of the activity in studying the controversial issues facing the dwellers of London in the 1830s.

Such a model might be used in any community. It could be used to recreate the influence of particular leaders in political decision-making situations such as political party caucuses, city council meetings, or state elections. It might also be used for showing some aspects of the nongovernmental power base of a community.

A second example of role-playing that might be used in a local history course is an exercise in negotiations entitled, "Should the Tea Be Landed in Boston?" [6] Students who live in Boston must always be aware of the important role their city played in early American history, and students all around the nation know at least something about the Boston Tea Party; but how many of them consider that the decision made in Boston was the result of choices made by the citizens of the city at that time and that these choices were not inevitable? The issue, whether tea taxed by the English Parliament was to be landed in Boston, was the same issue that faced colonists in Philadelphia, New York, and Charleston, South Carolina. The citzens of each of these cities faced precisely the same question, but responded differently in each place, depending on the choices the people felt they had available to them, as well as the ways in which they responded to the crisis.

In this particular activity, the students are given data cards explaining the background of six of the actual participants in the Tea Party, as well as a list of the options available to those individuals. Students are encouraged to develop other options through a study of local history materials available to them. A series of bargaining sessions takes place, and eventually a joint solution is developed. Throughout the exercise, the students are encouraged to utilize a "Calendar of Events," which is a record of activities that actually took place in Boston from October 21, 1773, until the actual "party" was held on December 16. The final question asked of the students is "Would you have joined the Tea Party?"

The purpose of exercises such as this one is to make students aware of the fact that historical events are not inevitable—there were no Tea Parties in the other cities—and that individuals can have a great amount of influence when political decisions are made. The activity could serve as a model for any number of local events bearing a relationship to national history. How did a particular community decide whether to recruit volunteer militia to take part in some of the Indian battles? Why did a particular town fight so hard to become the location of the land-grant college of the state? What made the citizens of a border state decide which side of the Civil War to support?

Some teachers will want to combine activities that teach about the economic, social, and political aspects of their community's development. Because a small unit of space is being examined, as compared to a national history study, students grasp the interrelationship of these aspects of human activities easier than they do when such activities are presented in the larger framework. When the alderman is also the owner of the grocery store and the leader of the civic improvement organization, it is easier for students to discern the motivations and understand the behavior of an individual opinion-shaper than when they are studying national figures. The practice of examining a history on a small scale makes the study of the larger picture more meaningful. This is one of the most important reasons for studying local history.

Part 3
A Local History Course

8
Setting Up a
Local History Course

A N increasing number of schools and colleges offer local history as a separate, elective course. Such existing courses reflect a number of basic approaches. Some are designed to have the students produce a written history of their community, which will be typed or printed and sold or otherwise distributed within the local area. Such a history may be added to, year after year. Some works of this kind are organized as chronological surveys, with emphasis on events that took place within the local community. Still others are cultural journalism courses, which tend to be concerned with folklore from the locality in which the school exists. There are other courses that are not chronological and are not designed to produce published works. These are topical courses, used in teaching historical methods that can be appropriately used in a later study of any historical problem. In such courses, students choose subjects of interest to them and spend much of their time doing independent research. Some courses combine these general approaches, and many courses change from year to year, depending on the strengths and interests of the students enrolled at any given time.

Types of Local History Courses

The Chronological Approach

In some schools, the local history course is a chronological survey, with the United States survey required as a prerequisite. It is usually offered as an elective. One of the best-known of such courses is that offered at Oliver Ames High School in Easton, Massachusetts.[1] Elected by half of the senior class each year, this course asks the students to work as much as possible from primary sources of information. Field trips and individual exploration of the community's resources make up much of the course work, but there are also extensive sessions in which the students examine slides of photographs, documents, town records, news clippings, and other sources. Each student is expected to spend a minimum of fourteen hours outside the classroom, working on an individual project due near the end of the semester. The units within this course give one a sense of the materials covered and the link that is made with national history. The units are "Geographic Background," "Indians of the Area," "First Settlers," "Background Sequences," "American Revolution," "Post-Revolution to 1850s," "The Civil War," "The Gilded Age," "1910 to 1945," and "Since World War II."[2]

A second example of a chronological course in local history is a senior seminar for advanced students taught at Chelmsford, Massachusetts. Students there researched the history of their community, organized their materials, wrote and proofread their copy, and produced a well-illustrated booklet entitled *From Settlement to Suburbia: A New History of Chelmsford.*[3] One particularly interesting aspect of this work is the parallels that the students drew between national social, political, and economic events and their local manifestations. At the university level, Brian Mitchell of the University of Lowell, at Lowell, Massachusetts, teaches a semester course on that city.[4] The units of his course are: "Pre-Industrial Lowell," "When Cotton Was King," "The Immigrant Experience," and "Twentieth-Century Lowell." The course work includes readings, guest speakers, slide presentations, and historical site visits.

Another example of the chronologically developed course is that of John D. Buenker of the University of Wisconsin at Parkside. The focus here is Kenosha, Wisconsin, and the immediately surrounding area. Units include: "Geography and Physical Growth," "The Peoples of Southeastern Wisconsin," "The Economic Evolution," "The Social Matrix (including ethnicity, class structure, and the status of racial minorities)," and "Government and Politics." [5]

The Topical Approach

Some local history courses do not utilize the chronological approach. Students are given a brief over-all introduction to the history of an area, but the greatest part of the course is devoted to research by the students themselves with guidelines provided by the instructor. Both of the authors of this book have developed such courses for their respective secondary and college-level students.

The high school course contains four units: "You and Your Place in Space," a several-days' look at the man-made environment of the city; "Getting Ready to Research," a four- or five-week unit introducing students to the use of local resources and the techniques needed for utilizing them (working with oral history, using microfilm and microfiche, making slide and videotapes, learning simple techniques of quantification, etc.); "Researching," an eight- or nine-week period in which students spend most of their time on projects, although they do meet individually with the teacher at specified times and as a class twice a week to hear guest speakers, see audio-visual materials developed by previous students, and take part in a few group activities; and, finally, "Reporting on Your Work," a two- to three-week unit in which students examine the projects done by other class members. All through the course, there are a number of field trips, walking tours, and sessions spent at the local historical society museum, which happens to be located within walking distance of the school. The students work on a great variety of individual topics.

The university course takes a different kind of topical approach. It is an undergraduate seminar in American urban history. The course is one of several seminars offered by the Department of History to give history majors at least one encounter with research using primary sources. After presenting a survey of urban development in the western United States, and in Colorado in particular, the instructor assigns the students a common historical problem. While the problem varies from year to year, it always requires the students to do local historical research. The students in one seminar, for example, were asked to explain why the rate of urban growth in Colorado from 1880 to 1900 was greater than the rate for the United States as a whole. Each student attempted to answer that question by examining the growth of one of the nearby towns during that period. In this course, the students work on a common topic, using different local communities as resources.

A second example of a university course taking a topical approach is one taught by Ted L. Underwood at the University of Minnesota at Morris.[6] Underwood's students also write local history as part of a seminar on historical research. Using local primary sources, students write papers of about twenty to twenty-five pages on some facet of local history. The final phase of these students' work is to write a three-page history of their work as historians. This helps them to evaluate the learning experience as a whole and also provides them with information needed to evaluate the finished product of the research. Underwood describes a problem that everyone who teaches such a course seems to have in common. A quarter or a semester is really a very short time for students to develop a valuable paper or project. Students sometimes do not discover until mid-way into the course that the topic they have chosen is not workable. They then have precious little time to start again and get a paper in on time. While one should keep in mind that false starts are common for anyone doing historical research, there are ways to minimize the problem in a classroom situation.

It is possible to encourage students to choose a topic on their own while also providing insurance that they will not waste too much time in the process. One way to do that is to set an early cut-off date for the students' selection of workable topics. By that date, they must not only have the topic defined, but must also demonstrate to the teacher that sufficient source material exists for completion of the project. If they have not been able to find enough sources for their topic, the teacher can let them select a topic from a list that he or she has already prepared for which sufficient sources do exist. That will reduce to a minimum the frustration Underwood describes, without wholly depriving students of the right to find their own topic.

The Cultural Journalism Approach

Without doubt, the most popular approach to using local history in the schools is that which has become known as cultural journalism. *Foxfire*, the magazine developed by Eliot Wiggington and his students, and Wiggington's own work describing his experiences are too well-known to need description. Countless schools now use the production of a magazine similar to *Foxfire* as a regular course offering, and even more of them use lessons or short units in the *Foxfire* mode.

Such works are not restricted to local history, for the contents of the magazines may range from ways to make cheese to ghost tales to the account of an island in American Samoa that was sold for three cigarettes. What the various magazines produced as school projects have in common is that they all use information gathered by students from the community in which they live. The courses are also designed to help students develop some specific skills. In working for the magazine, students learn to interview, record, transcribe, photograph, develop and print photographs, write stories, lay out stories, circulate and advertise a magazine. They learn to appreciate and understand the types of knowledge people in their own community need to have for daily survival, and they learn the folklore of the community. Occasionally, such a course is taught in a history or social studies department; more often, a course of the *Foxfire* type is offered by an English or communications department within a school. A number of good guides on ways to set up such a course are available.[7]

Developing a Local History Course
The Teacher's Responsibilities

Successful local history projects and courses are obviously not spur-of-the-moment enterprises. Local community studies of any kind, as Colin J. Marsh has put it, "do not just happen on a sunny afternoon." [8] A great deal of preparation by the teacher has to precede the excitement that comes from the student's encounter with the past. In fact, launching students into local history projects without a previous tilling of the ground is generally conceded to be a prescription for disappointment. One manual insists that teachers accept responsibility for at least the following:

1. A comprehensive list of topics for student research, which will help eliminate some of the frustration that students encounter in finding a manageable topic.
2. Providing a comprehensive list of community resources, including the type of historical information that students can expect to find in libraries, museums, local historical societies, and public agencies. This should be prepared as a handout.
3. Displays of projects completed by previous students, to serve as models, along with a thorough discussion of the pitfalls that other students have fallen into.
4. Plans for an attractive culminating activity as a goal toward which students can work and as a device for sustaining motivation. This means that student projects will receive visibility as local history displays; as presentations to student, parent, or community groups; or as markers for local historical buildings. More ambitious projects, such as self-guided historical walking tours or historical markers for hiking trails, could make a lasting contribution to the community.[9]

A guide for a state history course that incorporated local resources, produced by the Ohio State Department of Education, also urged teachers to seek financial support from the school district. "Some schools might be willing to pay expenses for the collecting of needed data or employ teachers during the summer to collect needed primary source materials," it suggests. "These materials could be duplicated for student use." [10]

Teachers must face the fact that local history projects and courses, like every other kind of instruction, require expenditures of money. Some of the important data about the community are very likely to be located out of the reach of students. The best-equipped libraries and the largest collections of archival material and photographs tend to be located in large cities. Even those students who live near these resources will probably find many collections restricted to use by adults. Access to rare materials is invariably limited to adult researchers. It will be necessary for the teacher to have such materials microfilmed or photocopied. A copying budget is essential for even a modest history effort. Although collecting of scattered sources will be necessary, that task should not be a major deterrent to any teacher who wants to utilize local historical resources. Every community, no matter how small or how recently developed, has some historical source materials close at hand.

More important than money is commitment. Fully exploiting the possibilities of local historical resources requires a long-term investment of time and effort. Community history programs tend to improve with age. Locating archival sources, identifying older residents who are important sources of oral history, and building up a core of other source materials is a continuing process. It is essentially a process of self-education. Eventually the experienced local history teacher will be the program's most valuable resource of all.

The successful use of historical source material also involves a commitment to work partiently and closely with the students. Even though students' projects require independent work after school hours, they should not be regarded merely as homework. The teacher will need to commit a great deal of class time to discussion and to helping with research.

Before the Course Begins

Developing a local history course differs in a number of ways from designing a traditional history course. There is much more involved than choosing objectives, activities, and evaluation methods and then searching for and ordering textbooks, supplementary reading, and appropriate audio-visual materials. Although the teacher of local history can manage without any particular formal training, he or she must do a good deal of reading and planning if the course is to be successful.

The first and most important task of the teacher is to survey and collect local resources—both actual materials and lists of people and places that might be useful for students to investigate.

While it is possible to teach the course with students using existing collections in public facilities, it is impractical to expect all the research to be done outside of school time.

Several months before the course is to be introduced, the teacher should visit a number of agencies to inventory their holdings and to set up arrangements for students to visit or do research at the agency. The following list suggests some of the important steps the teacher should take:

1. Check the school library to see what holdings already exist. See whether books about the community, the region and the state exist and whether they will be useful for your students to read. Check the pamphlet, map, and audio-visual files for useful materials. Ask the librarians if you can set up a special local history vertical file. Eventually, this file might be filled with photocopied journal and newspaper accounts of aspects of the town's history, and it might also become the repository for written student projects. Many librarians will help set up a cataloguing system for these files, and most will wish to catalogue the materials in the main card catalogue, as well.

2. Visit the public library and the local historical society, if there is one. Develop a bibliography of the important holdings of these agencies. This can be a student project, once the course begins, but the teacher must have a good sense of what is available at the start of the course. Either or both of these agencies are appropriate places to check for oral history collections, for photograph collections, and for ephemera—broadsides, scrapbooks, and other such materials. The public library may also be the repository of the municipal records. If that is so, the teacher should spend some time becoming familiar with the materials and with the cataloguing system so that that information can be passed along to students planning to do research at these institutions. Check for the availability of old newspapers, microfilm readers, city directories, census records, or other items. The librarians or curators will have many suggestions of materials that one might overlook. Many librarians will develop a list of their holdings for students and will give an orientation tour, as well.

3. Visit the city hall and the county courthouse. At both places, make lists of the holdings available for student use. If the

county seat is some distance from the school, be sure to ask about procedures for copying materials and for ordering materials by mail. Make sure the clerks in the various offices are aware of the program you are developing. Although these people are curators of public information, they are often overworked, and they are not always receptive to the requests of students. If they become interested in the program, however, they can be of great help.

4. Visit the local newspaper office. Find out whether it maintains copies of back issues, or issues of newspapers that predated it. See whether students will be allowed to use the newspaper's library and whether they will be given permission to copy old photographs. If the newspaper runs regular columns on local history, make copies of the articles that have appeared. Ask for the names and addresses of the writers and arrange interviews with these people. Not only will most of these people be happy to be on your list of classroom speakers, but they are also a good source of names of other people in the community who might either speak to the class or agree to be interviewed by students. During this visit, you might also wish to speak with the editor of the newspaper. Explain your intended project, ask about publicity for your program, and see whether students might eventually be allowed to write articles the paper would wish to publish.

5. Visit the state historical society and the state archives. Find out about the procedures for using their materials and check out the costs involved in copying materials. If these agencies are some distance away, you might also, on this first trip, wish to copy manuscripts of diaries, journals, letters, census records, and other materials certain to be of interest to the class. Eventually, if money becomes available, one would wish to copy all materials in these agencies that concern your locality.

6. Begin a photograph file. Slides are the most practical form of photographs for classroom use. They can be made into prints if students wish to use them in projects. You will want to use as many historical photographs as possible, in the early days of the course.

7. Check out the district and school equipment for media possibilities. See whether students will be allowed to check out cameras—still, movie, and video. Find out whether photocopy work

can be done at low cost to students. See whether the media center owns or will purchase a microfilm copier for you to use in your classroom. Find out how much help students might expect from the audio-visual technician and graphic artists, if these positions exist in your school district or campus media center.

8. Visit the local cemetery or cemeteries. Find out who is the caretaker and what organization is in charge. While you are there, take a few photographs of headstones, make a few rubbings, and take a few shots of the entire cemetery. You will want to use these when you introduce cemetery projects to the students.

9. Take a number of walks throughout the town. Identify areas that will make good walking tours for the students, keeping in mind that these walks will be developed for a number of purposes. Again, it is helpful if you take a number of photographs. Prints or slides can be examined at leisure, and they can be very useful in planning the directions for a particular walk. You may also wish to use them for debriefing exercises, after some of the tours.

10. Visit any historical sites in your vicinity. If there are curators, enlist their aid in developing a productive tour to the site. Try to plan exercises requiring some activity on the part of the students. Mere looking gives very little mileage.

11. Spend a couple of days just examining your materials and checking the lists you have developed. You will want to begin the course with topics on which you have the most data. As the course progresses and as students develop projects, you will soon find that there is not nearly enough time to cover all you would like to get through in the term. When you have a good sense of the types of materials available, you will want to think of the focus and approach you will want to use as you teach the course. This focus will depend, to a great extent, on the purposes of the course within the total curriculum and your own interests and philosophical attitude toward the discipline of local history. The units chosen will be a reflection of these concerns, but they will also be dictated, to a large extent, by the history of the particular area.

12. Ask for as much money as you think might possibly be forthcoming. It is possible to do such a course inexpensively, but copying and filming will be continuing expenses. Remind your

authorities that there will not be a need for textbooks, which will be a considerable saving. At the university level, students can be asked to contribute to photocopying expenses in lieu of buying textbooks.

13. Finally, check with local museums, historical societies, public libraries, historic preservation, and other agencies, to see whether they would be interested in a collaborative program of some kind. See Chapter 2 for a description of types of co-operative programs which now exist.

The Introductory Unit

While an introductory unit of a local history course can accomplish several purposes, it should, above all else, open up to the students the broad range of possibilities awaiting them. The introductory unit is the time for breadth and overview. Most of the research projects the students will be engaged in as time goes on will require a limited horizon, a sharpening and narrowing of focus, a honing in. Thus they need to have, at the outset, sufficient information about the history of the community to be able to ask interesting questions and to design an interesting project. Before they have committed themselves to a project, they need to know about the kind of research techniques that would be required for it. They need to know the kind of sources that would most likely be useful and whether those are available. The introductory unit should provide the broad base from which the students can begin to select more narrowly focused topics and appropriate techniques.

It is important for students to understand, early in the semester, that there are a great many ways to do research in local history. Their research can take the form of oral history interviews, reading old newspapers, collecting numerical data from census returns, or interpreting photographs—to mention only a few. While most topics will require a combination of research techniques and sources, some will require a greater concentration of time and effort in one type of source material. Different research techniques will require different skills and aptitudes. Some require mathematical aptitude; others rely more upon communication skills. The students need to know what is required of them before they commit themselves to a topic. They should know what kind of skills they will need and whether they have time to develop skills they do not already have.

During the introductory unit, the teacher should also introduce the students to potentially interesting aspects of the community's history. It is one of the axioms of historical investigation that one must know something about a topic *before* doing research. The more extensive one's knowledge, the more significant the research is likely to be. The same holds true for a student research project. It will be virtually impossible for a student to ask an interesting question about local history without some prior knowledge about the history of the community. The teacher may develop a list of feasible projects; but the larger the students' share of responsibility in developing the topic, the greater the motivation, and the better the outcome will likely be. Of course, a large part of the orientation to the community's history can be accomplished at the same time the students are introduced to research techniques and source materials.

Finally, the introductory unit should also be used to establish the proper learning environment for a local history course. The students should understand, from the outset, that in one major respect, this course will be different from any other history course they have ever taken. The content of this course lies outside the school classroom, in the historical sites, libraries, local museums, and newspaper files, rather than between the covers of textbooks. They will need to search actively for most of what they will learn in the course. That will require a different mode of learning from the passive, classroom-bound process most familiar to them. It is an active mode that will lead them in unpredictable directions; it is the mode of the researcher, the sleuth. This style of learning should be incorporated into as many course assignments and activities as possible from the very outset.

Seeing History in the Streets

To serve notice that the course will be focused on materials that lie beyond the school, the teacher should take the students on a historical walking tour no later than the second or third class meeting, or as early in the semester as possible. Even if the most historic sections of the community lie beyond walking distance of the school or the walking time permitted by a fifty-minute class period, an excursion into any area that has some old buildings will serve the purpose. The walking tour can also be used as an initial exercise in training the students to look for historical evidence in the man-made environment around them. Consequently, it should be a simple exercise in which the students look for historical evidence, rather than a narrative performance by the teacher acting as tour guide.

To give the activity a semblance of structure, the following checklist or some variation of it should be handed out to the students before they leave the classroom. They can fill it in individually, or work together on it in small groups, as they proceed on the tour.

1. Give the address of the oldest building on the tour route.
2. Give the address of the newest building.
3. List the evidence that helped you determine both of the above.
4. Identify a building now used for a different purpose from that for which it was originally constructed.
5. List seven building materials used in the construction of buildings on the tour route.

This particular list was developed for a walk through one of the oldest streets in the business district of a town. Little expertise was required to answer the questions. Several older buildings happened to have construction dates chiseled into their stone fronts. A building now used as a specialty shop has the word *BANK* embossed on its front. The building materials included a number of cast-iron store fronts, as well as brick, native sandstone, and later glass and aluminum fronts. In residential areas, there may be more guessing about the age of buildings, but historical accuracy is not the point of this lesson. For perhaps the first time in their lives, many students will be staring at buildings for clues to age and touching them to find out what they are made of.

Plate 8.1.   Only by touch could the student detect that this surface was made of cast-iron.

A debriefing exercise—or, at least, a chance to compare notes—is essential, if the students are to get full benefit from the walking tour. Part or all of the following class period should be used for that purpose. Is there a consensus about the oldest and newest buildings? On what basis was age determined—a date on a cornerstone, architectural style, building material used, location on the block, state of disrepair? Each student will probably be impressed and made somewhat humble by the number of things others noticed that he or she did not. Perhaps the most important lesson to be learned from the debriefing is that we see so little of the physical world around us, because our powers of observation usually are underdeveloped and little used. For example, the authors have experienced one such debriefing session in which the entire class of twenty students missed one of the most noticeable features of late-nineteenth-century commercial construction—the cast-iron front.

Through the Camera's Eye

The impact of the debriefing session can be further enhanced with the use of slides made from historical photographs of the tour area. The additional preparation that this requires is well worth the effort. The problem to be posed for students is identification of the buildings seen on the tour from the slides being shown. For commercial streets with even fifty to seventy-five years of continuous use, this is anything but an easy exercise. Commercial buildings go through a gradual but steady process of renovation and remodeling. Window lintels are changed, new fronts are added, old buildings are replaced. It may not even be an easy exercise for a residential area. Houses also change, as new rooms are added, porches closed in or removed, or trim taken off. But once again, the most striking lesson to be learned is that we notice so few clues and pay so little attention to those we do see. At the first showing of the slides, very few students will be able to remember whether any of the buildings in the slides still exist.

During this initial unit of the course, students should also be introduced to the variety of other uses of historical photographs. Since the purpose of these initial sessions is to help students select projects, slide series should be organized topically. A judicious mixture of slide series organized by teacher-selected topics along with "catchy, problem" slides that raise questions may be the best course. The selection of slides would depend upon the teacher's purpose and the extent to which it seems important to direct students toward an early definition of a topic.

Insurance Maps: A New Kind of Evidence

Insurance maps are an excellent complement to photographic evidence. Although they provide very different types of visual evidence, each form makes up for the shortcomings of the other. The residential area shrouded in trees when photographed from a bluff overlooking the town will have the shape of each house starkly outlined on the insurance map. Conversely, the map's austere information about a business block will be fleshed out in rich detail from the photograph of Main Street. Students cannot be expected to realize the potential of this kind of evidence, however, unless they have some experience using the maps.

One way to offer such experience is to set up a series of problem-solving situations in which the historical evidence—in this instance, the insurance map—provides clues to a solution. A two-day exercise using the insurance map in such a manner as described can be productive. One begins by making color slides from a page of a map such as those drawn by the Sanborn Map Company. The slides are photo-enlarged on a color photocopy machine. The four to six sections are then taped together to produce a map of a four-to-six-block section to the business district. One then makes a list of the number of residences and businesses located in the area covered by the map. Students are given this list, along with an outline map of the area. The students' task, usually done in groups of three or four, is to guess the identity of and then to draw in on their outline maps the items on the list. At first glance, the project will seem, to both teacher and students, an exercise in sheer guessing: how should the students know where the grocery stores were located in 1883? However, they probably will have a general idea that groceries were located off the main street, near the residential area. They will no doubt place the lumberyards off on the outskirts of the map, where the extensive land required for stocking a lumberyard could be had more cheaply. Each group of students will come up with slightly different organizations for their maps, and it is worth taking a few minutes for each of the groups to explain their reasoning. The students will then wish to know the "correct" answer, and there is one: the answer sheet is the insurance map.

When students are given the insurance map to compare with their own drawings, they will usually find that their guesses about the location of the grocery stores and the lumberyards are wrong. Grocery stores tend to be clustered on the main street, unlike the chain-store supermarkets located in dispersed shopping centers today. Even some of the lumberyards most likely occupied prime locations in the center of town. In the smaller towns of the nineteenth century, Main Street functioned as the town's shopping center. Farmers in from the countryside parked their

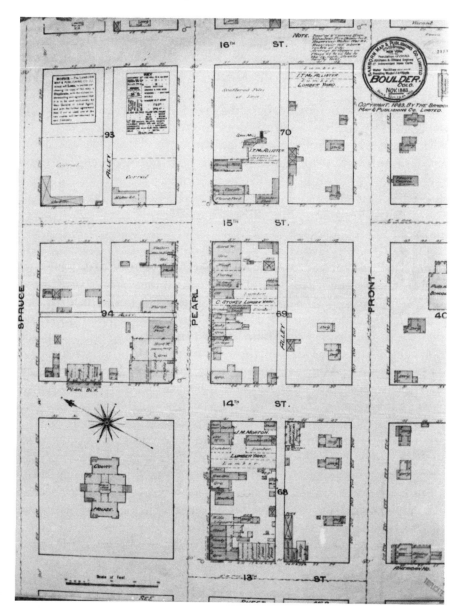

Fig. 8.1.   Sanborn fire insurance maps are available for most communities.

wagons along the street; townspeople walked the four or five blocks to the downtown area. Since people looked to the main street for convenience shopping, it was expected that a lumber store as well as a hardware, feed store, and so on, would be located nearby, as well.

Students learn from this experience that perceptions of the way space is used in the community in an urban area today can be misleading when applied to the community of the past. Students have a tendency to fill up the blocks of the downtown business district to make it similar to those of today. The amount of open space, the clustering along the front of the block that faced Main Street, with the rear of the blocks virtually unoccupied, surprises them.

A third exercise using insurance maps demonstrates the advantage of combining the two principal kinds of visual evidence—maps and photographs. In our particular example, a "bird's-eye view," whose 1874 date the class had already confirmed, was paired with the 1883 insurance map. Students could identify the buildings on Main Street built during that nine-year interval, to get some idea of the rate of growth. The pairing did provide a tentative answer to one question: Why was the lumberyard across from the courthouse? The lumberyard site was still vacant land in 1874, and if the yard was put up shortly thereafter, it was on the fringe of the business district. The business district had simply expanded beyond it by the later date. By comparing the 1883 map with slides of photographs made of the business district in the mid-1890s, students were able to see the results of continuing and even more rapid growth beyond that date. As the slide collection had very few photographs from the 1880s, the insurance map provided the missing link.

If one wished to extend this particular exercise a fourth or fifth day, it can also be profitable to use a set of slides with a business directory for the same time period. One can discover from the business directory that the businesses along one main street, for example, included four clothing stores, a meat market, two grocery stores, three book stores—one of which also sold musical instruments, while the other two also sold paint, station-

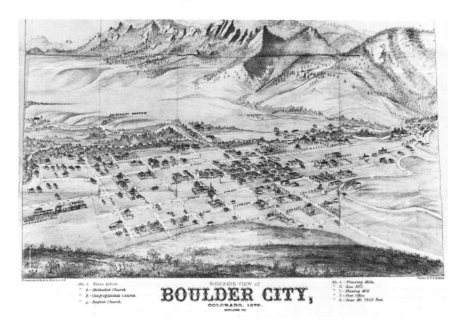

BOULDER CITY,
COLORADO, 1874.
BOULDER CO.

Fig. 8.2. Lithographs such as this one provide a comprehensive view of a town.—Boulder Historical Society. Reprinted by permission.

ery, and drugs—two real estate offices, a restaurant, a dressmaker, a saloon, a notary public, and a bank. From the photographs, one can match up the names of the owners of the businesses with the signs on the shops. A short walking tour along this street, with the students carrying along the photographs from the 1880s and the addresses from the 1883 business directory can prove enlightening and reinforces the lesson "Through the Camera's Eye."

There are any number of other activities one could use to orient students to the course. The important thing to keep in mind is that students do need an orientation to the types of materials and kinds of methods and techniques they will be using during the term. The work is very different from that which most of the students will have encountered in their previous history or social studies courses, and some set of activities making that explicit will go a long way in developing the sort of mind-set students will need to begin their study.

Research and Reporting

There are a number of important responsibilities for the teacher to consider as students research projects. Most were implicit in the section on teacher responsibilities, but a few specific tasks should be mentioned here. First of all, students must have a clear idea of the requirements of project work. They need to know approximately how many hours of work outside the classroom will be required, how much class time might be spent on the project, and what a finished project should look like.

All of these requirements will vary, depending on the age and the ability of the students, the focus of the course, the approach the teacher is taking, the proximity of needed resources, and the quality of such resources. The location of the school also has an important bearing on the way the course is arranged. If one is in a small town, where the school or college is located within blocks of the main street and the public facilities, one can expect that students' work will be greatly facilitated. On the other hand, some schools are located so far from research sites that only special Saturday workshops will make research in these locations possible. The teacher must decide whether he wants to make such a commitment and whether students can do so.

Students should be encouraged to report the results of their work and to share it with at least the other class members. A great many schools end up with published works that are circulated within the community. If teachers decide that that would be a productive culmination to the course work, they should be alert to the tremendous demands upon their own time that such a step will take. Students cannot be expected to do all of the work involved in so large an undertaking without a good deal of guidance. The time needed for the project must be made part of the course work. A number of publications provide guidelines for this type of publishing. Among the most useful are Thomas E. Felt's *Researching, Writing, and Publishing Local History*[11] and Pamela Wood's *You and Aunt Arie, A Guide to Cultural Journalism.*[12]

Perhaps the last words on this topic are: local history courses tend to take up most of a teacher's school time (even vacations tend to be spent taking photographs or wildly copying documents), and one's other courses and leisure time may suffer from that situation; student projects do not always turn out to be as complete or as thoroughly done as one would hope, and one must come to terms with that well-documented phenomenon; *but*, for many of us, the excitement of learning along with our students makes such an undertaking worthwhile.

Appendixes

Appendix A

Secondary School Library Tour Guide

1. Look in the card catalogue under (your state). Write down the call numbers for the general history books listed there.

2. Look in the card catalogue under (your state—your city). Write down the call numbers for the books listed there.

3. Pull some of these books from the shelves and, using the index as a guide, see if you can answer the following questions:

   (a). When was the town founded? _____

   (b). Why was it first settled? ___ _____

   (c). Who were the first settlers? _____

   (d). Why did they come? _____

   (e). What is the economic base of the town? _____

   (f). Is the town noted for anything special (e.g., is it a college town, the home of a large industry, the site of an army base, etc.) _____

   _____

4. Go back to the card catalogue. Look under the heading of biographies, including collected works. Which, if any, of the people listed are directly connected to this town?

   _____

5. Look again under the name of the state and check other listings that follow the name of the state—for example, natural history, religion, transportation. Which of these items might be useful to you? List them.

   _____

6. Look through *The Readers' Guide to Periodical Literature*. Check both the state and city names to see whether there are any articles about the city in the general magazines listed. Look up some of these and jot down the basic content. _____
   What other indexes and finding guides are available in your library? List them. _____

   _____

7. See whether there are past issues of the newspaper(s) of the town kept in the library. If there is an index, look up topics that interest you and skim several of the issues listed. If there is no index, skim several issues starting with the oldest and progressing to the present. What specific information did you pick up? _____ What kind of information is in every issue? _____ How could this help you in your project? _____

8. Move to the reference section of the library. See if your town is listed in any of the encyclopedias or almanacs. Jot down the basic information given. (You may have to look under the state heading.) _____

_____

If the town has 5,000 or more people, you should be able to find the population numbers for 1960, 1970, and 1980. Compare these figures. What do they tell you about the town? _____

_____

9. Examine the map of the state or community with the largest scale. What is the latitude and longitude of the city? _____

10. If there is an oral history collection in the library, check to see how it is indexed. Write down the bibliographic information for two tapes from the collection. _____

11. Check to see whether there is a picture file. Write down the way these are indexed. _____

_____

Developing A Research Strategy

Instructions for Students in a Local History
Course at the University of Colorado

For your research paper in this course, you will need to devise a research strategy that includes more than the subject card catalogue in Norlin Library. The object is to locate all the important materials pertaining to your topic whether or not they are listed in the card catalogue. The following exercise will, at least, get you started.

1. *Guides to Bibliographies:*

You will need to find bibliographies that contain lists (sometimes annotated) of articles and books about your topic. The following guide lists several such bibliographies:

Eugene R. Fingerhut. *The Fingerhut Guide: Sources in American History.* Santa Barbara, 1973.

Locate this guide and write the title of a bibliography that you found in it that might contain information on your topic in the space below:

2. *Bibliographies:*

The following are some bibliographies that you should consult for books and articles about your topic. In the space below each bibliography, list one title that may contain useful information. If none obviously do, include a closely related title instead.

O. O. Winther and Richard A. Van Orman. *A Classified Bibliography of the Periodical Literature of the Trans-Mississippi West.* Bloomington, 1961.

O. O. Winther. *A Classified Bibliography* . . . (Supplement to the above, for 1957–1967). Bloomington, 1970.

Marion J. Kaminkow. *United States Local Histories in the Library of Congress: A Bibliography.* Baltimore, 1975.

Clarence S. Peterson. *Consolidated Bibliography of County Histories in Fifty States in 1961.* Baltimore, 1961.

Virginia Lee Wilcox. *Colorado: A Selected Bibliography of Its Literature, 1858–1952.* Denver, 1954.

America: History and Life. 1964.

American Historical Association. *Writings on American History, 1902–1959.*

3. *Other Sources for Printed Materials:*

In addition to bibliographies, there are other resources to guide you to printed materials about your topic. Include at least one related source from each of the following, writing it in the space below the item:

Union List of Newspapers, edited by Winifred Gregory

University of Colorado Theses and Dissertations Catalogue File

Colorado Magazine Index

Now proceed to the Subject Card Catalogue.

SOCIO-ECONOMIC RANKING SCALE

White-Collar Occupations

I. High White-Collar

Professionals

Architect
Chemist
Clergyman
Editor
Engineer (except locomotive or
  stationary)
Lawyer

Pharmacist
Physician
Scientist
Social worker
Teacher
Veterinarian

Major Proprietors, Managers, and Officials

Banker
Broker
Builder, Contractor (with
  sufficient property)
Corporation official
Government official (upper
  ranks only)

Hotel keeper or manager
Labor-union officer
Manufacturer
Merchant (with sufficient
  property)

II. Low White-Collar

Clerks and Salesmen

Accountant
Advertising man
Agent
Auctioneer
Auditor
Baggageman
Bank teller
Bill collector
Bookkeeper
Canvasser
Cashier

Clerk
Collector
Credit man
Dispatcher
Insurance adjuster or salesman
Mail carrier
Messenger
Office boy
Salesman
Secretary
Typist

Semiprofessionals

Actor
Airplane pilot
Artist
Athlete
Chiropractor
Dietician
Draftsman

Librarian
Musician
Newspaperman
Optician, Optometrist
Osteopath
Photographer
Surveyor

Embalmer   Technician—medical, dental,
Entertainer   electrical, etc.
Journalist   Writer

Petty Proprietors, Managers, and Officials

Foreman   Proprietor or manager of a
Huckster, Peddler   small business
Minor government official   Railroad conductor
                                  Self-employed artisan

BLUE-COLLAR OCCUPATIONS

III. SKILLED (Apprentices in IV, Self-employed in II)

Baker   Machinist
Blacksmith   Master mariner
Boilermaker   Mechanic
Bookbinder   Millwright
Bricklayer, Mason   Molder
Carpenter, Cabinetmaker   Painter
Caulker   Paperhanger
Compositor, Printer   Patternmaker
Confectioner   Plasterer
Coppersmith   Plumber
Craneman, Derrickman   Roofer
Electrician   Shoemaker (except in factory—
Engineer (locomotive or   IV)
   stationary)   Silversmith
Engraver   Slater
Fireman (locomotive)   Steamfitter
Furrier   Stonecutter
Glazier   Tailor
Goldsmith   Tinner
Jeweler   Tool-and-die maker
Lithographer   Upholsterer

IV. SEMISKILLED AND SERVICE WORKERS

Apprentice   Janitor
Barber   Lineman
Bartender   Longshoreman
Brakeman   Meatcutter
Bus, cab, or truck driver,   Milkman
   Chauffeur   Motorman
Cook   Policeman
Cooper   Sailor
Deliveryman   Servant
Elevator operator   Soldier (except officers)

Factory operative
Fireman (stationary or city)
Fisherman
Gas-station attendant
Guard, Watchman
Hospital attendant

Stevedore
Switchman
Teamster
Waiter
Welder

V. UNSKILLED LABORERS AND MENIAL SERVICE WORKERS

Coachman
Gardener
Hostler, Liveryman

Laborer
Lumberman
Porter

SOURCE: Stephan Thernstrom, *The Other Bostonians: Poverty and Progress in the American Metropolis, 1880–1970* (Cambridge: Harvard University Press, 1973), pp. 290—292.

Appendix B

Recording Cemetery Data

Developed by Richard J. Riley, North Quincy, Massachusetts

Instructions for recording information on the "Cemetery Data Sheet".
All information MUST BE PRINTED.

1. SITE: Print the official site designation.
2. DATE: Note the date the sheet is completed.
3. RECORDER: Print your full name here.
4. TYPE: Place an "X" after the appropriate designation.
5. NAME: Record the full name of the person interred as it appears in the text of the epitaph/inscription.
6. MAP/LEDGER: Obtain the Engineers Map number of the Hancock Cemetery Ledger number and record it here.
7. DEATH DATE. Record this information, if available, using the form: day/month/year.
8. SEX: Place an "X" after the appropriate designation.
9. AGE: This information occurs on a small portion of the stones and should be recorded here. The age designation on some stones is AET.
10. STATUS: Place an "X" after the appropriate designation. If no indication of status is given in the text, place an "X" after "Other" and print "STATUS: None" under "NOTES."
11. STONE MATERIAL: Place an "X" after the appropriate designation. If "Other," note below.
12. DIMENSIONS: Fill in the appropriate information.
13. CONDITION OF STONE: Place an "X" after the appropriate designation and fill in the appropriate information.
14. COMMENTS: Provide any additional information relating to the condition of the stone that you feel may prove helpful.
15. CONDITION OF INSCRIPTION: Place an "X" after the appropriate designation.
16. COMMENTS: Provide any additional information relating to the condition of the inscription that you feel may prove helpful.
17. FOOTSTONE PRESENT: Place an "X" after the appropriate designation, and fill in the appropriate information.
18. STONE FACES: Place an "X" after the appropriate designation. "Stone" here refers to the headstone, and the direction it faces may be determined using a compass.

19. STONE SHAPE-OUTLINE: Place an "X" after the appropriate designation.
20. STONE SYMBOLISM: Place an "X" after the appropriate designation—refer to attached sheets. If the symbol is of a different type, describe it under "Other." Be as specific as possible in your description.
21. NOTES: Provide any additional information that you feel may prove helpful—for example: birth date as it appears in the text of the epitaph/inscription.

CEMETERY DATA SHEET

1. Site_____ 2. Date _____ 3. Recorder _____

4. Type: A. Gravestone __ B. Monument __ C. Tomb __ D. Other __

5. Name _____ 6. Map/Ledger _____

7. Death Date _____ 8. Sex: A. Male _____ B. Female _____ 9. Age _____

10. Status: A. Mr.____ B. Mrs.____ C. Miss____ D. Deacon____ E. Rev.____

            F. Lieut.____ G. Capt.____ H. Col.____ I. Dr.____ J. Master____

            K. Esq.____ L. Other____

11. Stone material: A. Slate ____ B. White marble ____ C. Marble ____ D. Granite ____

12. Dimensions: A. Height to ground _____ Inches B. Width _____ Inches

            C. Thickness _____ Inches

            D. Mass (L times W times H) _____ Cu. Inches

13. Condition of stone _____ 14. Comments _____

    A. Replacement stone ____   _____

    B. Good ____   _____

    C. Cracked ____   _____

    D. Broken ____   _____

    E. Tilted: (1) Yes ____ (2) No ____ (3) Angle of tilt _____

    F. Has stone sunk (1) Yes ____ (2) No ____

15. Condition of inscription   16. Comments _____

    A. Clear _____   _____

    B. Blurred _____   _____

C. Illegible _____ _____

D. Recut _____ _____

E. Newly cut _____ _____

17. Footstone present A. Yes _____ B. No _____

    C. Distance from headstone _____ Inches

18. Direction stone faces: A. North _____ B. N-East _____ C. East _____ D. S-East _____

    E. South _____ F. S-West _____ G. West _____ H. N-West _____

19. Stone shape—outline

    A _____ B _____ C _____ D _____ E _____ F _____ G _____ H _____ Other _____

    Comments _____

20. Stone symbolism

    1 _____ 2 _____ 3 _____ 4 _____ 5 _____ 6 _____ 7 _____ 8 _____ 9 _____ 10 _____

    11 _____ 12 _____ 13 _____ 14 _____ 15 _____ 16 _____ 17 _____ 18 _____ 19 _____ 20 _____

    Other _____

21. Notes: _____

    _____

    _____

    _____

    _____

EPITAPH/INSCRIPTION DATA SHEET

1. A. Gravestone _____ B. Monument _____ C. Tomb _____ Date_____

2. Name _____ Recorder _____

3. Stone material: A. Slate _____ B. White marble_____ C. Granite _____ D. Other _____

4. Death date _____ 5. Sex: A. Male _____ B. Female _____

    day   month   year

6. Dimensions: A. Height _____ B. Width _____ C. Thickness _____ D. Mass _____

7. Inscription cond: A. Clear _____ B. Blurred _____ C. Illegible _____

8. Ledger map number _____

9. Full inscription epitaph

    _____

    _____

John W. Lyan

James H. Boyle

PHOTOGRAPHS

If the recorder wishes to photograph gravestones, following are some hints for obtaining good results.

1. The best photographs will be obtained on a sunny day between 10:00 A.M. and 2:00 P.M.

2. To make a good photo-record, take two photographs, one of the whole gravestone and one of the details of the head or carving.

3. If photographs are taken of a stone, each print should be identified by the following information: Town, location, name of burial ground, and name of stone. A number should be assigned each gravestone photographed and that number recorded on prints and Form E.

Types of Pre 1830 Gravestone Shapes

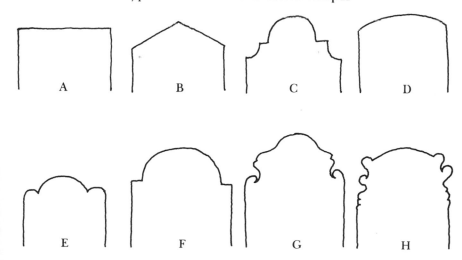

Types of Pre-1830 Gravestone Designs

Types of Pre-1830 Gravestone Designs, con't.

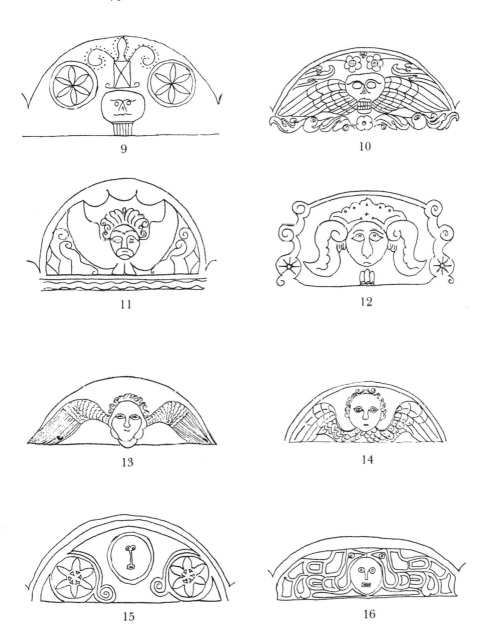

Types of Pre-1830 Gravestone Designs, con't.

17

18

19

20

BIBLIOGRAPHY

Forbes, Harriet M. *Gravestones of Early New England* Boston: Houghton Mifflin, 1927.
A standard work on the subject, particularly useful for identification and discussion of various carvers.

Ludwig, Allen. *Graven Images.* Middletown: Wesleyan University Press, 1966.
Striking and numerous illustrations, excellent discussion of symbolism and the religious aspects of mortuary art.

Deetz, James, and Edwin Dethlefsen. "Death's Head, Cherub, Urn and Willow." *Natural History*, March 1967.
The archaeological and social implications of mortuary art.

Deetz, James, and Edwin Dethlefsen. "The Doppler Effect and Archaeology." *Southwestern Journal of Anthropology* 2, no. 3.
The use of gravestones in developing explanatory models in archaeology.

Appendix C

The walking tour of two neighborhoods in Boulder, Colorado, that follows was prepared by Catherine Taylor, in co-operation with Historic Boulder and the Boulder Valley Schools, with funds provided by the Local Assistance Program of the State Historical Society of Colorado. Reproduced here with permission.

WALKING TOUR OF
TWO BOULDER NEIGHBORHOODS

THE PIONEER ERA

This walking tour will take about ninety minutes and will lead you through two Boulder neighborhoods—the Tourtellott-Squires Addition and the Mapleton Hill area. *Begin at the corner of Eleventh and Spruce.* This corner is a good point from which to view the natural setting of these neighborhoods. You are standing at the edge of the valley created by Boulder Creek. Looking to the north, you see Mapleton Hill, really a mesa or shoulder extending out from the mountains. University Hill is its counterpart across the valley. The homes you see as you look north represent a picturesque cross section of those that make up these two neighborhoods, ranging from the simple, white frame house on Pine in the older

Tourtellott-Squires Addition to the elegant Mapleton Hill homes set on their majestic sites.

Water In 1862, residents of pioneer Boulder made their first lasting mark across the face of Mapleton Hill when they constructed the "Farmer's Ditch" to carry Boulder Creek water to farms to the north and east of town. The ditch can be clearly seen in the detail of the 1874 "Bird's-Eye View of Boulder" below, on this page. It still runs behind the homes you see on the north side of Pine. You will encounter this man-made waterway several times as you walk through this area—a reminder that water is of great importance in this semiarid environment.

263

Religion   Like water, religion was often an early concern of pioneers. Just up the hill from where you are standing, settlers built Boulder's first church. The minister remarked, "What a help it would be for the county seat to have a substantial church on the hillside whose tower would be visible for miles down the valley." Boulder was at that time competing with Valmont to become the principal settlement in the county, and citizens were concerned about the future of their tiny town. When completed in 1870, the church stood alone on the grass-covered hill, with the Farmer's Ditch running behind it.

Congregational Church

A Pioneer House   *Walk west on Spruce to 1019 Spruce.* Here, set back from the street, is the Tourtellott-Squires House, built by two remarkable pioneer families. Jonathan and Maria Tourtellott and Frederick and Miranda Squires came to Boulder in 1860. Twin sisters Maria and Miranda ran a boardinghouse and restaurant a block south of here. Their husbands ran a bustling general store. They built this house in 1864 at a cost of $8,000, patterning it after farm houses in their native New England. Shortly after the house was finished, Boulder experienced a period of economic uncertainty. Squires said of that time, "The fine stone house we had just built was all that kept us from removing to Denver and going into business there."

Look closely at the stonework. Signs of a porch, since removed, can be seen on the front. On the east side of the house, note the rough fitting of the stones (an interesting contrast to the fine stonework on later Boulder homes, like those on Mapleton Hill), and the wooden beams used for lintels. A tour of the interior of this pioneer house reveals the thick walls, original panes of glass, and the simple woodwork from an early mill.

Pioneer House

THE RAILROAD ERA

By 1870, the future of Boulder seemed secure enough to warrant the businessmen of town's subscribing $200,000 to bring the railroad to Boulder. Tourtellott and Squires began to sell lots in their "Addition to West Boulder," land they had acquired from the government in 1866 for $1.25 per acre. The detail of an 1874 lithograph of Boulder, printed on the preceding page, shows the growth of the neighborhood as the Railroad Era begins.

Other resources from this period help us to identify which of these early houses still stand. Sketches from a book by Rocky Mountain Joe (J. B. Sturtevant) show some of the homes of merit in Boulder around 1880. A map from the same year tells us where some of these houses stood. For example, the map indicates that a Col. Van Fleet lived at Tenth and Spruce. *Walk across Spruce to see if this house is still standing on the southeast corner of Tenth and Spruce.*

Walk around to look at the east side of 1002 Spruce. Stucco was often applied to renovate and modernize older homes during the 1920s and 30s. Frequently, it masks original building materials and details.

Cross Spruce and walk west until you are in front of the houses at 1001 and 1003. Note the large cottonwoods here, reminders that we are still in the floodplain of Boulder Creek, where underground water is available for these thirsty trees.

Continue west, stopping to look at the house at 935 Spruce. This house was built by a Dr. Groesbeck in 1871. Soon afterward, the Wilder family purchased the house, and they lived here for more than fifty years. In 1872, the Wilder house and the Tourtellott-Squires house stood alone on this block. By 1922, every home you now see had been built. Note the difference between the 1880 drawing and the house as it appears today. Sometime during the Wilder family's long residence here, the second floor was enlarged and opened out.

Walk west to the corner of Ninth and look across Spruce to view the cottage at 910 Spruce. This small house is the only remaining hint of a row of modest Victorian laborers' cottages which once lined this side of Spruce.

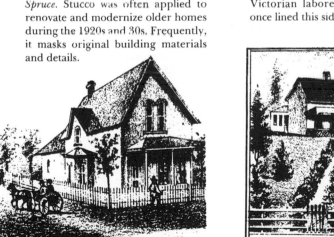

Cross Ninth Street, then turn right and walk north to Pine Street. Stop and look across to the brick house on the northeast corner, 903 Pine. This fine house was built in the late 1870s, and was for many years the home and office of a prominent Boulder physician named Earhardt. Note the windows and their stone trim, in a style that can be seen all over Boulder. Dimick, the architect and contractor who designed this house, also was responsible for Old Main on the university campus, and similar details appear on both buildings.

Now walk west on Pine to look at the houses at 827 and 835 Pine.

City Lots in a Small Town   These two frame houses are beautifully preserved examples of simple "town houses," built on deep, narrow lots. Homes of this basic plan were built along city streets all over the United States during the 1800s. Machine-milled lumber and the construction method known as "balloon framing" allowed builders to put up a house cheaply and quickly. Wooden siding encloses the framing skeleton; vertical boards or covers finish off the siding at the corners. These two thin houses fit

tightly on their fifty-foot lots. In the 1888 Mapleton Addition, twenty-five-foot lots were laid out. Why such narrow lots, when so much land was available? We can only guess that developers were eager to earn the profits of urban and suburban land development, and that purchasers were willing to recreate the close, urban feeling of the towns and cities they had left.

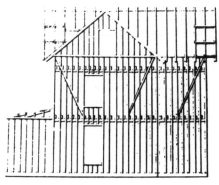

Plans for the "balloon-frame" skeleton of a typical town house, from an architectural pattern book of the 1880s.

Upward Mobility   The histories of the owners of these two simple homes tell us more about Boulder in the Railroad Era of the '70s and '80s: 835 Pine was owned in 1883 by I. T. McAllister, who had prospered as owner of a lumber mill. McAllister was then building himself a new, more impressive frame house at 1619 Pine.

827 Pine was built, and occupied for many years, by the Fonda family. George Fonda was one of Boulder's most enterprising citizens. His name can still be seen on the Pearl Street mall, atop the building he erected to house his thriving business. In 1901, Fonda built a house, easily seen from

here, on the southwest corner of Eighth and Pine. These two homes, built for the same family, provide an interesting contrast: 935 shows a modest simplicity. The larger house at 2135 Eighth expresses prosperity and a concern with "modern" style (the round stone arch at the front door and the Neoclassical columns were popular architectual details at the turn of the century). The boxlike hipped-roof shape of 2135 Eighth also provides an interesting contrast with the steep-roofed Victorian houses across the way.

A Victorian Gem *Cross Pine to view the house at 809 Pine.* This house was also designed by Dimick, but here he uses a different group of popular styles. The turret, veranda, and trim are typical of Queen Anne, a Victorian style that was new when this house was built in 1877. Look at the ins and outs of the walls of this house, and contrast this complex plan with the frame boxes at 927 and 935 Pine and the substantial, square box of the new Fonda house.

BIG HOUSES ON THE HILL

Revival Styles from the turn of the Century *Walk uphill on Eighth to Highland, crossing the Farmer's Ditch. Stop at the corner of Highland and look west to see two turn-of-the-century homes at 745 and 725 Highland.* These are examples of Revival styles that were popular at that time; 745 uses tall, Ionic columns in a Neoclassical Revival style; 725 combines Georgian and Colonial Revival elements. Other examples of Revival styles can be seen on Mapleton Avenue—columns are a good clue.

Continue uphill on Eighth toward Mapleton. As you walk past 745 Highland, stop and look back toward the south to see the spectacular view that this house enjoys—a reminder that we have climbed out of the creek bottom and up the side of the mesa that is Mapleton Hill.

A Man-made Environment *Continue north to Mapleton and cross to the island in the middle of Mapleton Avenue.* Stop here for a moment to survey this man-made environment. Originally a wind-swept hill covered only by native grasses, this area began to change when the Boulder Land and Improvement Company laid out lots and streets in 1888. A year later, the company obtained irrigation water and planted trees along the streets. These trees, now mature, create their own environment, especially in the summer, holding moist, cool air close to the ground.

Mapleton School *Now walk east on Mapleton, across Ninth Street. Stop and look back to the west to view Mapleton School.* Compare the school as it looks today with the photograph on the next page. This school was built in 1888 and served as a high school and administrative offices, as well as an elementary school. When first built, the school stood alone and prominent on this hill, facing Old Main across the valley. The land on which the school was built was then known as Squire's pasture. Many changes have taken place in the school since this photo was taken.

Pleasant View Hill The section of Mapleton Hill between Ninth and Broadway was originally known as Pleasant View Hill. The first homes were probably built here early in the 1880s. *Continue east on Mapleton until you come to the house at 1002 Mapleton.*

Walk further east on Mapleton to look at the houses around 1020. 1020 Mapleton is often called the "lion house" (look closely to find out why), and shows a

Mapleton School, as it appeared shortly after it was built. Some original features have been removed, while new additions have been made. As in so many cases, the original harmony of the design has been altered. Do you find the new harmony an improvement?

flamboyant combination of Greek and other Neoclassical details. Across Mapleton from 1020 are several homes of a much more modest character, dating from the 1880s. For example, the brick house at 1019 Mapleton was built in 1883 by Joseph Haffner, a furniture dealer.

The Shingle Style The house at 1012 Mapleton and its more famous neighbor at 1040 were built in the 1890s in the Shingle Style. Houses in this style have a shingle exterior which seems to be organic, wrapping its frame skeleton and enclosing part of a chimney, as on the house at 1012, or part of a tower, as on 1040. Each of these houses, especially 1040, has a wealth of original detailing and deserves a careful look.

This photo, taken about 1900, shows the W. H. Allison family. Note how the house has changed. The square, hipped roof we see now probably represented a modernization of the house, as well as providing more room. Again, the original design was altered. Which roof-line do you find more pleasing?

PROGRESSIVE BOULDER

Continue walking east on Mapleton, going downhill until you reach Broadway. Turn right on Broadway, and walk to Pine Street, crossing Pine to view the Congregational Church. This handsome stone church was built in 1908 to replace the pioneer church pictured on page 1. (Note that the tower on this church very nearly matches that on the original building.) Just after 1900, Boulder's growing tourist industry, spurred by the Sanitarium and Chautauqua, began to see the need for new and improved facilities. The congregation of this church raised $40,000 and hired a prominent Colorado architect to build this stone church. Their efforts were in marked contrast to those that built the pioneer church, based as they were on minimum cash and donated labor. The bell from the original church tower can be seen in the yard to the north of the church.

The Carnegie Library   *Walk west on Pine to view the old Carnegie Library building.* This is one of many libraries across the country built by funds donated by Andrew Carnegie. Boulderites waged a campaign to have this library built beginning shortly after 1900. The building is designed after a Greek temple. It is now used by the City Department of Parks and Recreation.

Filling in the Gaps   The house just to the west of the Carnegie Library building is an example of the bungalow style, which was popular in the first few decades of the twentieth century. In a neighborhood of old homes, these little bungalows, with their double gables and flaring porch piers, can be easily identified as the homes that were later additions, filling in the gaps between their older nieghbors.

HISTORIC PRESERVATION

Continue west to the corner of Eleventh, then turn left and walk downhill on Eleventh. Turn left again on Spruce and walk to the house at 1123 Spruce. This brick house is one of a growing number in Boulder's central area which is being converted to office use. When it was built in 1896, this was one of the finest residences in Boulder. Its carriage house, now converted to other uses, is still visible to the rear. Over the years, however, the house was allowed to deteriorate. The present owner took pains to complement the original design of the house when converting it for business use. This kind of adaptive reuse of older buildings is one important step in Historic Preservation.

This completes the circle and ends your walking tour of two Boulder neighborhoods.

NOTES

Notes, Introduction

1. The authors also reported on this development in *Teaching Local History: Trends, Tips, and Resources*, by Fay D. Metcalf and Matthew T. Downey (Boulder: ERIC Clearinghouse for Social Studies/Social Science Education, 1977). The San Antonio project is described in "High School Students Research History of German-English School in San Antonio," by Mary Mathias El-Beheri and Susan Clayton, *Unterrichtspraxis* 8 (Autumn 1975): 62–66.

2. David A. Gerber, "Local and Community History: Some Cautionary Remarks on an Idea Whose Time Has Returned," *The History Teacher* 13 (November 1979): 7.

3. G. Stanley Hall, editor, *Methods of History Study* (Boston: Heath, 1885), p. 161.

4. Robert E. Keohane, "The Great Debate over the Source Method," *Social Education* 13 (May 1949): 212–218.

5. Quoted in Robert E. Keohane's "The Madison Conference and the Committee of Seven: A Reconsideration," in *The Social Studies* 40 (March 1949): 107n.

6. Mary E. Cunningham, "A Survey of Current Practices in the Teaching of State and Local History," in *Teaching Local History in Today's World*, vol. 44, part II, Annual Proceedings of the Middle States Council for the Social Studies, 1946–1947, edited by George I. Oeste (Philadelphia: MSCSS, 1948): 6–9.

7. Ruth West, editor, *Utilization of Community Resources in the Social Studies*, Ninth Yearbook of the National Council for the Social Studies (Washington, D.C.: National Council for the Social Studies, 1938).

8. Howard R. Anderson, editor, *Teaching Critical Thinking in the Social Studies*, Thirteenth Yearbook of the National Council for the Social Studies (Washington, D.C.: National Council for the Social Studies, 1942).

9. *American Heritage* 1 (April-May 1947): frontispiece. The American Association for State and Local History was organized in 1940, with one of its principal objectives being "to encourage the use of state and local history in the schools" (*American Heritage*, new series, 3 [Spring 1952]: 1). The journal *American Heritage* was addressed primarily to history teachers until September 1949, when it was revamped to become a more expensive history magazine intended for a general audience. Although it continued to review books and audiovisual materials of interest to teachers, information about local history in the schools was thereafter limited to an "Education Page," which appeared sporadically through the year 1951. Its first editor, Mary E. Cunningham, was replaced in 1949 when the magazine's format was changed.

10. *American Heritage* 2 (December 1948): 99.

11. *American Heritage*, n.s. 3 (Fall 1951): 60.

12. *American Heritage*, n.s. 2 (Summer 1951): 56.

13. Ralph Adams Brown and William G. Tyrrell, *How To Use Local History* (Washington,

D.C.: National Council for the Social Studies, 1961); Philip D. Jordan, *The Nature and Practice of State and Local History*, publication no. 14 of the Service Center for Teachers of History (Washington, D.C.: American Historical Association, 1958); Clifford L. Lord, *Teaching History with Community Resources* (New York: Teachers College, Columbia University, 1964). The latter volume was the introductory volume of the Localized History Series, which Lord edited.

14. Mary E. Cunningham, " 'Junior' Historians," *American Heritage*, n.s. 1 (September 1949): 50; H. Bailey Carroll, *The Junior Historian Movement in the Public Schools*, Bulletin of the American Association for State and Local History (Montpelier, Vt.: American Association for State and Local History, 1947); Elizabeth Wallace, "The Pennsylvania Federation of Junior Historians," *Social Education* 9 (April 1945): 161–164.

15. Donald Dean Parker, *Local History: How to Gather It, Write It, and Publish It* (New York: Social Science Research Council, 1944) p. 24.

16. *The Study of History in Schools: Report to the American Historical Association by the Committee of Seven* (New York: Macmillan, 1899); the influence that professional historians of that generation had on the school curriculum is considered in "Historians and the Teaching of History: A Study in Leadership and Responsibility," by Erling M. Hunt, *Teachers College Record* 61 (March 1960): 290–300; and "Professions in Process: Changing Relations Among Social Scientists, Historians, and Educators, 1880–1920," by N. Ray Hiner, *The History Teacher* 6 (February 1973): 201–218.

17. *American History in Schools and Colleges*, The Report of the Committee on American History in Schools and Colleges of the American Historical Association, Mississippi Valley Historical Association, National Council for the Social Studies (New York: Macmillan, 1944), pp. 81–82.

18. Allan J. Lichtman and Valerie French, *Historians and the Living Past* (Arlington Heights, Ill.: AHM Publishing Corporation, 1978), p. 168.

19. Gerber, "Local and Community History," p. 13; David J. Russo, *Families and Communities: A New View of American History* (Nashville: American Association for State and Local History, 1974). For a still earlier tradition of New England local history, see Harvey Wish, *The American Historian: A Social-Intellectual History of the Writing of the American Past* (New York: Oxford, 1960), pp. 3–21.

20. *American Heritage* 2 (December 1948): 99.

21. Mary Sheldon Barnes, "The Teaching of Local History," *Educational Review* 10 (December 1895): 482.

22. John A. Neuenschwander, *Oral History as a Teaching Approach* (Washington, D.C.: National Education Association, 1976), p. 23.

23. For a recent example, see Michael H. Ebner, "Students as Oral Historians," *The History Teacher* 9 (February 1976): 196–201.

24. Catherine Taylor, Matthew T. Downey, and Fay D. Matcalf, "Using Local Architecture as an Historical Resource: Some Teaching Strategies," *The History Teacher* 11 (February 1978): 175–192; David R. Goldfield, "Living History: The Physical City as Artifact and Teaching Tool," *The History Teacher* 8 (August 1975): 53–56.

25. The most stimulating source of ideas for this approach to local history is *MISHAP*, the newsletter published by the Minnesota Social History Project, Saint Mary's College, Winona, Minnesota 55987.

26. *MISHAP* 1 (September 1978).

Chapter 1

1. Bonny Cochran, "Interview: Willa Baum," *Looking at Oral History* (September 1975), ERIC/CHess, p. 1.

2. Willa Baum, *Oral History for the Local Historical Society,* 2nd ed. (Nashville: American Association for State and Local History, 1974), pp. 32–35.

3. Baum, *Oral History,* pp. 25–28.

4. Baum, *Oral History,* pp. 37, 41.

5. Fred Schroeder, *Designing Your Exhibits: Seven Ways to View an Artifact,* American Association for State and Local History, Technical Leaflet no. 91, *History News* 31, no. 11 (November 1976).

6. E. McClung Fleming, "Artifact Study: A Proposed Model," *Winterthur Portfolio IX* (1975), pp. 153–173.

7. Matthew T. Downey, "Pictures as Teaching Aids: Using the Pictures in History Textbooks," *Social Education* 43 (February 1980): 93.

8. Robert U. Akeret, *Photoanalysis* (New York: Peter H. Wyden, Inc., 1973), p. 35.

9. Prudence Moylan and Walter Kelly, *Chicago Metro History Fair: A Handbook for Teachers* (Chicago: Chicago Metro History Fair, 1978), pp. 30–31.

10. Martin Sandler, *Teachers' Guide: In Search of America* (Lexington, Mass.: Ginn and Company, 1975), pp. TG-8, TG-9.

11. Ken Switzer, "Project QUESST," personal interview Social Science Education Consortium, Inc. Boulder, Colo., January 3, 1980.

12. Sam B. Warner, Jr., "Writing Local History: The Use of Social Statistics," American Association for State and Local History, Technical Leaflet no. 7, *History News* 25, no. 10 (October 1970), p. 6.

13. Norman H. Nie, et al., *SPSS: Statistical Package for the Social Sciences,* 2nd ed. (New York: McGraw-Hill, 1975).

14. Alice Eikenberry and Ruth Ellsworth, "Organizing and Evaluating Information," in *Skill Development in the Social Studies,* Thirty-Third Yearbook, edited by Helen M. Carpenter, (Washington, D.C.: National Council for the Social Studies, 1963), p. 89. Reprinted with permission.

15. Eikenberry and Ellsworth, "Organizing and Evaluating Information," p. 90.

16. Barry Beyer, "Pre-writing and Rewriting to Learn," *Social Education* 43 (March 1979): 188. Reprinted with permission of the National Council for the Social Studies.

17. Beyer, "Pre-writing and Rewriting," p. 189.

18. Arthur L. Smith, "Producing the Slide Show for Your Local Historical Society," American Association for State and Local History, Technical Leaflet no. 42, *History News* 22, no. 6 (June 1967).

19. Les Satterthwaite, *Graphics: Skills, Media, and Materials* (Dubuque, Ia.: Kendall/Hunt Publishing Company, 1977).

20. Charles Bennett and J. Michael Lenihan, "Process Guide for Student Involvement in Historical Research," Rhode Island State Department of Education (Providence, n.d.), p. 22.

Chapter 2

1. *Family, Work, Community: Museum Education Catalog of Teaching Materials,* Old Sturbridge Village, Sturbridge, Mass.
2. *Sonoran Heritage,* A Learning Library Program, Tucson Public Library, Tucson, Ariz.
3. Alberta Sebolt, *Building Collaborative Programs: Museums and Schools,* Old Sturbridge Village, Sturbridge, Mass. (1980), p. 15.

Chapter 3

1. James Deetz, "Material Culture," in *Experiments in History Teaching,* by Stephen Botein, et al., Cambridge, Mass.: Harvard-Danforth Center for Teaching and Learning, 1977), p. 17.
2. Gerald A. Danzer, "Buildings as Sources: Architecture and the Social Studies," *The High School Journal* 57, no. 5 (February 1974): 207. Copyright 1974 by the University of North Carolina Press. Reprinted by permission of the publisher. Danzer states that his perspective in this paragraph was developed through his reading of Vincent J. Scully, Jr.,'s work in this field.
3. Gerald Danzer, "Art and the City: Aesthetic Values and the Human Condition," material presented at the National Council for the Social Studies Annual Meeting, Atlanta, Georgia, November 26, 1975.
4. David C. Goldfield, "Living History: The Physical City as Artifact and Teaching Tool," *The History Teacher* 8 (August 1975): 535–556.
5. Goldfield, "Living History," p. 543.
6. Goldfield, "Living History," p. 548.
7. Catherine Taylor, "Local History Reflected in Two Boulder Neighborhoods," Kit #95 DIMC, (Boulder, Colo.: Boulder Valley Public Schools, 1977).
8. Catherine Taylor, unpublished classroom materials.
9. Angela O'Dowd, "Exploring Staten Island through Its Architecture," *Instructor* (August/September 1972), p. 137.
10. Danzer, "Buildings as Sources," p. 206.
11. Danzer, "Buildings as Sources," pp. 209–211.
12. Linda Ellsworth, "The History of a House: How to Trace It," American Association for State and Local History, Technical Leaflet no. 89, *History News* 31, no. 9 (September 1978).
13. "Field Guide to Old-House Styles," *The Old-House Journal,* 1974. (The address for this publication is 191 Berkeley Place, Brooklyn, New York 11217.)
14. John J.-G. Blumenson, *Identifying American Architecture* (Nashville: American Association for State and Local History, 1977).
15. Richard Rabinowitz, "The Crisis in the Classroom: Architecture and Education," *History of Education Quarterly* 14 (Spring 1974):115–123.
16. Mary Lohmann, *A New Look at History* (Old Lyme, Conn.: Old Lyme Bicentennial Commission, 1975).
17. Thomas J. Schlereth, "Historic Houses as Learning Laboratories: Seven Teaching Strategies," American Association for State and Local History, Technical Leaflet no. 105, *History News* 33, no. 4 (April 1978).
18. Schlereth, "Historic Houses," pp. 2–10.

19. Schlereth, "Historic Houses," p. 7.

20. Ralph Adams Brown and William G. Tyrrell, "How to Use Local History," How-to-Do-It Series, no. 3 National Council for the Social Studies, Washington, D.C., 1961, p. 3.

21. Danzer, "Art and the City," unnumbered.

22. Rhode Island State Department of Education, Division of Development and Operations, "Rhode Island Box," Providence, 1976, p. 140.

23. *Above-Ground Archaeology* (Washington, D.C.: The American Revolution Bicentennial Commission, n.d.), p. 2.

24. Frances A. Brayton, "School Loan Exhibits for the Local Historical Society," American Association for State and Local History, Technical Leaflet no. 16, *History News* 26, no. 8 (August 1971).

25. Chart adapted from Audrey Wilson, "Cemetery Studies: An 'Integrated' Resource Found Outdoors," Northumberland and Newcastle Board of Education Central Area, as reprinted in *Mid-South Humanities Project Institute Manual* (Murfreesboro, Tenn.: Middle Tennessee State University, 1979).

26. Harriette Merrifield Forbes, *Gravestones of Early New England and the Men Who Made Them, 1653–1800* (Boston: Houghton Mifflin, 1927), as quoted in David Weitzman, *Underfoot* (New York: Charles Scribner's Sons, 1976), p. 69.

27. John Reilly, "Everything You Wanted to Know About Carmel but Were Afraid to Look," *Social Science Record* 12, no. 1 (Fall 1974): 13–19.

28. Audrey Wilson, "Cemetery Studies."

29. Mary-Ellen Jones, "Photographing Tombstones: Equipment and Techniques," American Association for State and Local History, Technical Leaflet no. 92, *History News* 32, no. 2 (February 1977).

30. John J. Newman, "Cemetery Transcribing: Preparations and Procedures," American Association for State and Local History, Technical Leaflet no. 9, *History News* 26, no. 5 (May 1971).

31. Elsa Martz, "Cemetery Restoration as a High School Course," Gloucester Community Development Corporation, Gloucester, Mass., n.d. As cited in *Experiments in History Teaching*, by Stephen Botein et al. (Cambridge, Mass.: Harvard-Danforth Center for Teaching and Learning, 1977), p. 19.

32. "Graven Images," Stephen Botein, et al., in *Experiments in History Teaching*, p. 19.

33. Felicia A. Holton, "Death Heads, Cherubs, and Shaded Urns," *Early Man*, Autumn 1979, pp. 5–9.

34. Two other provocative studies by these authors are available and useful for background studies. They are: James Deetz and Edwin Dethlefsen, "Death's Head, Cherub, Urn, and Willow," *Natural History* 76 (March 1967): 29-37. "Death's Heads, Cherubs, and Willow Trees: Experimental Archaeology in Colonial Cemeteries," *American Antiquity* 31, no. 4 (1966).

35. Louis Untermeyer and Carter Davidson, *Poetry: Its Appreciation and Enjoyment* (New York: Harcourt, Brace, and Co., 1934), p. 429.

36. Epitaph for Molly Sanders, 1824–1880, Burlington Cemetery, Longmont, Colorado.

Chapter 4

1. David H. Culbert, "Undergraduates as Historians: Family History Projects Add Meaning to an Introductory Survey," *The History Teacher* 7 (November 1973): 7–17; Kirk

Jeffrey, "Write a History of Your Own Family: Further Observations and Suggestions," *The History Teacher* 7 (May 1974): 365–373; D. J. Steel and L. Taylor, "Family History in Schools: The Development of a New Approach to the Teaching of History," *The History and Social Science Teacher* 10 (Winter 1974): 17–24.

2. An alternative approach is presented in the American history textbook by John G. Clark, David M. Katzman, Richard D. McKinzie, and Theodore A. Wilson, *Three Generations in 20th-Century America: Family, Community, and Nation* (Homewood, Ill.: The Dorsey Press, 1977). The book examines recent American history through the lives of seventeen families.

3. Jeffrey, "Write a History of Your Own Family: Further Observations and Suggestions," p. 365.

4. Davis Bitton, "Family History: Therapy or Scholarship?" Paper delivered at the annual meeting of the Society of American Archivists, Salt Lake City, Utah, October 6, 1977, p. 4.

5. Jeffrey, "Write a History of Your Own Family: Further Observations and Suggestions," p. 367.

6. Bitton, "Family History: Therapy or Scholarship?" p. 8.

7. Project Probe, *Experiencing the Age of Homespun with J. Y. Brown* (Oneonta, N.Y.: Catskill Area School Council, 1968).

8. For the development of the field of family history, see Tamara K. Hareven, "The History of the Family as an Interdisciplinary Field," *Journal of Interdisciplinary History* 2 (Autumn 1971): 399–414; Allan J. Lichtman and Valerie French, *Historians and the Living Past* (Arlington Heights, Ill.: AHM Publishing Corp., 1978), pp. 153–168; and Michael Gordon, editor, *The American Family in Social-Historical Perspective*, 2d ed. (New York: St. Martin's Press, 1978), pp. 1–15.

9. Much of the scholarly work in the field of family history rests upon two basic methods of gathering data. The family reconstitution method involves the reconstruction of individual families, including dates of births, deaths, and marriages for every member, using a variety of local records. The second method utilizes manuscript census data to produce a "snapshot" of individual households at a single moment in time. The latter method does not necessarily identify every member of a family, but only those living within the household at the time the census was taken.

10. John Demos, *A Little Commonwealth: Family Life in Plymouth Colony* (New York: Oxford University Press, 1970).

11. For the importance of distinguishing between households and families, see Tamara Hareven, editor, *Family and Kin in Urban Communities, 1700–1930* (New York: New Viewpoints, 1977), pp. 1–10.

12. This packet, entitled *Households and Families,* is available from the Museum Education Department, Old Sturbridge Village, Sturbridge, Massachusetts 01566.

13. For a more comprehensive description of the federal manuscript census, see Barnes F. Lathrop, "History from the Census Returns," in *Sociology and History: Methods,* edited by Seymour Martin Lipset and Richard Hofstadter (New York: Basic Books, Inc., 1968), pp. 79–101.

14. Charles M. Dollar and Richard J. Jensen, *Historian's Guide to Statistics: Quantitative Analysis and Historical Research* (New York: Holt, Rinehart and Winston, Inc., 1971), pp. 13–14.

15. Information about household and family sturcture for various communities and sections of the United States can be found in Rudy Ray Seward, *The American Family: A Demographic History* (Beverly Hills: Sage Publications, 1978); Gordon, *The American Family in Social-Historical Perspective;* and Hareven, *Family and Kin in Urban Communities, 1700–1930.*

16. Tamara K. Hareven, "The Family as Process: The Historical Study of the Family Cycle," *Journal of Social History* 7 (Spring 1974): 323.

17. Hareven, "The Family as Process," p. 324.

18. See especially E. W. Bakke, *Citizens without Work* (New Haven: Yale University Press, 1940); Robert C. Angell, *The Family Encounters the Depression* (New York: Charles Scribner's Sons, 1936); Ruth Cavan and Katherine Ranck, *The Family and the Depression* (Chicago: University of Chicago Press, 1938); Winona L. Morgan, *The Family Meets the Depression* (Minneapolis: University of Minnesota Press, 1939); and Mirra Komarovsky, *The Unemployed Man and His Family* (New York: Dryden Press, 1940).

19. For a general review of the impact of the Depression on the family, see Glen H. Elder, Jr., *Children of the Great Depression* (Chicago: The University of Chicago Press, 1974), pp. 27–30.

20. Interview with Celeste Woodley, Boulder, Colorado, January 3, 1974.

Chapter 5

1. George J. Albert and Christian A. Castendyk, "Wales—A Case Study of a Small New England Town: A Teacher-Developed Kit," *Social Education* 39 (November/December 1975): 471.

2. Gene E. Rooze, "Local History Can Enliven Social Science Concepts," *Elementary School Journal* 69 (April 1969): 346–351.

3. *Teaching the Age of Homespun: A Guide Unit for 7th-Grade Social Studies* (Albany, N.Y.: Bureau of Secondary Curriculum Development, New York State Education Department, 1965).

4. *MISHAP: Newsletter of the Minnesota Social History Project* 1 (December 1978): 1–18.

5. Robert S. Lynd and Helen Merrell Lynd, *Middletown: A Study in American Culture* (New York: Harcourt, Brace and World, 1929, 1956).

6. Lynd and Lynd, *Middletown*, pp. 255–256.

Chapter 6

1. As one social historian, Tamara K. Hareven, has observed, "Until very recently, American social history was written from the perspective of the dominant culture. It dealt with elites rather than common people, with institutions rather than social processes, with attitudes rather than experiences." In *Anonymous Americans: Explorations in Nineteenth-Century Social History*, edited by Tamara K. Hareven, (Englewood Cliffs, N.J.: Prentice-Hall, 1971), p. vii.

2. Samuel P. Hays, "A Systematic Social History," in *American History: Retrospect and Prospect*, edited by George A. Billias and Gerald N. Grob (New York: Free Press, 1971), pp. 315–366.

3. Kathleen Neils Conzen, *Immigrant Milwaukee, 1836–1860: Accommodation and Community in a Frontier City* (Cambridge: Harvard University Press, 1976); Virginia Yans-McLaughlin, *Family and Community: Italian Immigrants in Buffalo, 1830–1870* (Ithaca: Cornell University Press, 1977); Josef J. Barton, *Peasants and Strangers: Italians, Rumanians, and Slovaks in an American City, 1890–1950* (Cambridge: Harvard University Press, 1975).

4. Anthony B. Penna, "Schools as Archives," *The History Teacher* 9 (November 1975): 19–28.

5. Mary Mathias El-Beheri and Susan Clayton, "High School Students Research History of German-English School in San Antonio," *Unterrichtspraxis* 8 (Autumn 1975): 62–66.

6. Gerald Cullen, "The Bicentennial and Local History," *Social Studies Journal* 5 (Winter 1975–76): 15–16. The use of oral history interviews as a technique for investigating the history of a school is described in Richard F. Newton, "Oral History: Using the School as an Historical Institution," *Clearinghouse* 48 (October 1973): 73–78.

7. Robert E. Gallman, "Trends in the Size Distribution of Wealth in the Nineteenth Century: Some Speculations," in *Six Papers on the Size Distribution of Wealth and Income*, edited by Lee Soltow (New York: National Bureau of Economic Research, 1969), pp. 2–6; Michael B. Katz, *The People of Hamilton, Canada West: Family and Class in a Mid-Nineteenth-Century City* (Cambridge: Harvard University Press, 1975), p. 30.

8. Gabriel Kolko, *Wealth and Power in America: An Analysis of Social Class and Income Distribution* (New York: Frederick A. Prager, 1962), p. 46.

9. Katz, *The People of Hamilton, Canada West*, p. 26.

10. For a careful consideration of that question, see Katz, *The People of Hamilton, Canada West*, especially pp. 71–72.

11. Katz, *The People of Hamilton, Canada West*, pp. 27, 76.

12. Stephan Thernstrom, *Poverty and Progress: Social Mobility in a Nineteenth-Century City* (Cambridge: Harvard University Press, 1964).

13. The principal conclusions of several of these studies are summarized in Stephan Thernstrom, *The Other Bostonians: Poverty and Progress in the American Metropolis, 1880–1970* (Cambridge: Harvard University Press, 1973), pp. 220–261. For a general survey and thoughtful criticism of this scholarship, see Michael Frisch, "American Urban History as an Example of Recent Historiography," *History and Theory* 18 (1979): 366–370.

14. Gideon Sjoberg, *The Pre-Industrial City: Past and Present* (New York: The Free Press, 1960), describes land use and other aspects of premodern cities. See also Emrys Jones, *Towns and Cities* (New York: Oxford University Press, 1966), which takes exception to some of Sjoberg's conclusions. For an analysis of land use in a preindustrial city in colonial America, see Sam Bass Warner, Jr.'s, section on Philadelphia in the 1770s in his *The Private City: Philadelphia in Three Periods of its Growth* (Philadelphia: The University of Pennsylvania Press, 1968), pp. 3–45.

15. Ian Davey and Michael Doucet, "The Social Geography of a Commercial City, Circa 1853," Appendix One in *The People of Hamilton, Canada West*, by Michael B. Katz, pp. 319–342.

16. In addition to the ethnic histories already cited in this chapter, the following books are representative of this literature. Oscar Handlin, *Boston's Immigrants: A Study in Acculturation* (Cambridge, Mass.: Harvard University Press, 1959); Moses Rischin, *The Promised City: New York's Jews, 1870–1914* (Cambridge, Mass.: Harvard University Press, 1962); Gilbert Osofsky, *Harlem: The Making of a Ghetto, Negro New York, 1890–1930* (New York: Harper Torchbooks, 1968); Allan H. Spear, *Black Chicago: The Making of a Negro Ghetto, 1890–1920* (Chicago: University of Chicago Press, 1967); Humbert S. Nelli, *Italians in Chicago, 1880–1930: A Study in Ethnic Mobility* (New York: Oxford University Press, 1970); Thomas Kessner, *The Golden Door: Italian and Jewish Immigrant Mobility in New York City, 1880–1915* (New York: Oxford University Press, 1977); Allen F. Davis and Mark H. Haller, editors, *The Peoples of Philadelphia* (Philadelphia: Temple University Press, 1973); Dean R. Esslinger, *Immigrants and the City: Ethnicity and Mobility in a Nineteenth-Century Community* (Port Washington, N.Y.: Kennikat Press, 1975); and John Bodnar, *Immigration and Industrialization: Ethnicity in an American Mill Town, 1870–1940* (Pittsburgh: University of Pittsburgh Press, 1977).

17. Conzen, *Immigrant Milwaukee*, pp. 14, 16.

18. Conzen, *Immigrant Milwaukee*, p. 34. The question why immigrants settled where they did is one of several questions raised in "Our Cultural Roots: A Classroom Exercise in Historical Geography," by Russel L. Gerlach, *The Journal of Geography* 75 (February 1976): 82–89.

19. Wilbur Zelinsky, *The Cultural Geography of the United States* (Englewood Cliffs, N.J.: Prentice-Hall, Inc., 1973), p. 29.

20. Zelinsky, *The Cultural Geography of the United States*, p. 29.

21. Barton, *Peasants and Strangers*, p. 54.

22. Milton M. Gordon, *Assimilation in American Life: The Role of Race, Religion, and National Origins* (New York: Oxford University Press, 1964), pp. 105, 106.

23. This technique was used by Kathleen Neils Conzen to map areas of ethnic dominance in Milwaukee. She defined areas of ethnic dominance as those contiguous cells in which 60 percent or more of the residents represented one ethnic group.

24. Madison Public Schools, *The Negro in the Social Studies Curriculum* (Madison: Department of Curriculum Development, 1968).

25. Shirla R. McClain and Ambrose Clegg, Jr., "Words, Records, and Beyond: Studying about Local Ethnic Groups through Primary Sources," *Social Education* 41 (May 1977): 382–388.

26. Carlos E. Cortes, "Teaching the Chicano Experience," in *Teaching Ethnic Studies: Concepts and Strategies*, edited by James A. Banks (Washington, D.C.: The National Council for the Social Studies, 1973), p. 194.

27. Dominic Candeloro, "Recovering the History of a Black Community," *The History Teacher* 7 (November 1973): 29.

Chapter 7

1. *Early Records of Gilpin County, Colorado, 1859–1861*, edited by Thomas Maitland Marshall (Boulder: University of Colorado Press, 1920), pp. 10–12; reprinted in Thomas Maitland Marshall, "Legal Beginnings and a Miner's Code," in *A Colorado Reader*, edited by Carl Ubbelohde (Boulder: Pruett Publishing Company, 1962), pp. 114–115.

2. *Boulder Daily Camera*, March 12, 1890.

3. Frederick L. Olmsted, Jr., *The Improvement of Boulder, Colorado*, Report to the City Improvement Association, (Cambridge, Mass.: Harvard University, March 1910).

4. "Introduction to Your Community," *Chicago Metro History Fair: A Handbook for Teachers* (Chicago: Chicago Metro History Fair, 1978), pp. 68–70.

5. Susan Smith Blocker, "The Elections of 1836 in Upper Canada: A Role-Playing Activity," *The History and Social Science Teacher* 13 (Spring 1978): 191–199.

6. Nona P. Lyons, editor, "A Negotiations Exercise: Should the Tea Be Landed in Boston?" *Social Education* 38 (February 1974): 137–152.

Chapter 8

1. Stephen Botein, et al., *Experiments in History Teaching* (Cambridge, Mass.: Harvard-Danforth Center for Teaching and Learning, 1977).

2. Francis Pratt and Frances Haley, "Finding Relevance in Your Own Backyard," *Profiles of Promise*, no. 10, ERIC/CHess, Boulder, Colo., n.d.

3. James A. De Vita, et al., *From Settlement to Suburbia: A New History of Chelmsford* (Chelmsford, Mass.: Chelmsford Public Schools, 1976).

4. Brian Mitchell, "The History of the City of Lowell," *Experiments in History Teaching* (Cambridge, Mass.: Harvard-Danforth Center for Teaching and Learning, 1977).

5. John D. Buenker, "History of Racine and Kenosha Syllabus," *The Newberry Papers in Family and Community History* (Chicago: Newberry Library, 1978).

6. Ted L. Underwood, "Undergraduates as Historians: Writing Local History in a Seminar on Historical Research," *The History Teacher* 7 (November 1973): 18–23.

7. The best introduction to the *Foxfire* concept is Eliot Wiggington, *Moments* (Washington, D.C.: Institutional Development and Economic Affairs Service, Inc., 1975).

8. Colin J. Marsh, "Whatever Happened to Community Studies?" *Clearinghouse* 24 (February 1976): 262.

9. Thomas L. Dynneson, *Planning Local History Projects for Elementary and Secondary Students* (n.p.: West Texas Council for the Social Studies, 1976), pp. 2–3.

10. *Frontier Ohio: A Resource Guide for Teachers* (Columbus, O.: State Department of Ohio Education, n.d.), p. 13.

11. Thomas E. Felt, *Researching, Writing, and Publishing Local History* (Nashville: American Association for State and Local History, 1976).

12. Pamela Wood, *You and Aunt Arie, A Guide to Cultural Journalism* (Washington, D.C.: Institutional Development and Economic Affairs Service, Inc., 1976).

INDEX

Adams, Herbert Baxter, 3
American Association for State and Local
  History: founding of, 271n9;
  mentioned, 5, 54, 185
American Heritage: as a journal for history
  teachers, 271n9; mentioned, 5
American Historical Association:
  Committee of Seven, 6
Anniversary booklets: as local history
  sources, 56–57
Antiquarianism. *See* Parochialism
Architectural features: and influences of
  the arts, 34; identification of, 100–105;
  mentioned, 85, 89–90
Architectural walking tours, 1, 13, 15
Architecture: books and articles
  describing, 68–70; teaching appreciation
  of, 100–101; as social history source,
  101, 106–107
Artifacts: analysis of, 33–35; in
  "Grandma's trunks," 82, 112; reflecting
  world views, 85; traveling kits, 114; the
  automobile as a cultural artifact,
  174–179

Barnes, Mary Sheldon: early advocate of
  local history, 12
Baum, Willa: on techniques of oral history
  research, 26
Bird's-eye views, 63, 92, 98, 240
Black history: local sources for, 205–206
Buildings: studying form and function of,
  86–90, 95–97; as sources for local
  history, 95; research methods, 97
Business directories: as local history
  sources, 58, 93, 240–241
Business histories: as local history sources,
  56

Cemeteries: records, 60; books and articles
  about, 70–71; as city parks, 88; as

sources of demographic data, 115–116;
  symbology and inscriptions, 117,
  121–126, 260–262; tombstone rubbings,
  119; photographic techniques, 119–120,
  259; recording data about, 120,
  255–258; restoration of, 120–121
Census records: for teaching about social
  mobility, 15, 191–192; used in
  Minnesota Social History Project, 15,
  144; sources of data on occupations, 40,
  162–165; as sources for local history,
  61–62; using manuscript census returns
  for family history, 139–143; sampling
  techniques for manuscript census
  returns, 141; uses for economic history,
  158–159; using manuscript census
  returns for women's history, 165–169;
  used for teaching about social structure,
  187; uses for ethnic history, 198–199;
  used for teaching about black history,
  205; mentioned, 24
Chicago Metro History Fair: directions for
  photograph analysis, 37; co-operative
  project with Chicago schools, 81; model
  for a community survey, 211–213
Cities: as artifacts, 86–90; teaching about
  urban form and texture, 87–88
Citizenship education: as rationale for
  local history, 12
City and county histories: as sources for
  local history projects, 54
City and county offices: as repositories of
  local history data, 24
City and county records. *See* Public records
City directories: used in the classroom, 15;
  as sources for local history, 58; sources
  of data on occupations, 162–163, 191;
  used for teaching about social mobility,
  191–192; as sources for social
  geography, 193; for teaching about
  black history, 205; mentioned, 16, 24, 98

281